Republicans Buy Sneakers Too

ALSO BY CLAY TRAVIS

On Rocky Top: A Front-Row Seat to the End of an Era

Dixieland Delight: A Football Season on the Road in the Southeastern Conference

Republicans Buy Sneakers Too

How the Left Is Ruining Sports with Politics

Clay Travis

BROADSIDE BOOKS
An Imprint of HarperCollins*Publishers*

HarperCollins books may be purchased for educational, business, or sales promotional use. For information, please email the Special Markets Department at SPsales@harpercollins.com.

FIRST EDITION

Library of Congress Cataloging-in-Publication Data has been applied for.
ISBN 978-0-06-287853-3

18 19 20 21 22   LSC   10 9 8 7 6 5 4 3 2 1

For Fox, Lincoln, and Nash, the three best sons any dad could ever want

Contents

Republicans Buy Sneakers Too

Introduction:
The First Amendment
and Boobs

SHOULD I PUT THE HOUSE ON THE MARKET?
—Lara Travis, via text to me on September 15, 2017

Every husband knows it's never a good sign when your wife texts you from inside the house.

Yet that's the text I received from my wife moments after CNN had ended a live interview with me where I said I believed in only two things completely—the First Amendment and boobs.

I'd gone on CNN from the third-floor office in my home to talk the intersection of sports and politics, specifically the statement by ESPN's Jemele Hill that Donald Trump was a white supremacist who had surrounded himself with other white supremacists.

I'd nestled into the chair in my home outside Nashville, Tennessee, a city I'd been born and raised in, turned on the camera and connected to the CNN studio in Atlanta, and stared into the camera to share my opinions. It was the third straight day I'd been on CNN or CNN Headline News. As part of that discussion on a Friday afternoon in September, I'd expressed my love for the First Amendment and boobs—a phrase I've been using for years that was, to me, more gripping than just saying I was a First Amendment absolutist—and the female host, Brooke Baldwin, reacted with pearl-clutching indignation.

How dare I, a man, have the temerity to appear on CNN and say I liked the First Amendment and boobs? When I'd refused to apologize for what I'd said, she'd abruptly ended the interview, igniting an immediate media firestorm.

The firestorm didn't bother me, I absolutely love being in the middle of media firestorms, it's where I'm most content, but my wife wasn't happy with me.

As every husband knows, when momma ain't happy, ain't nobody happy.

Moments before I'd done the CNN interview, I'd told my wife that our busy week was almost over. When I finished the CNN and Fox News hits—we were taping Fox News for a Saturday show—we could take our three boys, ages nine, seven, and three, out for pizza and relax before the weekend's college football and NFL games. I'd even told her that things were going spectacularly well with Outkick and that our surging ratings on radio and online readership might lead to a White House invite before long.

My wife, whom I met in our first year at Vanderbilt Law School, had voted for Hillary Clinton and wasn't that excited about visiting the Donald Trump White House. However, I'd been arguing with her that whether you voted for the president or not you had an obligation to go to the White House if you were invited to go there.

I thought I'd been making some headway.

Now I had to trudge downstairs from my upstairs office where I worked all day, to talk to her. When I arrived downstairs, she was not happy with me: "I think you're going to get fired," she said.

This has been my wife's fear for over a decade, that my insistence on saying exactly what I believe and not tempering my opinions to avoid offending anyone in our perpetually offended society, was going to eventually get me fired.

That the online mob was going to line up, put me squarely in their sights, and before everything was done, I'd be unemployed. I had partly protected myself, due to her fears, by founding my own company,

Outkick the Coverage, and creating a burgeoning sports media empire predicated on total and complete creative freedom. What I sold to my audience every day was four things: that I was going to be smart, original, funny, and authentic.

Since the company's founding in 2011—and many years before that even—I'd found myself in the center of many media firestorms.

But this was going to be a different level of attention than ever before.

"I'm not going to get fired," I told her. "This is the best thing that's ever happened for my career. The people who love me will love me that much more, and the people who hate me will hate me that much more. All of that is great for what I do; love and hate are just two sides of the same coin. The CNN host overreacted, and I didn't do anything wrong."

She rolled her eyes.

"Why didn't you apologize?" she asked.

"For liking boobs and the First Amendment?"

"What are you going to tell our boys?"

"I'm not going to have to tell them anything. They're going to like boobs too; it's biology."

She rolled her eyes again.

"Look," I said, "there's nothing to worry about. CNN has already invited me back on their shows for Monday." (This was true, in the immediate aftermath of my appearance on the show, CNN had left me a phone message inviting me back on their network on Monday.)

My phone, which had been blowing up with reactions from friends, family, and coworkers for the past twenty minutes, buzzed anew.

It was my boss at Fox Sports Radio.

"We're getting some pressure to fire you from the radio show," he texted. "Call me."

"What's that?" my wife asked.

"My friends like boobs too," I said.

But I left her and went back upstairs to my office.

I've been fired a bunch of times before. The first time I got fired was in college when I didn't show up for work on Sunday at Abercrombie & Fitch because I went to a Denver Broncos and Washington Redskins game instead. I was fired from the first congressional campaign I worked on, as Democratic congressman Jim Cooper's driver and body man, because I wrecked the congressman's wife's Volvo sedan, and then took a trip to New York City without giving proper notice.

At the website Deadspin, where I'd been hired as an editor, I'd quit over not having complete creative control over the articles under my name. At the sports website FanHouse, back in 2011, they shut down the entire website, and I suddenly didn't have a writing job. That one really stung because I had a contract extension on my boss's desk and I'd convinced my wife, who lived in perpetual fear that I was going to be fired at any moment, that we were close to having it made.

At long last, I was going to be paid at least $100,000 a year to write about sports.

Boom, it was right there and then, double boom, I was unemployed and fired with two months of severance from a $40,000-a-year writing job and two young kids to take care of.

When you've been fired before, you're always prepared to be fired again.

Even still, the irony wasn't lost on me. Was I really going to be fired from my national radio show for saying I loved the First Amendment and boobs? Had the country gone so insane that admitting you liked boobs, in conjunction with the First Amendment, was now unacceptable to say on television?

I picked up the phone and dialed my boss at Fox Sports Radio. "Okay," he said, "it's not good."

My name is Clay Travis and I make a living writing and talking about sports. I never really thought I would make a living doing this, but back in 2004 I started writing online about sports while I was a practicing attorney in the United States Virgin Islands, and my audience, which at the time was literally zero, just kept growing.

Over the ensuing fourteen years, I'd produced millions of words of written content, a couple of books, and I'd found out I was pretty good at sports talk radio and TV. So as I sit here writing this book at the age of thirty-eight, I've written a couple of books, graduated from Vanderbilt law school, also added a second graduate degree from Vanderbilt University in creative writing, hosted the top-ranked local radio show in the country in Nashville, Tennessee, and now host—at least for the moment, anyway—one of the most listened-to national sports talk-radio shows in the entire country, which airs each morning, Monday through Friday, on nearly three hundred affiliates nationwide in all fifty states and on satellite radio from 6 to 9 a.m. eastern.

Oh, and I also hosted my own TV show on FS1 a couple of years ago.

Along the way, I also managed to marry a former Tennessee Titans cheerleader I met in law school, father three sons, and found a website, OutkicktheCoverage.com, which millions of people now read, watch, or listen to each month. If you're not familiar with the phrase "outkick the coverage," it has a dual meaning. In football it's when a punter kicks the ball too far for his special teams unit to cover the kick, allowing a favorable return. In life, it's when a man ends up with a woman who is far too good-looking for him.

So things were going pretty well for me in the fall of 2017 when sports and politics suddenly became so inextricably intertwined it was impossible to escape either. We'll get to all of that later—as well as how we got to these politically charged times in sports and how we get back to sports being about sports and not politics—but for now let's go back to a seminal moment in my career when my point of view on everything changed forever—when racial protests suddenly erupted in November of 2015 at the University of Missouri.

I still remember exactly where I was when news of the Missouri football team's protest reached me—I was flying back to Nashville from Los Angeles on a Sunday afternoon. During the 2015 college football season, I'd been hosting a Friday night college football show for FS1 and news had been percolating all weekend about a student protest on the University of Missouri's campus.

The University of Missouri, which had joined the Southeastern Conference in 2012, was struggling through a difficult 2015 season, which would ultimately be the final season for their legendary coach Gary Pinkel. Pinkel's team, beset with significant injuries all season long, was then sitting at 4–5.

What had been a relatively disappointing, but somewhat quiet, football season was about to change: the football team had just announced they would not play unless the demands of a hunger-striking student were met.

What were those demands and why were students protesting and living in tents on the campus's quad?

Media evidence about the particulars motivating the protest was glaringly absent, but the protest was directed, in general, at racism and lack of inclusion at the university.

This surprised me on its face because I knew Missouri had recently elected a black and gay man student body president and because I knew the school, and its alumni and fans, had embraced Michael Sam, the first openly gay football player in SEC and NFL history.

Sure, every school has its issues and every student is not the same on any campus, but the University of Missouri did not seem to have a culture of exclusion or to be, as many of the protesters were stating, openly racist and discriminatory toward minorities.

The story fascinated me because everyone I saw on my social media feed as I scrolled through it during my Southwest flight was praising the protesting students for their bravery and the football team for taking a stand on behalf of the hunger striker. The football team was saying they would not play unless the university met the demands of the protesting students.

This was a blockbuster story, one that threatened to tear apart the college football season for a team in a major conference. Yet rather than blindly praise the football team for their political activism—which I was seeing was the default clichéd response of every sportswriter I followed on social media—I wanted to know what was at the heart of the Missouri protests.

Why were they so angry at the school's president and administrators? What had these officials done to permit racism to flourish at Mizzou?

What I found when I investigated the protest was shocking. There were three incidents that students, who had taken over the quad at the center of Mizzou's campus, were protesting: a poop swastika that had been found inside a campus bathroom (Yes, you read that right. This was a Nazi swastika made out of poop and scratched on the wall of the bathroom by an individual of unknown race and sex. Heck, we still didn't even know if it was a student who did it or the race or political persuasion of the person); a racial slur that had been allegedly uttered by a nonstudent walking through campus; and an alleged racial slur that had been uttered by a mysterious person in a red truck off campus.

That was it.

This was the sum total of the incidents that had led Missouri's football team to refuse to play.

That struck me as odd. Why should the president of a university be responsible for nonstudents uttering a racial slur on campus, for an unknown person making a poop swastika in the bathroom, and for an alleged racial slur, with no witnesses, happening off campus?

Plainly, racism is bad and shouldn't exist, but it's not like a president can stop racism from existing. Especially when, you know, the racism might not even be perpetrated by any students. As if that weren't enough, we don't even know if the poop swastika was intended as an endorsement of Nazism or a repudiation of it. (After all, if one of you showed up at a book signing and said you'd made a portrait of me with your feces, I wouldn't be sure if you were a fan or not, but I would be sure you were crazy. I certainly wouldn't consider it an honored and reasoned endorsement of everything in this book.)

I know I'm getting old now and that it's been just over fifteen years since I graduated from a university, but I went to college in Washington, D.C., and it's hard for me to even fathom what the president of my university would have said in 2001 if I'd demanded a meeting because someone off campus had said something mean to me. He probably would have laughed at me and told me to get thicker skin. And if he'd said that, he'd have been right. College kids all need to get tougher and stop whining so much about microaggressions and triggering words in books.

Regardless of what my own opinion was, as a result of two racial slurs from nonstudents and a poop swastika from an unknown perpetrator, some of Missouri's black students had taken over the quad of the main campus and were protesting racism on campus. Included in this protest was a hunger strike by a grad student. Now the Missouri football team was saying it would refuse to play until these students' demands were met.

At this point, I asked another question no one else in the sports media was asking. What were the student demands? What did these Missouri activists want? Fortunately, those demands had been placed online in a handy document.

The demands were, frankly, ludicrous. Many of them were flat-out illegal, such as firing white faculty members and replacing them with black faculty members, but the most absurd of all was a demand that the university president climb onto a table in the school cafeteria, denounce his white privilege in front of the entire student body, and then resign from the university.

When I read the demands, my mind was blown. Really? These were the protesters that the sports media were lionizing? Yes, these protesters—and the Missouri football team supporting them—were being praised as heroes by the sports media.

As I looked more and more into the protest, I became convinced of how absurd and without merit it truly was. I also saw something else: the sports media weren't just treating the protest as legitimate, they were praising the students and players for their bravery.

Their bravery?!

I felt like I was living in an upside-down universe. Everywhere I looked, the Missouri football team and the Mizzou protesters were being praised. How could so many people in the sports media be so blindly supporting something so ridiculous?

In over ten years of writing and talking about sports, I'd never given much thought to how politics impacted sports stories before the Missouri protests, but this story gave me pause. Why were so many in the sports media unwilling to call out the absurdity of the Missouri football team's actions? Hell, why was their legendary coach not able to stop the protest from spreading? What was going on here?

That's when it hit me. The sports media covering Missouri—and the head coach of the football team as well—were afraid of calling out the stupidity of the protest because they were afraid they'd be called racist if they didn't support a black protest on campus.

This wasn't about right or wrong; it was about white men being afraid of being publicly branded as racists.

As the media coverage of the "brave" protesters grew, my sense of disconnect with reality also grew—how was no one else aware of what was going on here? As I started to write articles at Outkick about the protest's sham nature, my Twitter feed exploded with charges of racism. I saw something crazy. Since I was a white guy, many people on social media honestly believed I wasn't permitted to disagree with black student protesters.

At first, the accusations of racism were jarring. I'd lived thirty-five years without ever being called racist. Now, as the racism accusations continued to pour down upon me, I quickly noticed something else.

No one was disputing what I was saying or writing about the protest or its illegitimacy and its absurd goals; my opponents were calling me racist in an effort to scare me into silence.

That is, they weren't disputing my factual statements or the logic behind my arguments, they were trying to shame me into silence by accusing me of being racist.

These protesters were cognizant of something I was learning. The fear of being called racist is so prevalent that most white people in prominent positions in sports media today would rather report the fabrication than examine the facts and report the truth if it meant being publicly branded a racist.

My world was rocked by this realization. What kind of world were we living in where sharing factual statements was now considered racist?

The racism charges were so powerful that the media didn't challenge the protesters, and the pressure grew to such an extent that Missouri's president and chancellor were forced to resign due to their "racial insensitivity."

Whatever that meant.

The football team returned to the field, and the protesting students were hailed as heroes, social justice warriors who had forced an entire university to bend to their will.

To me, they looked like something else entirely: little terrorists.

The University of Missouri had just negotiated with terrorists and allowed them to win.

The media coverage of the student protesters remained glowing. ESPN would make a movie, produced by Spike Lee, lionizing their behavior and also reward the football team an honorary ESPY for their courage. However, as the information about what had happened trickled out, led by sites like Outkick, something equally remarkable happened: the market eventually reacted, and the truth started to emerge.

Aided by a viral video of the protesters on the Missouri quad refusing media access to the protest and demanding "muscle" to block the media, the masses finally revolted against the artificial image being sold by the sports media.

This wasn't a brave protest against racial injustice; it was a bone-headed attack upon innocent university administrators by students who had faced no actual wrongs. The football team hadn't made Missouri's situation better: they'd poured jet fuel on a raging conflagration of inept protesting and turned what should have been a nonstory into a national referendum on the insipid nature of many campus protests.

In the process, it turned out, the protesters had nearly killed the University of Missouri.

By the next spring, it was clear Mizzou had a major problem: students were choosing not to enroll. Just months after the protest, freshman enrollment plunged by nearly 25 percent for the entering class in 2016.

How bad was that enrollment decline? It was similar to the impact of Hurricane Katrina on Tulane University in New Orleans.

Think about this for a minute: the disastrous Mizzou protest was as crushing to Missouri enrollment as the New Orleans hurricane had been to Tulane.

The worst wasn't over. The next year freshman enrollment dropped again, leading to a 35 percent overall drop in freshman enrollment within two years. Worse than that? It was the best students, who had other options of where to go to college, who were choosing not to come to Mizzou, meaning the overall quality of the university was collapsing right as the school needed top students the most. Ultimately the university would have to shut down seven dorms and fire over four hundred employees as a result of the protests and their negative impact on the school's brand.

The University of Missouri's bungled response to student protesters ended up costing the school hundreds of millions of dollars and thousands of students.

The most amazing thing about the protest's impact is that it led to fewer black employees and fewer black students at the university. That is, the black students protesting at Missouri led to Mizzou's black enrollment plunging from 10 percent of overall students to 6 percent in the space of two years, and led to many black employees losing their jobs too.

If actual racists had wanted to cut minority enrollment and employment at Missouri, they could never have accomplished in years of effort what these fake protesters did in the space of a single month.

How did it all happen?

Simple, the sports media was afraid to do its job and hold the protesting students accountable because so many were afraid of being called racist if they reported the truth. The protest was a sham and its goals were illegitimate, but that didn't matter.

I spent a great deal of time thinking about this story in the aftermath of the protest. It was in my wheelhouse at the time, an SEC football school—I'd literally written *the* book on SEC football in 2007, *Dixieland Delight*—succumbing to modern left-wing political protest to the massive detriment of the school.

How was it that the marketplace had so desperately failed the University of Missouri? The media existed to tell the truth, yet I'd seen very little actual truth-telling. As a result, Missouri's response had been calamitous, and hundreds of millions of dollars had been lost along with hundreds of jobs.

From an economic perspective, the Missouri protest was the single most devastating event to happen to any university in the 2010s . . . so far.

I'd been right there to see it all happen in real time.

What was actually happening and why? These were questions I began to increasingly grapple with. More alarming, I started to wonder this: How many other stories like Mizzou that weren't true had I allowed myself to believe? Was the Missouri protest an outlier or had the country, and sports, begun to go insane?

What could and should I do about stories like these in the future? How could I help to ensure that no school ever again went through what Missouri went through in the fall of 2015? This book is one answer.

But more important, so was my goal with the Outkick website, radio, Periscope, and Facebook shows.

I resolved to investigate every story on my own and not allow media misperceptions to ever drive my opinions again. If sometimes that led to me being called names or attacked for my opinions, I could handle that.

Many years earlier, my hero had been another Tennessean, the frontier explorer Davey Crockett, who made his life's mantra "Be sure you're right and then go ahead."

That was now my goal.

I'd become a First Amendment warrior, I'd shout my opinions as loudly as I possibly could, and I'd ensure that I was never afraid to say what I believed because it made some people uncomfortable.

Fortunately, I had the kind of job that allowed me to do this, to be outspoken about what I believed was right regardless of the consequences. Sure, I might get fired again someday, but I'd been fired before. I wanted to be the voice for many people who felt like me but didn't have the same freedom to speak as loudly as I did.

I resolved to tell the truth in public no matter the consequences.

I know many of you reading this book right now have had similar moments of your own when you've seen sports or politics or media, in general, be covered in a way that's fundamentally inaccurate.

For me, the Missouri protest was my red pill moment, the instant when the way I viewed the media, and particularly the sports media, changed forever.

If the Missouri protest could be founded on fake racism allegations and allowed to flourish to the point where it nearly destroyed a university, what else was happening out there in the world of sports that was also rooted in a fake reality?

It was time for me to take the red pill and see the world as it truly was, not as I'd wished it had been.

If you're reading this book and not familiar with the red pill metaphor, there's a scene in *The Matrix*, early in the movie, when the Keanu Reeves Neo character is confronted with two options by his guide Morpheus, played by Laurence Fishburne: he can take a blue pill or a red pill. If he takes the blue pill, he wakes up in his bed, and nothing has changed in his life. If he takes the red pill, as Morpheus tells him, "You stay in Wonderland, and I show you how deep the rabbit hole goes."

In the fall of 2015, I took the red pill in the wake of the Missouri protest, and it changed my life.

This book is the result of that decision.

If you're willing to, take the red pill with me now, and keep reading. Just beware, if you do, your life will be forever changed by the time you finish this book.

Some of you might want to put down this book right now and take the blue pill instead.

If so, it's a decision you can certainly make, and it's a decision many make every day.

I hope you enjoy the fake sports news on ESPN for the rest of your life.

For the rest of you, buckle up, here we go.

1

Stick to Sports (or at Least Leave Out One-Sided Politics)

After I took the red pill, I realized sports stories like what had happened at the University of Missouri weren't uncommon in our modern-day sports universe.

In fact, they were everywhere.

The left-wing sports media was using sports to advance their own political agendas and disguising it inside their sports coverage.

This was completely jarring to me because I'd never been a conspiracy theory guy. In fact, I wasn't even a Republican; I was a Democrat. I'd volunteered on Bill Clinton's 1996 presidential campaign, worked for Al Gore's 2000 presidential campaign, voted for John Kerry in 2004 and Barack Obama in 2008 and 2012. Hell, I even donated money to both men. As if that weren't enough, I'd worked on Capitol Hill for multiple years in a Democratic congressman's office, but I'd mostly kept my own personal politics out of my writing.

When I published *Dixieland Delight*, my 2007 book about SEC football, I ensured that a photo we selected of a Tennessee football game didn't feature me with a Harold Ford Jr. sticker on my Tennessee Vols polo. Back in 2006, the year I traveled around to all twelve SEC football stadiums in the same season to write about why SEC football mattered so much to Southerners, Ford, the Democrat, and Bob Corker, the Republican candidate, had been battling for the state of Tennessee's open Senate seat.

I didn't want to inflict my politics on anyone who might read the book—or my CBS Sports article—because I thought my politics didn't matter at all for a story about SEC football.

In so doing, I was following my Southern grandma's advice. Born in 1912, her first statement upon meeting one of my college girlfriends from New York had been, "By God, she's a YANKEE, CLAY!" She always told me: "You don't talk about politics or religion when you don't have to talk about politics or religion."

I figure all y'all reading this book have made up your own minds already about abortion and guns and gay marriage, and you probably don't need a guy writing about sports to come around and tell you why you're right or wrong about all those opinions.

What I loved about sports, and in particular SEC football, was the degree to which it united all of us in the South, regardless of what our political beliefs, education, religion, or prior backgrounds were. When your team wins or makes a great play, you don't think about the political beliefs, race, ethnicity, or religion of the people you're celebrating with. I'm telling you, if you go below the Mason-Dixon line and talk about SEC football, you better be ready for strong opinions, but you also better be ready for the best damn time you can have at a sports event anywhere in the country.

We don't expect everybody to root for the same college football team we do, but we damn sure expect that you'd better be rooting for an SEC team somewhere in the SEC footprint.

Unless, hell's bells, you're a goddamn Yankee. (Part of me is glad my grandmother died without having to know her only grandson was going to marry a Yankee from Michigan. A Big Ten fan to boot. I think she would have disowned me. Related: I'm also pretty sure I'm the last generation of Southerners who will be able to remember having a grandmother who would tell stories about the things Yankee soldiers did during the War of Northern Aggression. "They took our cows, Clay!" my grandma would exhort when she got really fired up. By "our cows" she meant her grandmother's cows in 1864 in Chattanooga, nearly fifty years before she herself would be born.)

But my grandma was right. Avoid politics and religion if you can. All they do is create division.

And, guess what, for most of my life that's exactly what happened. Sports was our national connective tissue, the place we all went to escape the serious things in life. It didn't matter if you were a neurosurgeon or a janitor; everyone's opinion on sports was equal. Even better, sports was the one place where we could all go to escape the partisan rancor afflicting our country elsewhere.

You might not agree on who the president should be, but we could all agree that Alabama football fans were the dumbest in the entire country. (Unless, that is, you were an Alabama fan and tried to argue, incorrectly, that Auburn or Tennessee fans were dumber.)

Sports united us and the games themselves entertained us. They helped to keep us sane amid an increasingly insane political and global environment.

Until, that is, everything changed and ESPN, the most powerful source in sports media, decided to turn into MSESPN, the nation's most far-left-wing mix of politics and sports, and every other sports media entity followed their lead.

Sports had suddenly become politics by any other name. The puzzle we face now is why this ridiculous thing happened in the first place.

I'm the exact same age as ESPN; we were born in the same year, 1979.

I was born in Nashville, Tennessee, the first child of two parents who worked as state employees, and ESPN was born in Bristol, Connecticut, a sleepy and unsuccessful launch bereft of any grand news coverage.

My formative years as a sports fan echoed with an ESPN soundtrack.

When I was nine years old, my dad finally got cable for the house and my personal relationship with ESPN began. Up until that point my dad had been too cheap to add cable. Of course, my dad was a bit of a Luddite when it came to all technology. When he finally agreed we could get cable, he also insisted that we could not get a remote control because he was convinced not standing up to change the channel would make us too lazy. We had an old gray and white cable box with a rotating dial-up top. A year or so later we bought our second television for the house, this one for the living room, and when my dad found out the television came with a remote control, he asked if the store could keep the remote because he didn't want my sister and me to grow up lazy. The store said they couldn't keep the remote and so the Travis household, reluctantly in my dad's wary eyes, embarked upon our long slouch toward Sodom and Gomorrah.

As a result, I remember standing in front of the old cable box and turning the dial around our old television—our TV was from around 1965—to see all the new channels we had.

I paused on ESPN, channel 11 on the Nashville-area cable box.

"You will love that channel," my dad said, "all they do is talk about sports."

"Just sports?" I asked, excitedly.

"Just sports," my dad said.

And he was right, I was in heaven.

Up until that point we'd watched the local news for sports highlights. Near the end of a half-hour local news show, you'd get a couple minutes of sports, often just a score, almost never an actual highlight of a game. And that was if I was still awake when a game ended, mostly on the weekends.

Otherwise, I'm old enough to remember getting a newspaper and turning to the box scores to see who won the night before. As I scanned all the baseball box scores, my stomach would tremble with nervous anticipation, paper gently shaking in my palms: Had the Cincinnati Reds won or not? Had my favorite player, center fielder Eric Davis, hit a home run or stolen a base?

I even remember waking up early some mornings and riding to the gas station with my dad to get the newspaper so we could find out whether the Tennessee Vols, my favorite team, had won a big basketball game or not. Those days seem totally antiquated now, a vestige of an era that my kids, who start off every morning now by asking Alexa who won games they weren't able to stay up for, will never believe happened.

But ESPN changed my viewing habits with a new show called *SportsCenter.*

Soon the newspaper and local news were cast aside and I had new habits. The first thing I did when I woke up in the morning was put on ESPN, always to see the highlights from games that had ended the night before after I'd gone to bed.

Within six months I pulled my dad aside. "Dad," I said, "I love this channel."

"Me too," my dad said.

ESPN was every sports fan's dream, a channel it was impossible not to love. The channel was so popular that cable companies were terrified not to carry it; the threat of a mass revolt was real. When cable companies balked about the cost of ESPN, the channel always won. Sports fans had to have their games. ESPN knew exactly why it existed, for sports fans to be drenched in the coverage of their favorite sports teams. It filled a niche that fans were desperate to have filled. The sports zealot, at long last, had a home on television.

And it wasn't just that you loved the channel—you came to love the talent on the network too.

When I was ten years old, I met ESPN anchor Chris Berman in a Cincinnati hotel lobby. Berman was coming off the elevator in a hotel that was too expensive for my dad and me to be staying in. My dad believed that any hotel room that cost more than $80 was flagrant extravagance. "We're just going to sleep there, Clay," he would say. As a result, we would go to a couple of baseball games every year in

Cincinnati and stay across the river in Kentucky, where rooms were cheaper. But we would drive into the city and stake out hotel lobbies to try and get baseball players' autographs. That involved sitting in the lobby and hoping to see players emerge from the elevators.

One day ESPN's Chris Berman, already famous for nicknaming baseball players and saying "Back, back, back" on highlights of would-be home runs as the ball took flight across the night skies, came out of an elevator in the downtown Omni.

I rushed up to him, every bit as excited to see him as I would be to see any major league baseball player. Berman was gracious, posing for a photo and signing an autograph.

Meeting Berman, one of my idols at the time, was one of the proudest moments of my youth.

"Dad," I said, looking at his autograph on a Cincinnati Reds game program against the Los Angeles Dodgers, "can you believe it?!"

We were both in awe. Chris Berman, the same person from television, had just graced us with his presence.

So long as ESPN offered something fans couldn't get elsewhere, more sports than anyone else could offer, the rise of the company was assured, and throughout the 1990s and into the early 2000s, ESPN was a sporting King Kong, an unchallenged behemoth running roughshod over all competitors.

ESPN was also studiously apolitical.

I don't remember any analyst being overtly political, even when overtly political events, like the O. J. Simpson murder trial, happened. The network covered sports news; it rarely, if ever, editorialized or debated the news of the day from a political perspective.

Indeed, it's wild to think about now, but can you imagine ESPN's current race-baiting debate shows discussing O. J. Simpson? Good Lord. The network would have insisted Simpson was framed by racist white police officers. And probably given him an ESPY for courage too.

The network's one dalliance with politics was a disaster, taking place in 2003, when ESPN's *Sunday NFL Countdown* made the decision to bring on Rush Limbaugh as a commentator on their pregame show.

Limbaugh, then and now one of the most listened-to radio broadcasters in the country, appeared on the ESPN pregame show and set off a massive controversy when he had the gall to say that the sports media was rooting for Donovan McNabb to succeed because he was a black quarterback. As a result, McNabb, in Limbaugh's opinion, was receiving more credit for his play because the sports media was desirous of seeing a black quarterback be successful.

Limbaugh made the comments on the show alongside two black men, Tom Jackson and Michael Irvin, and two white guys, Steve Young and Chris Berman.

I went back and watched this clip on YouTube, which is posted with a handy transcript reflecting what Limbaugh said along with what the other people on the show said in reaction to him. Most of you have probably forgotten this episode or never even knew it happened.

Here's the transcript:

RUSH: I've been listening to all of you guys, actually, and I think the sum total of what you're all saying is that Donovan McNabb is regressing, is going backwards—

TOM JACKSON: Mmm-hmm. (Nodding)

RUSH:—and my . . . I'm sorry to say this, I don't think he's been that good from the get-go. I think what we've had here is a little social concern. I think the media has been very desirous that a black quarterback do well.

TOM JACKSON: Mmm-hmm. (Nodding)

MICHAEL IRVIN: (Nodding)

RUSH: I think there is a lot of hope invested in McNabb, and he got a lot of credit for the performance of this team that he didn't really deserve. The defense carried this team, I think.

TOM JACKSON: But Rush—But Rush somebody went to those championship games.

RUSH: Oh, they "went."

TOM JACKSON: Somebody made those plays that I saw running down the field, doing it with his legs, doing it with his arm. He has been a very effective quarterback for this football team over the last two or three years—

RUSH: Yeah, but you take . . .

TOM JACKSON:—and they didn't have any more talent then than they do now.

RUSH: Oh yes they did: on defense. On defense, they did.

MICHAEL IRVIN: (Nodding)

TOM JACKSON: (Nodding) Oh, on defense they did. I'm talking on the offense side of the ball.

RUSH: Well, that's what I'm saying. I think he got a lot of credit for the defensive side of the ball winning games for this team.

STEVE YOUNG: But I'll tell you what. I'll say it even more strongly, Tom. When they're winning, nobody makes more plays—

TOM JACKSON: Right.

STEVE YOUNG:—with his arm than Donovan McNabb. That guy is one of the best in the league at making plays, but making plays does not win championships. Running the offense does. So at some point—

TOM JACKSON: Gotta run the offense.

STEVE YOUNG:—I think that Koy Detmer looks like a better option because he'll go in there, drop back, and throw the ball correctly.

CHRIS BERMAN: Isn't it odd that last year with the broken leg I know it was Arizona but the one time he was in the pocket he looked great. Right?

STEVE YOUNG: He had to run that offense.

TOM JACKSON: So Rush, once you make that investment though, once you make that investment in him, that's a done deal.

RUSH: I'm saying it's a good investment. Don't misunderstand. I just don't think he's as good as everybody says he has been.

MICHAEL IRVIN: Rush has a point.

STEVE YOUNG: Well, he [McNabb] certainly hasn't matured.

MICHAEL IRVIN: Rush has a point.

Looking back on this 2003 transcript fifteen years later, I think the most outlandish thing anyone said on the show was Steve Young's suggestion that Koy Detmer—*Koy Detmer!*—might have been a better option for the Eagles at quarterback than Donovan McNabb. McNabb would go on to have a not-quite hall of fame career with the Eagles and later we would work together on air at FS1. I liked him, found him to be an engaging easygoing guy who would have likely been a fun teammate.

The immediate aftermath of Limbaugh's comments was fascinating to see. As you can see in the transcript above, no one aggressively counteracted what Rush said. Having done quite a bit of television in my career, I can tell you it's unlikely Limbaugh's suggestion that McNabb's race might be impacting media coverage of him would have appeared unprompted on the show. Television is like a play, everything is scripted, virtually nothing is left to chance. ESPN knew what Limbaugh was going to say and so did his coworkers.

That's why ESPN initially defended Limbaugh's comments. ESPN vice president Mark Shapiro said: "This is not a politically motivated comment. This is a sports and media argument. Rush was arguing McNabb is essentially overrated and that his success is more in part to the team assembled around him. We brought Rush in for no-holds-barred opinion. Early on, he has delivered."

But that defense began to crumble as the media tempest grew. Eventually, ESPN issued a new official statement: "Although Mr. Limbaugh today stated that his comments had 'no racist intent whatsoever,' we have communicated to Mr. Limbaugh that his comments were insensitive and inappropriate. Throughout his career, he has been consistent in his criticism of the media's coverage of a myriad of issues."

Later that same night, with public attention growing, Limbaugh announced he had decided to resign: "My comments this past Sunday were directed at the media and were not racially motivated. I offered an opinion. This opinion has caused discomfort for the crew, which I regret. I love 'NFL Sunday Countdown' and do not want to be a distraction to the great work done by all who work on it. Therefore, I have decided to resign." Limbaugh's decision to resign came with pressure building from Jesse Jackson as well as then Democratic presidential candidates Wesley Clark, Howard Dean, and Joseph Lieberman, all demanding he be fired, and other political figures threatening boycotts of ABC and ESPN if they didn't fire Limbaugh.

In demanding his firing, Jesse Jackson said, "It is wrong and painful to give someone like Mr. Limbaugh appraisal power over the African American players in the NFL."

Which is an insane statement because, you know, that's literally what every fan does about every player in the NFL, regardless of race. We all appraise who we think is good or bad every single game and every single season. Heck, that's the entire purpose of fantasy football, appraising players and determining who is worthy of being drafted or not. It's also why Limbaugh was hired, to give his opinion on NFL coaches and players.

The next week Limbaugh's exit was discussed by the *Sunday NFL Countdown* crew. Interestingly, Tom Jackson didn't focus on race; he was more insulted that Limbaugh's comments dealt with something other than football: "He was brought here to talk football," Jackson said. "And he broke that trust. Rush told us the social commentary for which he is so well known would not cross over to our show, and instead, he would represent the viewpoint of the intelligent, passionate fan."

Chris Berman, by that time the face of ESPN, claimed he'd never even noticed Donovan McNabb was black. "I'm angry for the hurt it's caused African Americans. I'm angry for the hurt it's caused all people. I've never looked at Donovan McNabb as a black quarterback, ever. Ever."

Looking back on this controversy now, what did Limbaugh say that was so wrong or hurtful? It's indisputably true that much has been made of the lack of black quarterbacks in the NFL. Certainly, throughout my entire life as a sports fan there hasn't been a year that has gone by without articles being written about the plight of the black quarterback. That's true even in 2018 when the report that Heisman trophy–winning quarterback Lamar Jackson was asked to run routes as a wide receiver at the NFL Combine—the same thing that was asked of white Heisman trophy winner Tim Tebow at tight end and white Heisman trophy winner Eric Crouch, who was flipped to safety—was taken as evidence by many of NFL racism and discrimination against black quarterbacks.

As if that weren't enough, in the days before the 2018 NFL Draft a columnist at the New York *Daily News* wrote an opinion piece with this headline: "If Lamar Jackson were white, he'd be the first quarterback drafted." This opinion was written despite the fact that in the twenty-first century alone Michael Vick, JaMarcus Russell, Cam Newton, and Jameis Winston, all black quarterbacks, had been drafted number one overall. Further, since 2001, the year Michael Vick became the first black quarterback to be drafted number one overall, there have been eleven white quarterbacks drafted as the first overall quarterback, six black quarterbacks, and one Native American.

Significantly, there were no public protests or calls for advertiser boycotts of the New York *Daily News* when the newspaper published the opinion piece arguing that Lamar Jackson, who would ultimately be drafted with the final pick of the first round, was being held back because of his race. It was fine to interject Jackson's race into this discussion as evidence of how he was being discriminated against, but woe unto anyone who argued that because of this legacy of discrimination there might be some sportswriters who were rooting for a black quarterback to succeed to prove the racists wrong.

Yet if you've been allowed to say racism is holding back black quarterbacks for decades, including as recently as this year's draft, couldn't you also say that some sportswriters and sports commentators are rooting for black quarterbacks, McNabb and others, to prove they can play quarterback at a high level? Isn't that argument, made by Rush Limbaugh earlier in the twenty-first century, probably still true today? That many football commentators would root for McNabb, and other black quarterbacks, to succeed because they want the stereotype that black men can't play quarterback to be proven wrong once and for all?

As an aside, anyone arguing that race is a dispositive factor in whether someone succeeds or fails at quarterback is an idiot, but that's not what Limbaugh was arguing. He was merely pointing out something that I believe is true, the sports media is mostly made up of liberal sportswriters who, at least in this instance, want to see ugly racism proven wrong and want to see McNabb succeed. Isn't this exactly what happened with Tiger Woods in golf? When Jim Nantz intoned on Tiger's first winning putt at Augusta in 1997, "A win for the ages," wasn't he explicitly making this clear, that he wanted a black golfer to win at a country club with a long history of racism in a sport that was ultimately bedecked with inequality?

Indeed, isn't what Limbaugh argued just the flip side of what liberal sportswriters have argued for decades: that racism is holding back black quarterbacks? And that because these same sportswriters are desirous of seeing a black quarterback succeed, and to combat this legacy of racism, they might be less critical of McNabb than they might be of a white quarterback with similar stats and performance?

Looked at in this context, it's incredible that Limbaugh was forced out at ESPN for saying what he did. He didn't say race was a hindrance to McNabb or that McNabb might not be successful because he was black, he said his race might be a benefit to McNabb in terms of his media coverage and that as a result McNabb wasn't being criticized the same way a white quarterback might be criticized. For that Limbaugh was effectively fired, becoming the first, but not the last, conservative scalp at ESPN.

Donovan McNabb would never win a Super Bowl, but Russell Wilson would, in Super Bowl XLVIII. I was there in person to see Wilson become the first black quarterback to win the Super Bowl since Doug Williams. Interestingly, Wilson's race never became a major story surrounding that Super Bowl, but two years later when Cam Newton took the Carolina Panthers to the Super Bowl to play Peyton Manning's Denver Broncos, Newton's race took center stage in ESPN's coverage.

What did many talking heads at ESPN argue? That many people in America weren't rooting for Newton because he was a black quarterback. Which was, you know, the exact opposite of what Rush Limbaugh had argued in 2003. So it was permissible to argue, by 2018, that people weren't rooting for Cam Newton because he was black or weren't drafting Lamar Jackson because he was black, but Rush Limbaugh was fired in 2003 for saying the media was rooting for McNabb because he was black.

At ESPN, over the space of fifteen years, race could be discussed, but only as a hindrance for a black quarterback, never as a benefit.

Not surprisingly, no one at ESPN was there to argue that many might also be rooting for Cam Newton to win a Super Bowl because of his race. Due to the contretemps surrounding Limbaugh, the lesson ESPN had learned was this: you don't provoke national outrage by arguing far-left-wing sports perspectives. It's only when you argue anything moderate or center right that the outrage police swoop in and demand retribution. Left-wing opinions on sports were acceptable, conservative and moderate opinions on sports were unacceptable.

But that would be in the future, when ESPN had a new president.

Back in 2003, Rush Limbaugh's foray into sports media editorializing, even if it didn't become explicitly political, didn't make then ESPN president George Bodenheimer happy. "We believe he took the appropriate action [by resigning] to resolve this matter expeditiously," Bodenheimer said.

It was 2003 and Bodenheimer, who was still building ESPN's business, didn't want to get bogged down in politics because ESPN's business was thriving and growing rapidly. Why inject politics into sports and alienate viewers in any way? It was far smarter and more lucrative to just stick to sports and make billions.

Which is exactly what ESPN was doing, even if most viewers didn't realize it. The ESPN business was surging and had been for several decades. ESPN, in fact, was well on its way to becoming the most lucrative media business in world history.

There was no reason to mix sports and politics when sports alone was such a good business.

I didn't know it growing up as a fan of the network, but ESPN wasn't just the top cable sports network in the world. It was also a hell of a business.

Billions of dollars were pouring into ESPN's corporate coffers thanks to acolytes like my dad and me. The NFL, Major League Baseball, the NHL, the NBA, the major college leagues, all of them needed ESPN to get their product distributed to the sports-starved masses.

From its beginning as a tiny cable station in the remote hinterlands of Bristol, Connecticut, ESPN expanded and rose in power, gobbling up millions of subscribers and billions of dollars along the way.

By the time I entered college in 1997, ESPN was a cultural leviathan. We all dreamed at George Washington University that our men's basketball team would be on ESPN or ESPN2. On those rare occasions when the home games were televised nationally on the cable networks, something interesting happened: the crowds were the biggest of the season.

When ESPN came to town, it was an event, a sign your team mattered in the larger sports stratosphere.

We made signs and recorded the games in our dorm rooms, slowed them down on replay to scan for ourselves in the crowd. "There we were on TV!" Our parents would call from home and say the same thing: "We saw you on TV!"

Being on ESPN was a sign you and your team had made it, but technology was also evolving rapidly.

During my first college semester, back in 1997, I realized there was this thing called the Internet and it was a sports fan's dream. I was homesick that first year in college, and I could follow my favorite local teams by getting on the Internet and reading the latest news about them.

Before long I was getting most of my news and scores online.

I remember occasionally seeing the sportswriters I'd read online in George Washington's racquetball court that would be disguised as a press room. I'd think, "Oh my God, that's Andy Katz from ESPN.com!" Or, and this one is even funnier now because he's become a good friend, "That's Dan Wetzel from SportsLine.com!"

It wasn't as if these guys were famous—their readership was probably tiny because the Internet audience at that point in time was tiny too—but to me they were rock stars.

God forbid if I'd ever seen Tony Kornheiser or Mike Wilbon, the top sports columnists at the *Washington Post* in the late 1990s—I would have lost my mind.

Significantly the sports world was rapidly changing thanks to the proliferation of the Internet and the rapid democratization of sports rights. And sports information, which had been ESPN's primary reason for existence, was becoming democratized too. Suddenly we were awash in all the sports news we could possibly consume. Even if we hadn't all realized it yet, ESPN's informational monopoly was dying.

I still remember the first time a friend of mine had sports scores on his cell phone. We were sitting at a college basketball tournament and my friend pulled out his new cell phone. "Guys," he said, "I can get sports scores on this."

We all gathered around him like he'd just discovered fire.

"Look," I said, pointing to the top twenty-five scores being flashed on the monitor in the arena, "his scores are more updated than the arena's scores!"

Suddenly the phones we'd all been using to call each other had very little to do with making actual phone calls. Shortly thereafter I had my own phone, and I would never again do something I'd spent decades doing—watching the scores scroll along the bottom of the ESPN ticker to see who'd won a game.

Before long it wasn't just scores on our phones: we had access to everything in the palm of our hand that we'd previously needed televisions, newspapers, and computers to access. With everyone able to watch highlights on their phones the moment they happened, why did ESPN's peripheral programming around the actual games need to exist? Where once sports highlights had been the reason ESPN existed, now those same highlights were available everywhere. Suddenly, just like with MTV when music videos went to YouTube for free, sports highlights weren't enough for ESPN.

If sports highlights weren't compelling and unique original content any longer, then ESPN had no business reason to exist; it was just a middleman, bringing games to the masses. And what happens to middlemen in most businesses? They get eliminated.

Before I explain why ESPN's business model was so threatened and how that led to a rapid politicization of their content, let's first discuss what ESPN's business model actually looked like during all those years when it was growing from zero subscribers in 1979 to 100 million subscribers in 2011.

And to do that, let me tell you a story about NBA point guard Mike Conley.

2

ESPN and Mike Conley

When the 2016 NBA season began, four players in the history of pro basketball had made $30 million a year: Michael Jordan, Kobe Bryant, LeBron James, and Memphis Grizzlies point guard Mike Conley.

That is, three of the ten greatest players in the history of the game had made $30 million a year, and a solid, if not spectacular, six-foot-one, 175-pound point guard entering his ninth NBA season also made $30 million a year. Conley, who joined the NBA at the age of nineteen after his freshman year at Ohio State, was drafted fourth overall and during his professional career had averaged 13 points, 5.5 assists, and 2.8 rebounds a game. He had never made an NBA All-Star team in his nine seasons.

That leaves us with a fascinating question: How did a relatively average player like Mike Conley end up signing a five-year, $154 million contract? A contract that paid him similarly to the top players to ever play the game?

I'll tell you. He hit free agency at the perfect time, just as the NBA was flush with cash from a television contract paying the league $2.66 billion a year: $1.47 billion from ESPN and $1.19 billion from Turner Sports. The TV contract, a staggering sum of money committed just as the cord-cutting era began to assault the cable and satellite industries, boggled the sports industry's minds. The NBA had received triple—triple!—its prior television deal.

Overnight, every player, even a guy like Mike Conley, was swimming in cash.

Okay, you might be thinking, but surely ESPN and Turner Sports were paying a rational sum of money for the NBA's television package, right?

You'd be wrong.

Before we explain why that's the case, let's first dive into the economics behind twenty-first-century sports on television.

ESPN is the most lucrative business in the history of media, valued at $50 billion as recently as 2014 by *Forbes* magazine.

How did ESPN attain that level of valuation? Well, ESPN owes its money to a dual-revenue-stream business structure; it makes 75 percent of its money from cable and satellite subscriber fees and 25 percent of its money from advertising.

It surprises many people to learn that their cable and satellite bills are a collection of bundled charges for individual channels. That is, while you may have two hundred stations and not realize it because your bill isn't itemized, each cable or satellite channel is being paid a carriage fee by a cable or satellite company. Effectively you are paying for every cable channel you receive in your bundled package even if most viewers don't realize it. Now, most of these charges are relatively small—AMC costs viewers roughly a quarter a month, for instance. However, a handful of channels, those featuring sports, are quite expensive.

ESPN is far more expensive than any other channel on cable.

In fact, here are the ten most expensive channels per month in cable packages according to a summer of 2018 analysis from Kagan, a media research group within S&P Global Market Intelligence.

1. **ESPN, $8.14**
2. **TNT, $2.28**
3. Disney Channel, $1.58
4. **NFL Network, $1.58**
5. Fox News, $1.57
6. **USA Network, $1.24**
7. **TBS, $1.10**

8. ESPN2, $1.02

9. CNN, $0.86

10. SEC Network, $0.78

The seven networks highlighted above each feature major sports, four of them full time. (The USA Network features the WWE.) FS1 and the Big Ten Network are the thirteenth and fifteenth most expensive cable channels as well, both of which feature sports full time.

Do the math here and you learn an interesting fact—every year, ESPN receives nearly $100 from every single cable and satellite subscriber in the country. That's whether you watch the channel or not. So you, who are presently reading this book and probably a sports fan, are paying nearly $100 a year for ESPN and so, interestingly, are your aunt Gladys and your uncle Hugh, neither of whom have watched sports all year.

That's where 75 percent of ESPN's revenue comes from. Effectively, ESPN receives close to the same amount of subscription money as Netflix and HBO each month, only unlike with Netflix or HBO, most cable and satellite subscribers have no idea what they pay for ESPN and, significantly, no one is electing to sign up and pay ESPN this amount of money.

Add on advertiser revenue and ESPN also pockets another several billion a year.

What does ESPN do with all this money? It buys sports rights, which in turn—it hopes—ensures that people will keep watching ESPN and as a result that their carriage fees will remain through the roof and advertisers will keep ponying up cash.

Hence the NBA deal.

As part of the NBA's collective bargaining agreement, players and owners split revenue, and that windfall of TV money was then redistributed to the players.

That's how Mike Conley becomes a $30 million man, just like Michael Jordan, Kobe Bryant, and LeBron James before him.

So everything's great; money's pouring in from two sources, and it seems that this sports gravy train should continue for years ahead, right? However, as noted ESPN mascot-head-wearer Lee Corso would say, "Not so fast, my friend." ESPN makes its money by renting the content that others produce—sports games—and distributing them to the masses. This makes ESPN the sports equivalent of Blockbuster Video. And just like Blockbuster Video, it is slated for economic collapse and obsolescence, which I'll explain later in the book. For now, all you need to know is that Mike Conley's contract wasn't supported by any legitimate economic reality. It was the product of a sports bubble, one fueled by ESPN's broken business model.

Of course, ESPN, the NBA, and others may argue that Conley's contract, as a result of the NBA's huge new television deal, is simply a function of market realities. That ignores the fact that sometimes markets break and, for a time, can behave irrationally. We saw it with NASDAQ stocks during the tech-stock boom in the early 2000s and in the recent subprime housing collapse that nearly torpedoed the entire global economy. We saw it with tulips in Holland in the seventeenth century (really, read up on this if you haven't before), and we'll see it again and again throughout human history. If anything, social media may make bubbles more likely today than in past years. After all, bubbles are the product of frenzy, excitement, and the masses losing their heads. If that doesn't perfectly describe our present era on social media, what does?

Indeed, the story of Mike Conley's contract, in many ways, epitomizes the sports industry's own bubble. In Michael Lewis's book *The Big Short*, about the collapse of the subprime mortgage industry and the near collapse of the American economy, the principals in that book, who are soon to make billions betting against the American housing market, experience a sudden realization at a strip club in Florida when a stripper confesses to having five houses and a condo. Don't worry, she tells the investors; she's only paying interest.

When I saw Conley's contract and realized it made him among the four highest-paid players in the history of the NBA, it set off the same kind of alarm bells for me as the stripper had for the investors in Lewis's book. I had to examine the underlying economics of his salary to understand how Conley's salary could possibly be justified.

What I found was staggering.

ESPN was a bubble poised to burst.

There was no rational way to justify what ESPN was paying the NBA. None at all.

Remember, it's not ESPN paying the NBA for its games, it's us, the cable and satellite subscribers. ESPN and TNT are just taking our money and passing it along to the NBA. Moreover, the vast majority of cable and satellite subscribers are paying for the NBA, but they'll never watch a single NBA game.

The data is staggering when you unpack the economic realities underpinning this deal. To pay for the new NBA rights deal, every single cable and satellite subscriber—and there are about 86 million of us with ESPN in 2018—chips in roughly $3.10 a month or $37.20 a year. (Since the NBA only plays eight months a year, you're actually paying $4.65 a month for the eight-month season. Remember, the NBA Finals are on "free" TV. To reach this number I'm simply dividing the NBA's new TV contract by the number of cable and satellite subscribers.)

Given that every single cable and satellite subscriber is paying $37.20 a year for the NBA, how many people watch the most popular of these games? The Western Conference Finals on TNT in 2016 were a scintillating seven-game series that saw the Golden State Warriors surge back from a 3–1 series deficit to beat the Oklahoma City Thunder. It was the highest-rated playoff series in TNT history, and an average of 9.9 million people watched each game. The 2018 Western Conference Finals also went seven games and featured the Golden State Warriors triumphing over the Houston Rockets. That series averaged just over 10 million viewers per game.

Which sounds like a lot.

But another way of looking at that would be by saying 76 million cable and satellite households didn't watch this series. That is, nearly 90 percent of cable and satellite subscribers with TNT didn't care to watch two of the best Western Conference Finals in NBA history. That's pretty common; sports fans are a vocal, and lucrative, minority of the overall American population.

And that's the Western Conference Finals, which produced a good product. ESPN broadcast the much less exciting Eastern Conference Finals in 2016 and ratings were dismal. An average of just 5.5 million people tuned in for the Cleveland Cavaliers' closing out of the Toronto Raptors. That means 79 million households, or 92 percent of all cable households, didn't watch the highest-rated NBA series on ESPN that year. (The NBA Finals are on ABC, which everyone gets for free. The NBA Finals ratings in 2016 were outstanding, but, again, it's on broadcast television, which doesn't require a cable or satellite subscription to watch.) The 2018 Eastern Conference Finals between the Cleveland Cavaliers and the Boston Celtics also went seven games, but only 9 million viewers a game tuned in for this series. Even with the best possible matchup going the maximum number of games, not that many people watched.

Putting those NBA viewership numbers into context, more people watched the NFL Draft and the Pro Bowl than watched an average NBA Eastern or Western Conference Finals game on TNT or ESPN.

The cable bundle's a great deal for us sports fans because the 90 percent of people who don't watch the Eastern or Western Conference Finals are subsidizing the cost of our sports on cable. I love watching the NBA; I'm happy I only have to pay $37.20 a year to do it.

Would I be so happy to be paying that $37.20 a year for the NBA if I was like the vast majority of Americans and never watched the league?

I doubt it.

This means nearly all of Mike Conley's salary is being paid by people who will never watch him play basketball.

It also means ESPN has created the biggest bubble in the history of media. If only those of us who watched had to pay for these games, we'd be paying roughly $400 a year.

What does economics teach us again and again about bubbles? Eventually, they pop. And ESPN's bubble has popped, only most haven't realized it yet.

ESPN executives have, however, seen the math, and they know the reckoning is coming, that the bubble has popped. What do I mean by "seen the math"? Let me explain.

In 2012 something alarming began to happen at ESPN: after thirty-two years of steadily increasing subscriber numbers, ESPN began to lose subscribers.

At first, the decline was small, barely noticeable. After all, a bit of fluctuation was perfectly normal, right?

Two thousand twelve was also an important year for ESPN because challenges loomed on the horizon for the network. After years of owning the cable business by themselves, Fox, NBC, and CBS were finally going to get into the cable sports business too.

Over the next several years all three media companies would launch their own cable sports challengers for ESPN.

What did ESPN do to combat these challengers? It doubled down on sports rights, arguing that the best possible way to protect its advantage on cable was to ensure it had the rights to the best possible games.

As a result, rights fees for sports on television skyrocketed, and soon ESPN had constructed a powerful moat surrounding its cable business castle.

Those yearly rights fees added up in a hurry over the next several years: $2 billion to the NFL for *Monday Night Football* and one playoff game, $1.47 billion for the NBA, $700 million to Major League Baseball, $608 million for the College Football Playoff, $225 million to the ACC, $190 million to the Big Ten, $120 million a year to the Big 12, $125 million a year to the Pac-12, and hundreds of millions more to the SEC.

Consider this: it wasn't just the NBA that ESPN had overpaid for, the network's NFL *Monday Night Football* package and a single wild-card playoff game cost ESPN $2 billion a year.

Two billion a year!

That means ESPN was paying over $100 million per *Monday Night Football* game by 2017. That also means the average cable and satellite consumer was paying $23.26 a year just for *Monday Night Football* on ESPN in 2017. Eighty-five percent of cable and satellite subscribers never watch the weekly *MNF* game either. Sound familiar? It's happening to every sports property ESPN owns.

What's worse than overpaying? Overpaying and not being able to afford to overpay again. By the late fall of 2017, ESPN was signaling to Wall Street that it was unlikely to be able to afford the NFL when its deal expired in 2021. Yep, the "Worldwide Leader in Sports" could no longer afford the most popular sport in the country.

By 2017, ESPN was in serious trouble, paying $7.3 billion a year in rights fees, more than any media company in America was paying for content. Even more alarming, unlike the other companies paying billions in rights fees like Netflix or Amazon, ESPN didn't own any of its content. It was just renting from the leagues.

If the NFL ever took *Monday Night Football* back, unlike Netflix, which would own *Stranger Things* or *House of Cards* forever, ESPN would be left with nothing at all to show for the billions in dollars in costs it had turned over to the NFL. The NFL even retained the rights to ESPN's broadcasts in future years to air on its own network.

In an era when all that mattered was owning original content, ESPN produced nothing of any lasting value that it retained at all save for the *30 for 30* documentary series.

But with 100 million subscribers in 2011 and billions in sports fees, ESPN had made its bet: outspend the competition for the best sports rights and nothing could go wrong, right?

Wrong.

Unfortunately for ESPN the subscriber decline began to accelerate, and when the subscriber losses hit 5 million, alarm bells went off inside ESPN headquarters in Bristol.

Why were so many ESPN subscribers disappearing? What did that mean for the future of the company? ESPN, which had looked so strong in 2011, suddenly started to look much weaker by 2016. Indeed, in a *Wall Street Journal* article in the spring of 2018 ESPN acknowledged it had gotten the impact of cord-cutting completely wrong. Back in 2014, ESPN's research department argued that cord-cutting was unlikely to become an issue for the company. The research department was horridly wrong. As a result, ESPN continued to wildly overpay for sports rights based on inaccurate business forecasts. Later, ESPN executives would have a name for those who had gotten things so wrong. "They were flat-earthers," said one former executive to the *Wall Street Journal*.

Getting the massive decline in subscriber numbers was particularly troubling because the only asset ESPN had was its distribution ability. All the leagues knew that ESPN could reach their audiences better than they could. But even that was changing rapidly. Leagues were realizing they could easily find their target audiences online on Facebook or Twitter. The highlight died. Conversations moved to Twitter. ESPN still owned all the sports rights, but it needed tonnage. It needed to fill all the time slots in the day that used to be dominated by *SportsCenter*, and it needed to make money off those shows too.

With billions guaranteed for sports rights fees in the years ahead and a declining subscriber base, ESPN suddenly faced a scary reality. Its business model was under attack on two fronts. The cost of the sports it rented and put on the air was surging just as its subscriber revenue was collapsing.

ESPN's goal had been to create an impenetrable moat surrounding its castle, but now the moat was starting to flood the castle just as the castle suddenly realized its powerful foundation was also built on quicksand.

By the fall of 2017 and the spring of 2018, according to Nielsen cable

and satellite channel estimates, ESPN was losing over 15,000 subscribers a day due to cord-cutting, the death of older subscribers, and,
probably, password sharing. Many subscribers were also turned off by
the political nature of ESPN's programming and were abandoning it
in droves as well. But we'll get to that in a moment.

In 2011, at the height of its business, ESPN had 100 million subscribers. Since then they'd lost 14 million subscribers, an average of
roughly 2 million lost subscribers a year, with the numbers increasing
in recent years.

In fact, if ESPN's subscriber defections continued at the same rate
as from 2011 to spring 2018, the network, which finished 2017 with
roughly 86 million subscribers, could begin losing money within four
years.

Here's what those subscriber numbers would look like if they continued at the present rate of decline:

> 2018: 83 million subscribers
> 2019: 80 million subscribers
> 2020: 77 million subscribers
> 2021: 74 million subscribers

Each of these lost subscribers represented somewhere in the neighborhood of $110 a year in lost revenue for the company. When ESPN lost
a subscriber—remember, it typically lost a subscriber not just on ESPN,
but also ESPN2, ESPNU, ESPNews, and ESPN Classic as well—that
lost revenue was unlikely to return, and it added up over the years.

ESPN was also unable to offer its own direct-to-consumer streaming option because of the cable and satellite carriage deals it had signed.
Unlike, say, HBO, which could offer a direct-to-consumer option for
cord-cutters, ESPN was contractually prohibited from offering ESPN
directly to consumers. (ESPN+, a direct-to-consumer streaming option,
launched in April 2018, but it only featured the programming not good
enough to put on television.) In other words, you couldn't subscribe to

ESPN directly and get the cable network programming without a cable or satellite subscription.

Let's pretend you're an ESPN executive. You see your subscriber numbers plummeting—ESPN was losing over 15,000 subscribers a day by the fall of 2017 and over 16,000 a day in April of 2018—at the same time your costs for that programming are skyrocketing. What do you do? Especially when those lost subscribers are costing ESPN $1.83 million a day in future subscriber revenue as of April of 2018. Add up all those 16,000-plus lost subscribers in April alone and ESPN lost $55 million in future revenue in one month in the spring of 2018.

That's a two-fronted war that's slowly encircling your business.

You better find a new way to win that war.

Except your ratings are also plummeting for your original programming as well. This means you're faced with an intractable problem—your business is dying and the entire purpose of your business for decades, sports highlights, are now available everywhere. Just as MTV lost relevance when YouTube became the de facto host for music videos, social media now distributes every sports highlight instantaneously.

Whereas in the past someone like me who grew up watching ESPN would put on *SportsCenter* in the morning before school to find out who actually won a game and see the highlights of that contest, now social media–savvy fans are receiving the highlights sent directly to their phones the moment they happen. They don't even need to seek them out; the highlights are coming straight to their devices as notifications. And the youngest generation of all? My kids, as I mentioned earlier, wake up in the morning and ask Alexa who won the games.

Seriously, Alexa!

What do you do if the entire premise of why your business exists, to serve sports fans highlights and breaking news, suddenly disappears?

You desperately seek relevance in the modern social media age. What does that relevance look like today? It's sports opinions, or the hot-take culture. Making people care about your sports opinions could increase ratings and help to save your business if, as seems likely, eventually the teams and sports leagues will have direct relationships with the sports fan rather than use ESPN as a middleman. Remember, at the end of the day ESPN is renting the games. With the highlights now prevalent everywhere online, the only thing they own that rates at all on a daily basis is their sports opinion shows. That's where they can make up the money they are losing elsewhere.

However, you face another problem—sports opinions don't move the needle on social media either, because social media is filled with sports opinions. It's incredibly hard to have an original sports opinion in 2018 on social media that makes people take note.

After all, how many times can you debate Michael Jordan versus LeBron James? (The answer is every day if you're Skip Bayless, who has now debated Michael Jordan versus LeBron James, always finding James lacking, for 14,643 consecutive days.)

Okay, what about breaking news, you might think?

Another brick wall.

The news cycle moves so rapidly that the minute sports news breaks it's everywhere. Most fans don't even realize who broke the news. If sports news has limited value and sports opinions about that sports news are also commodified in a world awash in sports opinion, what do you have left to move the ratings needle and try to save your business?

You have sports opinions mixed with politics.

And that's what ESPN aggressively moved into as its business collapsed.

Sports opinions mixed with politics would be their savior, their raison d'être.

Sports opinions mixed with politics seems sexy because it plays well on social media. Unfortunately for ESPN, it's ultimately self-defeating because you may win a daily battle but you're losing the overall war. You're alienating a large percentage of your audience that just wants sports. Hell, most of us come to sports to escape the political obsession currently infecting every aspect of American life.

Faced with a business crisis, ESPN looked to Twitter and Facebook to save it and saw that sports mixed with politics was an untapped terrain that could offer ratings promise. Whereas in years past sports networks had treated athlete political opinions like Hollywood treats actor and actress opinions, as distractions unworthy of serious contemplation, ESPN suddenly decided to treat every athlete as if they were Muhammad Ali opposing the Vietnam War.

Wedding sports and politics was ESPN's desperate sporting gambit, a Hail Mary designed to increase ratings and save a collapsing business.

Best of all, it offered something ESPN didn't have—relevance.

ESPN decided that combining sports and politics would make it matter in the modern era, but ESPN also realized something else: wedding sports and politics from a conservative perspective might alienate the advertisers it relied upon. This is where the Rush Limbaugh example comes in. No advertiser has ever pulled out of a sports show because that show was too liberal, only if that show was too conservative.

The network made the decision not just to embrace sports and politics, they decided to marry sports to left-wing politics.

A big part of this decision came via John Skipper, the president who followed George Bodenheimer. Skipper was a far-left-wing liberal, and his values immediately rolled throughout the company. He promoted talent who advocated far-left-wing political positions and obsessively valued diversity over ratings. In fact, and this is a remarkable detail, before he "resigned for substance abuse issues" over an extortion claim relating to his use of cocaine, Skipper replaced ratings bonuses for ESPN management with diversity bonuses instead.

ESPN management was now rewarded not by serving viewers, but by ensuring diversity was promoted over ratings success. This is, put plainly, a horrible way to run a business, but the tone had been set. Even if you weren't a far-left liberal, you learned that the best way to keep your job was to embrace far-left-wing politics.

Voilà, in the space of a few years' time ESPN tossed aside decades of apolitical coverage and became MSESPN, the progressive voice in sports and politics—lean forward and catch a football.

Initially, it worked.

Mentions of ESPN surged on social media as the network embraced the social justice warriordom of Michael Sam, Caitlyn Jenner, and Colin Kaepernick. Executives added more steam to the MSESPN connection, even—and this is flat-out amazing—allowing *SportsCenter*'s presenting sponsorship on many nights to be sold to MSNBC!

As all this happened, my sports audience began to revolt. I'd open Twitter, and my readers and listeners and viewers would have attached a new segment, a new clip; one left-wing political absurdity after another continued to pile up until a full-scale fan rebellion began.

Why, my fans asked, does ESPN feel the need to lecture me about progressive politics when I just want to watch sports?

So much for just being able to come home, pop open a beer, and escape the country's problems. Now, instead of coming home from work and finding out the latest news on the NFC West and seeing a breakdown of the latest league highlights, which many fans still wanted, you got a panel debate on how heroic Colin Kaepernick was for taking a knee during the national anthem.

Facing the collapse of its subscription business and with sports rights fees still surging at the exact moment that sports highlights—the core reason for ESPN's peripheral programming surrounding the games—became available for free everywhere, ESPN panicked and went fully political and turned sports into politics by any other name. Out were sports highlights, in was constant coverage of athletes' political opinions and a perpetual sports culture war.

It wasn't just praising the athletes either; it was elevating the talent that most fervently connected left-wing politics and sports. Jemele Hill, Max Kellerman, Sarah Spain, Bomani Jones, Michelle Beadle, Pablo Torre—the more left-wing your politics, the more you got on television.

Every single one of these ESPN employees received their own television show. And as a result, lines between reporting and opinion vanished. Everyone at ESPN rushed to become as far-left-wing as possible to serve the new, clear business imperative—give me MSESPN, and I'll give you contract extensions, raises, and TV shows.

This sudden far-left-wing, liberal lean received rave reviews in the sports media, which was insanely left-wing itself, much more so than even the regularly attacked left-wing media in politics and news. In 2017, The Big Lead, a popular sports website, surveyed media members to find out how they'd voted in the 2016 election between Donald Trump and Hillary Clinton.

While the nation was nearly evenly divided, the sports media was not.

According to an anonymous survey of prominent sports media members on that site, 80.4 percent voted for Hillary Clinton, 9.8 percent didn't vote, 5.9 percent voted for a third party, and just 3.9 percent voted for Donald Trump. That means 96.1 percent of the sports media didn't vote for Donald Trump.

That's staggering when you consider that Trump received nearly half of the overall vote in the country and won thirty states in the electoral college.

It wasn't just that the sports media didn't like Donald Trump. Only 6 percent of the respondents in this survey even identified as Republicans; fully 94 percent of all sports media surveyed by The Big Lead weren't willing to even consider voting for a Republican.

I probably don't need to remind you, but Donald Trump actually won the election, opening a huge chasm between who sports fans vote for—sports fans are even more likely to vote Republican than the American public in general—and who the media who report and talk about sports support. That left-wing solidarity among sports media members leads to one of the scariest things in modern American life, groupthink.

The political groupthink was staggering. ESPN employees gave Hillary Clinton 270 times more money than they gave Donald Trump in the 2016 election. Hillary Clinton received financial support from 217 different employees, Donald Trump received financial support from 2, totaling $102. Putting those numbers in context, the American news media, which is routinely decried for its liberal bias, gave 27 times the money to Hillary Clinton that it gave to Donald Trump. ESPN gave 270 times as much to Hillary Clinton as to Donald Trump. Based on these public donation figures, ESPN is 10 times as biased toward the left as the news media in general.

Wow.

According to a study by Deep Root Analytics, the sports audience noticed this leftward turn, with Republican voters abandoning ESPN en masse from 2015 to 2016. Indeed, it was the Republican voters leaving the network that contributed to a tremendous ratings decline in ESPN's original programming.

Now despite the numbers cited above, it's not that no one in sports media votes Republican either; it's that those who do are terrified to admit it publicly for fear of losing their jobs. Don't worry guys and gals, I'm not going to out anyone working at ESPN who votes Republican. However, many of the most prominent sports people you see on TV have privately sought me out to say thanks for embracing a marketplace of ideas and talking about the far-left-wing environment at ESPN and in sports media in general.

Think about this for a moment: hundreds of ESPN employees publicly supported Hillary Clinton and lamented her loss in election night social media posts. Many of them, including top ESPN executives on the business side, sent tweets suggesting the world was coming to an end. Indeed, the number-two man at ESPN right now, Connor Schell, publicly retweeted that Donald Trump was elected because "Trump supporters openly voted for the oppression of LGBT's, minorities' and women's rights." In subsequent tweets, Schell said the president should be taunted over losing the popular vote, encouraged people to share pictures from the women's march and compare them with the inauguration crowd to ridicule the president, tweeted encouragement to everyone to get involved in politics to combat Trump, and praised San Antonio Spurs coach Gregg Popovich for attacking Trump.

Now certainly Schell is entitled to his own political opinions, but if you were working at ESPN and were a Republican or a Trump supporter, how comfortable would you be sharing those opinions if the man who decided whether you had a job or not was publicly on the record as hating Donald Trump? That's especially the case when your company was in the process of laying off hundreds of employees and when the directive from Disney CEO Bob Iger to then ESPN president John Skipper was favoring far-left-wing politics. (Iger made this point explicitly clear in a spring of 2018 *Vogue* magazine profile about his decision to run ESPN in a progressive, left-wing manner. Why would he do this? Iger told *Vogue* he was preparing to run against Donald Trump as a Democratic candidate for president before a purchase of 21st Century Fox assets made that impossible.) Do you really want to risk your job by coming out against the candidates favored by your bosses?

As a result, not one single ESPN employee publicly celebrated Donald Trump's election or announced he or she had voted for him.

Not one!

ESPN's embrace of far-left-wing politics had so chilled political discourse in sports media that even people making millions of dollars a year to appear on your televisions were afraid to admit they'd voted for Trump. Because they feared losing their jobs if they did so.

Why did they have this fear?

Because hundreds of employees were being laid off at ESPN in 2016 and 2017 and also because of what happened to Curt Schilling, a conservative former ESPN baseball analyst, in the spring of 2016.

Before we get to the firing of Curt Schilling, let's first examine the question "When did ESPN's left-wing bias first reveal itself and alter the trajectory of the company's history?" I believe it started with the first openly gay football player in the NFL, Michael Sam.

3

Dragging the Sports Media Left

On May 10, 2014, ESPN televised the final day of the NFL Draft.

As part of their coverage, they placed a camera in the residence where Michael Sam, a defensive end from the University of Missouri, who had recently announced he was gay, waited to see whether or not he would become the first openly gay player drafted by an NFL team.

For several weeks ESPN had obsessively chronicled the story and now, with live cameras following his every move, Sam stood talking on his cell phone in a salmon-colored shirt with his boyfriend alongside him.

Watching live at home, I texted a friend. "Watch," I said, "this is totally staged. ESPN is going to show Michael Sam kissing his boyfriend when he's drafted."

"You're probably right," my buddy texted back.

It was plain as day, ESPN wanted the controversy, they wanted the shot, they wanted Michael Sam's homosexuality to be inescapable to all their viewers.

On the television screen ESPN played up the drama: "There you see him on the phone, and there you see the raw emotion," an ESPN announcer intoned from Radio City Music Hall in New York City. Sam leaned over, overcome with emotion and his boyfriend cradled him, gripping his hand tightly. Upon hanging up the phone, Sam embraced his boyfriend and as the cameras rolled Sam kissed his boyfriend on the lips, just as I'd predicted he would.

Almost immediately I noticed something interesting on Twitter, left-wing sports opinionists celebrated the kiss and then went looking for someone to say something "inappropriate" about ESPN televising the kiss. In other words, it wasn't just that sports media on social media embraced Sam; it was that they wanted to find someone who didn't embrace Sam so they could rain down their derision upon that person.

An angry sports media mob was out circulating and woe unto anyone who didn't celebrate Sam's moment. This had been the real point all along. Not the kiss, but covering the supposed "backlash."

It didn't take long for an athlete to send out a tweet that the left-wing sports media found unacceptable.

Miami Dolphins defensive back Don Jones tweeted "OMG" and "Horrible," two tweets that rapidly went viral. Jones didn't want to see two men kiss on the sports network he was watching. Many viewers felt the same way as Jones, but they weren't employed in the NFL, and they weren't public figures.

It didn't matter how many NFL players said the "right" thing, the sports media pounced on Jones, turning his two tweets into a major news story.

This would become an all-too-common template: an event occurs, most people respond one way to the event, but one or two people don't respond that way. Then those one or two people's responses, representing a tiny minority of the overall responses, become major news stories.

Reprisal for Jones's nonwork-related commentary on his personal Twitter account was swift.

Jones was banned from Miami Dolphins team activities and suspended from playing football until he underwent sensitivity training. Almost immediately, he began issuing abject apologies.

"I want to apologize to Michael Sam for the inappropriate comments that I made last night on social media," Jones said in a statement. "I take full responsibility for them, and I regret that these tweets took away from his draft moment. I remember last year when I was drafted in the seventh round and all of the emotions and happiness I felt when I received the call that gave me an opportunity to play for an NFL team and I wish him all the best in his NFL career."

Jones also apologized to the Dolphins and their fans: "I sincerely apologize to Mr. Ross, my teammates, coaches, staff and fans for these tweets. I am committed to represent the values of the Miami Dolphins organization and appreciate the opportunity I have been given to do so going forward."

Not content with this apology, the Dolphins also issued an official statement from head coach Joe Philbin: "We were disappointed to read Don's tweets during the NFL Draft. They were inappropriate and unacceptable, and we regret the negative impact these comments had on such an important weekend for the NFL. We met with Don today about respect, discrimination and judgment. These comments are not consistent with the values and standards of our program."

Now, many of you reading this may agree with Jones's apology and the Dolphins actions, but I'm interested in pointing out something more intriguing: Why is this a story at all? There are roughly 1,700 NFL players. Jones isn't remotely famous. In fact, I bet that most of you have never heard of him before.

While you, as I do, may feel that gay people deserve the right to be married and in loving relationships like anyone else, was Jones's Twitter commentary really that egregious in the grand scheme of things? Is a relatively anonymous NFL player writing "OMG" and "Horrible," when two gay people kiss on a sports broadcast, worthy of a team suspension and national news stories everywhere? I would feel differently if Sam had been drafted by the Dolphins and Sam was set to become Jones's teammate, but that wasn't the case here. Indeed, Sam wasn't even drafted by the same conference or division, meaning the two players weren't even likely to compete against each other.

This represented one of the first times I noticed a substantial trend: sports media members using news stories to advance their own political beliefs. Increasingly, the sports media became hawkish in searching out "appropriate" and "inappropriate" personal beliefs on social media and then turning those reactions into stories.

The trend became commonplace in sports media: find someone who disagrees with something you believe politically and shame them for that belief by turning their opinion into a news story. Again, why is an otherwise anonymous Miami Dolphins player's reaction to Michael Sam on Twitter legitimate news? Furthermore, is it unacceptable for an NFL player to believe that homosexuality is a sin or for an NFL player not to want to see two men kissing when he's watching a sports event on television?

Based on the standard the Dolphins laid out, that seems to be the case.

If so, think about how absurd this standard is, you can be convicted of felonies and go to prison for those felonies and remain eligible to play in the NFL, but if you tweet that you don't like seeing two men kiss on television, you can't play in the NFL? That's insanity.

Why in the world do NFL teams and the sports media care what an individual player thinks about gay marriage or two men kissing on a sports broadcast? Simple, because they've all bought into the idea that sports and politics are indistinguishable.

Why couldn't the Dolphins have just released this statement: "We disagree with the opinions expressed by one of our players on his private Twitter account in his private life, but we aren't in the business of punishing opinions we disagree with outside of work hours."

That's what teams and leagues should do. In fact, I think it's what all employers should do.

If you feel strongly as an owner about your player being on the wrong side of an issue you care deeply about, you can privately meet with him and suggest why he's wrong, but even that, in my opinion, is strange and unseemly behavior. Do you really want employers requiring employees to have the same political opinions as their bosses in order to keep their jobs? And do you want those same employers monitoring every comment on social media to ensure compliance as well? I don't.

If you're reading this book right now and you think that's perfectly appropriate, would you feel the same way if the ownership was insisting on conservative political beliefs? What if an owner believed abortion was murder? Wouldn't you think it was problematic if a player had to attend an abortion seminar designed to convince him his opinion that women should have the right to choose was wrong?

What if you were Muslim, Jewish, or an atheist and you were forced to attend Christian church services with the owner until you agreed to adopt his religious belief?

Again, when you've taken the red pill, you start to look around and ask yourself this question: Why does everyone have to have the same opinion on gay relationships in order to play football? Doesn't that begin to look a bit Orwellian? Even stranger, why are people with traditional beliefs the only ones who have to attend training to cleanse them of their prior opinions?

I am far more troubled by our modern-day fixation on "acceptable" and "unacceptable" opinions than I am by the opinions themselves. Because the NFL might well have considered approving of gay marriage to be an unacceptable opinion a generation ago.

We'll return to Michael Sam in a moment, but this would rapidly become a prominent trend in sports—forcing people you disagree with to apologize for their opinions, often after asserting the opinions at issue were racist, sexist, or "insensitive," whatever that means.

Sports Illustrated writer Andy Benoit saw it happen to him. He had the audacity to tweet that most women's sports weren't worth watching when an *SI* colleague tweeted a Women's World Cup goal and mocked him for not watching the event. That's an opinion that most American sports fans of both sexes share if you go by the ratings for what they watch. Most women's sports are much less popular than men's sports on television. In fact, the ratings are not even close, even in sports that are the same. Around 400,000 people watch a WNBA Finals game, compared to roughly 18 million who watch an NBA Finals game. Why are the numbers so different? Because male athletes are bigger, stronger, and faster playing their sports than women athletes are playing theirs. That's not sexism; it's biology. (Unless, of course, you want to argue biology itself is sexist, which many left-wing sportswriters would, no doubt, love to argue.)

Benoit's tweet went viral with left-wingers on social media. How dare a man not like women's sports as much as men's sports?! *Saturday Night Live* even did a skit about it, ridiculing his opinion in the process. Benoit was forced to tuck his penis between his legs and apologize. He fell on the sword with this tweet: "I got carried away responding to playful ribbing . . . and in my stupidity, overcompensated by saying something ignorant and extreme. 100% mistake on my part, for which I'm deeply sorry."

Why do you have to be "deeply sorry" for not liking women's sports as much as men's sports? Or believe that opinion is "ignorant and extreme." Choosing to watch men's sports instead of women's sports is literally what tens of millions of people, both men and women, do every single day.

In 2015 the Tampa Bay Buccaneers announced a women's football clinic. Twitter was outraged, and articles poured forth ridiculing the Bucs for doing what many teams had done before them. Then something curious happened. There was a clear disconnect between the social-media faux rage and the real reaction at the Bucs ticket office. The event sold out immediately. Women loved the opportunity to attend the clinic.

It turns out much of the social media outrage was just fake public posturing, and that social media didn't remotely reflect the real world, an idea we'll return to in later chapters.

Yet this trend would continue again and again; an online left-wing sports media mob takes aim at someone's sports opinion for not being politically correct enough.

Witness John McEnroe, who in 2017 wrote a book about tennis and was so sexist he had the gall to say Serena Williams was the best women's player ever. Then this interview with a female NPR host went viral, and he was considered a sexist pig:

NPR host: We're talking about male players, but there is, of course, wonderful female players. Let's talk about Serena Williams. You say she is the best female player in the world in the book.

McEnroe: Best female player ever—no question.

NPR host: Some wouldn't qualify it, some would say she's the best player in the world. Why qualify it?

McEnroe: Oh! Uh, she's not, you mean, the best player in the world, period?

NPR host: Yeah, the best tennis player in the world. You know, why say female player?

McEnroe: Well because if she was in, if she played the men's circuit she'd be like 700 in the world.

NPR host: You think so?

McEnroe: Yeah. That doesn't mean I don't think Serena is an incredible player. I do, but the reality of what would happen would be I think something that perhaps it'd be a little higher, perhaps it'd be a little lower. And on a given day, Serena could beat some players. I believe because she's so incredibly strong mentally that she could overcome some situations where players would choke 'cause she's been in it so many times, so many situations at Wimbledon, the U.S. Open, etc. But if she had to just play the circuit—the men's circuit—that would be an entirely different story.

To his credit, McEnroe refused to back down amid the uproar, but I talked to several professional men's tennis players who said McEnroe had been far too kind. Serena wouldn't even be able to make most top college men's teams, much less beat professionals. She was nowhere near a top 700 men's player. The men tennis players are stronger, faster, and quicker than even the best women players. It would be no contest: Serena wouldn't even win a set against most top men's college players, much less the best professionals in the world.

Yet John McEnroe was savaged for sharing his factual opinion about Serena's talents: she was the best women's tennis player ever, but nowhere near as good as a men's player.

How about Kid Rock performing at the 2018 NHL All-Star Game? Surely no one could be upset by that decision, right?

Wrong.

The top story at ESPN.com was about the "controversy" surrounding Kid Rock's selection. This story offers a textbook example of left-wing sportswriting about political issues disguised as legitimate sports news.

First, let's start with the headline at ESPN.com: "NHL aware of backlash over Kid Rock performing at All-Star Game, standing by decision."

The headline itself tells us that nothing is changing. That is, the NHL is doing what the NHL was already doing, having Kid Rock perform at its all-star game.

There is no substance to this story, and the headline tells us this before we read a word.

Let's continue with the opening paragraph of that story:

"The National Hockey League said Thursday that it's aware of the backlash over Kid Rock performing at the 2018 All-Star Game in Tampa, saying that the decision to hire him was 'purely based' on his entertainment value and history as a hockey fan."

The opening paragraph here tells us that the NHL picked an entertainer to entertain because he's an entertainer.

That seems like a logical NHL decision.

However, the league is also "aware of the backlash" over their decision to pick Kid Rock.

One of the real issues with social media today is that it only takes a couple of hundred people, or even fewer, on Twitter obsessively tweeting about something to constitute a "backlash" if the news media agrees with what these people are saying. The truth of the matter is there is no decision that a league, a team, a politician, or an entertainer can make in America today that doesn't immediately provoke "backlash" on social media.

Another way to classify "backlash" would be to say that everyone on social media doesn't have the exact same opinion as a league, a team, a politician, or a famous person might have on every single subject.

If you doubt me, go look at the reaction to every draft pick made by a team or every coaching hire. There are always people who disagree with the draft pick or the hire. That's because there has never been a time when opinions are more easily shared with the masses than the present day. But that isn't as powerful of a lede for a story because fans know this. "Some Fans Disagree with the Decision Made in the NFL Draft" isn't a very powerful headline.

Instead, there's a "backlash" on social media, which is just another word for "disagreement," and this disagreement is used to justify the entire story's premise. (Interestingly, the sports media would never base a "backlash" storyline on a string of sports talk radio callers because they would view that as an absurd and unrepresentative snapshot. So why use Twitter without a second thought? Especially since, unlike Twitter, we at least know a sports radio caller is a real person.)

What is the backlash here?

Well, it's a few people on social media, many of whom are anonymous, stating they disagree with the decision to pick Kid Rock to perform at the NHL All-Star Game.

Let's pause here for a moment and think about this. Can you imagine how little of a life you must have to be upset at the *decision of which artist is going to perform at an All-Star game?!*

I mean, seriously, of all the things for a sports fan to be upset about, this is the hill you choose to die on, which musical act is performing at the NHL All-Star Game?

This is where your antenna should go up if you're an objective media member or fan. "Wait a minute," you should think, "do NHL fans really dislike Kid Rock this much, or am I using an artificial basis for the premise of my article?"

Once an ESPN writer decides this is a story, the NHL is asked about the "backlash" and the NHL can't say no comment when ESPN asks them about this made-up backlash, and they can't admit they haven't seen the fact that everyone doesn't agree with them because that would make them look out of touch. So they say they are aware that everyone on earth didn't agree with the Kid Rock decision, and that they didn't pick him for political reasons but just because he's an entertainer who likes hockey.

So that's what they said.

Somehow that's a lead story on ESPN.com.

Let's continue with the second paragraph of the ESPN story. (Remember, this is a story that editors have deemed to be a top story for the day in sports, what some people online think about Kid Rock performing at the NHL All-Star Game.)

"The 47-year-old singer has drawn attention in the last year for endorsing President Donald Trump, his history of displaying Confederate flags at concerts, criticism of NFL quarterback Colin Kaepernick's protests during the national anthem and anti-transgender comments made during a concert."

Wow, so conservative political opinions aren't allowed now for entertainers at sporting events? Because that's what this paragraph is designed to do, paint Kid Rock's politics as unacceptable to the masses, thereby disallowing a major sports league from being connected to him at all.

Even though, and this is a key point, the majority of NHL fans vote Republican, disagree with Colin Kaepernick's protests during the national anthem, and probably don't think you're a hero if you change your gender. To be fair, NHL fans as a group probably don't have a strong opinion on the Confederate flag since most of them are from the

North and the North won the Civil War, making the Confederate flag the equivalent of a participation trophy to them.

Kid Rock's "controversial" political stances are supported by the league's fans. (One thing I noticed once I took the red pill is that none of my left-leaning opinions are ever labeled as controversial. No one has ever written, "Travis, whose controversial belief that abortion and gay marriage should be legal and the death penalty should be impermissible . . ." It's always my "conservative" opinions that are labeled as controversial.)

Now it would be one thing if all entertainers were subjected to the same "backlash" coverage, but that doesn't happen in the sports media. Only players, coaches, or artists with conservative political opinions provoke a "backlash" in the minds of the left-wing sports media covering a nonsports story like this.

For instance, ESPN itself picked Kendrick Lamar to perform at halftime of the college football national title game between Georgia and Alabama.

Kendrick Lamar's selection, like any decision on entertainment, certainly provoked a "backlash" on social media. Many college football fans aren't Kendrick Lamar fans and would have preferred another musical act instead. Or to have the school bands perform. (Interestingly, many of these fans may well have preferred Kid Rock.)

Unlike the average hockey fan, who probably likes Kid Rock and supports his politics, college football fans in the South, who voted for Donald Trump by an overwhelming margin, certainly don't support Kendrick Lamar's far-left-wing and liberal politics.

Yet I didn't see MSESPN or any other sports website cover the "backlash" over Kendrick Lamar's selection.

But if they had covered this backlash, do you know how that story would have run? They would have painted the fans who were upset about Lamar's selection as being racist because, as the mainstream media has taught us, anyone from Alabama and Georgia who disagrees with anything involving a black person is racist.

The far-left-wing sports media at ESPN could have very easily written the exact same opening paragraph about the college football playoff's selection of Kendrick Lamar receiving a backlash and quoting the college football playoff leaders as saying Lamar was picked purely based on his entertainment value and status as a well-known football fan and the decision had nothing to do with politics.

The next paragraph of that Kendrick Lamar article could have just as easily said: "The thirty-year-old rapper has drawn attention in the last year for criticizing Donald Trump, his condemnation of the Confederate flag, his praise of quarterback Colin Kaepernick's protests during the national anthem, and his antipolice comments made during concerts."

Those articles weren't ever written.

Why not?

Because this is a transparent example of a journalist who doesn't agree with the selection of Kid Rock using his "objective journalism" to discredit the selection while attempting to cover this as an actual news story.

Here's the paragraph from the ESPN home page story that seeks to justify the story's very existence as a legitimate piece of news.

"The NHL's decision to have him perform at the All-Star Game was widely criticized on social media this week. It's the second time in recent months that a Kid Rock appearance created controversy in the hockey world, as the Detroit Red Wings were criticized for having him open their new arena with a concert in August 2017."

Again, *social media criticism isn't a legitimate hook for news stories.*

Nor is citing social media criticism as a "controversy" or a "backlash."

Literally everything is criticized all day long on social media. By this logic, there is a perpetual backlash to everything.

If this writer wanted to write an opinion piece that Kid Rock was the wrong choice for the NHL because of his political opinions, have at it, fire away with that opinion. I may not agree with the opinion, but at least it's clearly an opinion, not an opinion being disguised as news by hiding in the skirts of anonymous social media "backlash."

This article is an illegitimate left-wing opinion piece disguised as sports news, and here's the even wilder thing—editors at ESPN read this article and elected to promote it as one of the top stories in all of sports.

Why?

Because those editors at ESPN agree that Kid Rock's political opinions are unacceptable and they, just like the writer, want to broadcast that opinion, which has been disguised as news, to as wide an audience as is possible.

Now I just happened to dissect this story about Kid Rock, but after taking the red pill I saw stories like this everywhere. The biased sports media was picking sides. They weren't even picking sides fairly. They were disguising opinion-based journalism as real news.

None of these examples we've discussed here are actual sports stories. They reflect what has become all too commonplace. There were now acceptable and unacceptable opinions—I could find countless other examples—where if you strayed outside the left-wing talking points you were assaulted by the sports media zealots until you apologized or dialed back your commentary.

Sometimes, the left-wing sports media came after you even if you'd done absolutely nothing wrong at all. In January 2017, ESPN tennis analyst Doug Adler was calling one of Venus Williams's Australian Open tennis matches for ESPN's online viewers.

During the match, as Williams charged the net, Adler used the phrase "guerrilla effect" to describe Venus charging to the net to win a point. The comment would likely have gone unnoticed but for someone clipping the comment off the website and sharing it on social media. Shortly thereafter a left-wing tennis reporter for the *New York Times* shared the clip on Twitter, writing: "This is some appalling stuff. Horrifying that the Williams sisters remain subjected to it still in 2017." Except, you know, the phrase "guerrilla tennis" has been used for decades and was the tagline for a popular tennis commercial featuring Andre Agassi and Pete Sampras in which the duo played tennis on a New York street.

Plus, if you used your brain at all, was this really the actions of a racist? Had Adler been practicing sleeper-cell racism—pretending not to be racist while calling over a decade's worth of tennis matches—so he could one day call Venus Williams a gorilla on an online broadcast of a second-round Australian Open match whose viewership likely measured in the hundreds?

If anything, Adler's word choice is far from racist since if he were racist, and thought Williams resembled a gorilla, he probably wouldn't use the phrase "guerrilla effect" because he'd be afraid of being discovered to be a racist. (By the way, when is the last time someone described an animal by appending the word "effect" after it? If you describe someone as behaving like an alligator, you wouldn't say they were slinking underwater like an alligator effect, you'd say they were slinking underwater like an alligator.)

That didn't matter for the sports media and the mob online; Adler was publicly branded a racist. Worse, the stink of publicly being branded a racist scared others from coming forward to defend him. Rather than defend him against the left-wing sports media mob, ESPN fired Adler after demanding that he apologize for his word choice. (Adler would come on my morning radio show and share his story. Friends of his at ESPN suggested he reach out to me because I was the only person in sports media they believed wouldn't be afraid to have him on air. It wasn't that anyone believed Adler was racist, it was that many were so afraid of becoming targets of the online left-wing mob themselves that they didn't even want to be connected to him and end up being publicly branded as racist as well.)

Adler has now been out of work for nearly two years and has a lawsuit pending against ESPN. "It is," he told me, "the worst thing that has ever happened to me in my life."

Adler was so crushed by the left-wing mob that tore him apart online and by ESPN's refusal to defend him despite decades of evidence that he wasn't racist that he couldn't sleep for months. The stress over publicly being branded a racist and losing his job, according to his doctors, caused him to have a heart attack.

Adler nearly died despite doing nothing wrong.

Worst of all, the truth didn't matter, Adler was gone, the victim of a word that sounded like another word, a homophonic racist.

As if that weren't enough, in the spring of 2018 another Disney employee, Steve Harvey, went on ESPN's *SportsCenter* before game three of the NBA Finals between the Cleveland Cavaliers and the Golden State Warriors and called the entire Golden State Warriors team gorillas. "You can't stop all them boys," Harvey said live on ESPN. "They've got too many gorillas on the team. They coming to play, man. They got eight-hundred-pound gorillas on they team."

Disney, the parent company of ESPN, which fired Adler for using the phrase "guerrilla effect" during a Venus Williams match and employed Harvey via the *Family Feud* TV show he hosts, did nothing at all to Harvey for actually calling the entire Golden State Warriors team, made up of almost all African-American players, gorillas. The social media outrage from the sports media? Nonexistent. Thank God for double standards, because without them Disney and ESPN would have no standards at all. But isn't this where an unbiased sports media should stand up and defend Adler? Other than me, there was not one single prominent member of the sports media who took note of the double standard.

All the biased, far-left-wing sports media coverage happened in the wake of the Michael Sam story, which is, I believe, when ESPN's turn to the far left, which would be copied by the rest of the sports media, really happened.

Back on that draft day in 2014, Michael Sam had become the 249th player selected in the NFL Draft, but he nearly received more media attention than all the other draftees combined in the days ahead.

For the next several months ESPN obsessively covered Sam's every move; never before had a seventh-round draft choice received this much attention. Many sports commentators even compared him to Jackie Robinson.

Except, you know, everyone could see that Jackie Robinson was black and no one would have known who Michael Sam slept with if he hadn't told us. But beware—if you argued anything other than that Sam was the most important sports figure since Jackie Robinson, you were a homophobe.

For the first time sports fans began to email and tweet me about ESPN's round-the-clock coverage: "Why," one emailer asked me, "is Michael Sam being covered like he's Tom Brady?"

While the network had fallen victim to celebrities before—as Tim Tebow, Johnny Manziel, and LeBron James could attest—the celebrities ESPN previously obsessed over were typically top athletes; never before had a practice-squad player received his own reporting team.

It was a harbinger of things to come, the first time ESPN allowed a nonstar to dominate its sports coverage, and not just a nonstar but one that fit into ESPN's liberal agenda.

Goodbye ESPN, hello MSESPN.

However, if you thought the Michael Sam coverage was excessively left-wing, you hadn't seen anything yet.

Up next was Caitlyn Jenner.

For many both inside and outside ESPN, the decision to award Caitlyn Jenner an ESPY for bravery and courage was the moment when the network stopped covering sports and officially became a left-wing ideological and political channel.

By the summer of 2015, ESPN had lost 8 million subscribers and its ratings were tanking for all nonlive-event programming.

The network needed something to galvanize attention and bring in viewers. Luckily there was a deal to be made. Caitlyn Jenner, born Bruce Jenner, was going to announce her transition to womanhood on Diane Sawyer's ABC program. Why not couple that decision with giving Jenner the 2015 ESPY for Courage?

The ESPYs, begun in 1993, were ESPN's answer to the Oscars, a large gathering of sports celebrities where the network presented awards for the year's best achievements in sports. In 2015 the top award, named after tennis great Arthur Ashe, went to Jenner for having "the courage to embrace a truth that had been hidden for years, and to embark on a journey that may not only give comfort to those facing similar circumstances, but can also help to educate people on the challenges that the transgender community faces," according to a top ESPN executive.

Anyone in the sports media who questioned the award was publicly shamed online.

The decision, to me, was nakedly political and partisan, a clear decision by ESPN to wed sports and left-wing politics. Look, I'm all for people making decisions that make them happier, but what made Caitlyn Jenner a hero? Deciding to put on a dress and become a woman made you heroic? What kind of world was ESPN living in to believe that sports fans shared this opinion?

Did Tom Hanks and Robin Williams deserve the Congressional Medal of Honor for pretending to be women on television? Hell, could you even make the movie *Mrs. Doubtfire* today? What in the world, my audience wanted to know, was happening in the sports world? Why was ESPN trying to socially engineer sports to its own political persuasion?

Jenner, who last participated in athletics in the 1980s, also allowed ESPN to dodge the truly difficult issues with her honoring. What would the reaction have been if Jenner were a present-day athlete, a dominant, gold-medal winner, who suddenly decided to become a woman at the peak of her athletic ability? Would she have deserved to compete as a woman? I suspect most of you would have an issue with that. Certainly the Olympics would as well. However, if we aren't going to have men and women compete against each other in the Olympics, allowing someone to choose their gender violates the spirit of competition. After all, no women would likely ever win a medal if men decided to identify as women for their competitions. Honoring Jenner long after her career ended allowed ESPN to avoid these potential pitfalls.

ESPN never addressed any of these challenges of the gender-fluid lifestyle. As is, Jenner accepted the award on ABC—it was the first time the ESPYs had ever aired on ABC instead of ESPN—in front of a massive television audience, the biggest to ever watch the ESPYs.

As Jenner addressed the huge audience with the Kardashian family beaming from the front row, ESPN executives rejoiced. This was the exact kind of political statement they believed the network needed to maintain its cultural relevance. Hosannas poured in from the left-wing sports media, praising ESPN for its brave programming decision.

But all was not well.

What, many asked, did Jenner have to do with sports at all? Jenner hadn't been active in sports for over thirty years. Why was ESPN needlessly interjecting itself into America's culture wars with a person who wasn't a sports figure at all?

The answer was all too simple: for ratings.

ESPN had become MSESPN.

And the rest of sports media was following ESPN right over the political cliff.

4

The Social Media Trap

I began this book telling you that in September of 2017 I almost got fired from my radio show for saying I liked the First Amendment and boobs live on CNN.

As we begin this discussion of social media's impact on sports, my own experience in the center of a social media hurricane is a perfect one to take you inside how stories like this play out.

In the immediate aftermath of my appearance on CNN, my phone exploded. As I told you, one of those texts came from my wife downstairs in our house. She was terrified of what the outcome was going to be.

I wasn't.

Because the truth of the matter is this—I love being in the center of a media hurricane. I find it energizing, invigorating, and the modern-day equivalent of playing three-dimensional chess. While other people are losing their heads, I'm coolly analyzing the situation and making the smartest moves to maximize my advantage.

I hadn't misspoken, I'd been saying I loved the First Amendment and boobs for a couple of years. I'd even said it the day before on CNN's *Headline News* with another female anchor at CNN. She'd laughed off the line, as Brooke Baldwin would have as well if she'd had an ounce of honesty. Instead of blowing up the interview and adopting a posture of false outrage, she should have addressed the substance of my argument, not the rhetorical flair. And, by the way, how could CNN claim to be astonished I used the line when I'd used the line *on their own airwaves the previous day*?

Regardless, as a media hurricane enveloped me, I stayed calm.

Public relations executives told me to stay quiet, but I did the exact opposite. I understand modern media better than most PR executives do. PR executives always recommend giving in to the mob and apologizing, which is like trying to get rid of sharks by throwing them more chum.

Rather than stay quiet, I immediately did a live Periscope and Facebook show to tell my side of the story. As part of that story, I announced we would be selling "First Amendment and Boobs" t-shirts at Outkick. And that we'd be donating the proceeds to breast cancer awareness.

A few minutes after my show, my phone rang. It was CNN leaving a voicemail message inviting me back on the air on Monday. This was pure gold.

I tweeted out this invitation from CNN, creating a new uproar. How could CNN claim to be upset if they had already invited me back on the network? CNN executives, evidently unaware of the fact that a producer from one of their shows had invited me back on the airwaves, issued a false denial of my invitation. I took to Periscope to play the live voicemail of my CNN invitation back on their airwaves. Later on Friday night the same CNN producer texted me to cancel the interview, so I screenshotted her text message to me and shared it with my entire audience.

What was fascinating about the CNN interview offer was that the mainstream media who'd reported that my invitation on CNN was false never issued any correction of their falsehood. The more time I spent as a member of the news media, the more often I noticed something alarming—the media got an awful lot of facts wrong.

While I was out there fighting a war to protect my side of the story, PR people were checking social media, and they were afraid that some people online were reacting negatively to my statements on CNN.

So what if there was an even bigger collection of people, many of whom are reading this book right now, that loved what I'd said on CNN and the fact that I wasn't backing down and issuing a false apology to try to sate the mob?

That didn't matter, there were people upset online, and they were demanding blood. They wanted me fired for saying I liked the First Amendment and boobs, and some people in positions of power were endorsing the decision. It looked like they might be winning.

Within three hours of my statements on CNN, my name and bio had been pulled off the Fox Sports Radio website. When a tipster sent me the link to the website, I could only laugh. The irony of a First Amendment absolutist losing a job because of fear related to a social media campaign being led by crackpots was positively detectable.

As the day progressed it looked like I might be fired from my radio show, yet another victim of the far-left-wing social media mob.

However, I'm a fighter, and while others would have apologized and begged for forgiveness, I doubled down on my response with my job on the line. Why should I apologize for saying something I believed? Especially when, as was the case here, the response from CNN and the other guest on the show was clearly rooted in faux rage, aka false social media outrage.

As the story grew, the CNN host, Brooke Baldwin, took to the CNN website to write a histrionic piece about our interview. Included in her article were these phrases: "I've been a journalist for 17 years—the past seven spent at CNN hosting a live show. I've seen and heard some things. But when I first heard 'boobs' from a grown man on national television (in 2017!!!) my initial thought bubble was: 'Did I hear that correctly?? There's no WAY he just came on my show and said what I think he said . . . DID HE?' And I let it hang.

"The thing is—this is not okay. Speaking to women like this is unacceptable. It is 2017. Why is this even happening?"

That was the crux of her argument, that I should speak differently to her than I should a male anchor. Isn't that the very definition of sexism, the idea that my speech should be altered based on the sex of the person

I'm speaking to? Shouldn't I do what I always do, speak the exact same way to men and women in public settings?

This became even more ridiculous when Brooke Baldwin had the lawyer for Stormy Daniels, the porn star who alleged she had a sexual relationship with Donald Trump, on dozens of times and quizzed him in graphic detail about the alleged sexual encounter. I mean, come on, could you really claim to be offended by my statement when you were dissecting the president's sexual encounter with a porn star like it was a Super Bowl–winning play?

Even wilder, CNN devoted hours and hours of coverage to Hugh Hefner's death. If anyone believed in the First Amendment and boobs more than me, it was Hefner, whom CNN praised as a true American hero. CNN and its hosts weren't actually outraged, they were pretending to be outraged to garner social media attention.

This was also true of the other guest, Keith Reed, a former ESPN editor. Reed expressed outrage at my statements as well, but within a few hours, my social media defenders had combed through Brooke Baldwin and Reed's past online history to determine that both were full of crap.

It turns out Reed, who was offended by my saying I liked boobs, had a Twitter feed full of graphic endorsements of women's asses and boobs. I mean, you can't even make this stuff up, the guy pretended to be outraged by my liking boobs while he'd been tweeting how much he liked asses for years. Maybe, after all, he was offended that I was more of a boob man than an ass man.

Meanwhile, Baldwin had laughed when her CNN cohost Don Lemon told Kathy Griffin live on air that she had a great rack and discussed his nipples. On New Year's Eve of 2017, Baldwin told Don Lemon she had bigger balls than he did live on CNN. (Outkick would later get its revenge on New Year's Eve of that same year when two of our fans staged a fake marriage proposal in a New Orleans bar and then sprang up, grabbed the microphone and the woman screamed in

Baldwin's face that they loved boobs, B-double O-B-S, spelling it out on air just as she had.) It turned out that Baldwin herself had said far worse than I had on CNN's own airwaves.

Even still, as the day progressed, the odds of me being fired vacillated.

I continued to fight the battle, insisting that I'd done nothing at all wrong. Eventually, I got on the phone with top executives and made my case that if they fired me for saying I loved the First Amendment and boobs the backlash from that decision was going to be far worse—and make this story far bigger—than it already was.

For several hours my radio show hung in the balance—would I be fired or not?

My phone continued to buzz incessantly until it turned hot to the touch, like it had been sitting outside in the sun all day. Slowly, as the afternoon hours moved into evening, I began to win the argument. Reasonable minds became aware that firing me for saying I loved the First Amendment and boobs would make me a free speech martyr. Public opinion, now divided, would move back squarely on my side.

By late that night, my position on the Fox Sports Radio webpage was restored. My bosses at Fox Sports Radio, including Don Martin, Scott Shapiro, and Julie Talbott, had lined up squarely behind me. So did the head of Fox Sports, Eric Shanks. For all of their support in the midst of this media maelstrom, I was, and remain, grateful.

Fox Sports, which was being pressured to condemn me, released a tepid statement on Friday night that quickly vanished into the oncoming weekend of new football games. That statement read as follows: "In response to Clay Travis' appearance on CNN today, his comments were inappropriate. Clay Travis has not worked at Fox Sports for six months and is a syndicated talent of Premiere Networks."

For their part Premiere Networks, who had stood behind me steadfastly throughout the day, released a statement saying I'd be on the show Monday and would face no punishment.

Until this book was released, very few people knew how close I came to being fired from my radio show for what I said on CNN. I like to think I won an important battle against the far-left-wing social media proponents of faux rage, that the First Amendment and boobs were still okay for an American white male to publicly admit that he liked. (All of you can breathe a sigh of relief.)

After a daylong battle to keep my radio show, I wasn't going to be fired for what I'd said on CNN.

I was, however, banned forever from appearing on CNN, adding my prior banning from ESPN to the hit list, which meant I'd now become the only media person in America who was banned from appearing on both CNN and ESPN. Plus, when you really get down to it, why was I banned by CNN and ESPN? Because I said and wrote things that upset the liberal orthodoxy, because the things you've read in this book aren't commonly said, because the First Amendment only matters to CNN and ESPN if you're saying what they want to hear. Even if many in the liberal and far-left-wing media claim that they embrace diversity of thought and opinion, the fact that I'm banned for my opinions on those two television networks tells you everything you need to know about our modern era.

As my radio job hung in the balance, I stepped back and considered the larger picture of the modern-day social media era—what I'd done was feed the beast, provided a video to allow another battle in the ongoing culture war to be fought. Before long, what I'd said didn't matter because I'd become a signpost in our modern culture war; people today fight not over specific facts or incidences, but over whether those facts and incidences confirm or conflict with their existing worldview.

Social media is just one large blame factory, a race to determine who is right and who is wrong. I was in the center of that blame factory, either a hero or a villain depending on what you already believed.

What I'd said and who I was didn't matter; I was just another battleground, a proxy to allow the never-ending fight to continue.

The most ironic angle, to me, of the entire imbroglio was that many on the left wing asserted that the reason I'd said what I said was because Donald Trump had been elected president. That Trump's election had somehow emboldened me to suddenly like boobs. Did they really believe that if Hillary Clinton had been elected, I would have stopped liking boobs? Hell, I worked on Al Gore's presidential campaign in 2000, and let me go on the record right now and make it clear: I liked boobs then too.

Furthermore, the entire premise of the outrage industry was entirely artificial. Were any women really surprised that men liked boobs? Victoria's Secret has turned the bra into its own version of the Manhattan Project, extracting billions of dollars out of making women's boobs look bigger and better than they did in other bras. Every year billions of dollars—billions with a *b*—are spent on boob jobs in this country.

Yet me joking about the First Amendment and boobs was a sudden cultural battleground.

Come on. It was all far-left-wingers grabbing their pearls, like Brooke Baldwin, and pretending to be outraged when they knew what I said wasn't outrageous at all.

As I was in the tempest, I was cognizant of the fact that my own social media fracas tied in with the larger social media explosion that has changed sports media substantially in the past several years. Indeed, one of my theories, which I established in the prior chapter, is that ESPN's desperation over its collapsing business model pushed it to left-wing politics to retain relevance as its revenue and ratings collapsed. It's also important to note that it wasn't just ESPN moving left in the sports media: CBS, NBC, and Fox Sports were all doing the same thing. While I believe ESPN led the charge, FS1, CBS, and NBC have also all promoted sports figures embracing left-wing politics and mixing it with sports.

By the fall of 2017 even though I'm relatively middle of the road in my political leanings compared to everyone else in sports media,

I appeared far right. That's not because I'm a far-right-winger, a term regularly applied to anyone who thinks socialism is a bad idea, it's because the sports media has become so far-left-wing that someone in the middle, even someone, like me, who leans a bit left of middle on social issues, and a bit right on fiscal issues, seems like a far-right-winger.

When I went to the wedding of a law school classmate in the fall of 2017, I asked several friends there whether sports had gone insane politically or I had. Every single guy and girl attending the wedding whom I'd gone to law school with—you get to know everyone's politics pretty well in law school—said what I wrote and said in 2018 sounded the exact same as what I wrote and said back in law school in 2004. Only back then I was a Democrat and now I call myself a radical moderate. I haven't changed at all; social media has just caused everyone else to go insane. And here I am, the most reasonable person in sports. (Who also happens to have the best hair.)

Why did this happen? I think ESPN—and the sports media that followed ESPN's lead—started paying way too much attention to social media. The most active Twitter users skewed left, but they weren't ESPN's target audience. Heck, most of those people weren't even sports fans. But they were loud, and they seemed very powerful online.

Effectively, ESPN stopped serving the average sports fan and began to cater to the sports fan on social media. Out was ESPN's target audience of a guy who wanted to drink a beer and catch up on sports news; in was the social justice warrior who wanted to complain about white privilege and systemic racism online—all while not actually watching sports on television. (The most absurd thing about far-left-wing social justice warriors interjecting politics into sports is that most of them aren't actually sports fans. Go look at video from a Colin Kaepernick rally some time. Those are not the people spending all day Sunday watching football. They just want to be mad about something online.)

Of course, social media was just a part of the rapidly evolving media environment everyone, myself included, faced in the modern era.

What's also fascinating about our modern era is how similar it is to the media eras we would have seen hundreds of years ago, particularly in the days long before radio and TV and the Internet popularized viral stories on social media. Let's pause here for a moment and let me take you way back in time, to the earliest days of America as a country, when the mass distribution of ideas was still in its infancy. Because I think modern-day social media is very similar to what early American media was like. As Rustin Cohle on HBO's *True Detective* memorably intoned: "Time is a flat circle."

For most of American media history, there was no concept of unbiased, neutral journalism. Newspapers endorsed political candidates and savaged their opponents in print. If you think politics is rough now, go read what was written about Andrew Jackson's wife when he ran for president in 1828 or what was said about Abraham Lincoln during his 1860 and 1864 presidential campaigns. Newspapers, which in their most basic business models are a method to deliver advertisements to readers, were the first mass-distributed method of political discourse in this country. (Leaving aside pamphlets like Thomas Paine's *Common Sense*, newspapers were our first mass-distributed pop culture.) Newspapers didn't begin as "impartial" and "unbiased" recitations of the day's news; they began as ribald, rollicking, bitterly partisan broadsides for or against particular political candidates, parties, and policies.

It wasn't until near the beginning of the twentieth century that any notion of "unbiased" news took root in the popular conception. What did "unbiased" news offer from a business perspective? Something for everyone. Instead of only selling newspapers to Republicans or Democrats or Whigs or Tories, you could appeal to every single person in an entire community. The notion of "unbiased" news wasn't a creation demanded by journalistic ethics to ensure an educated American populace; it was a newspaper business model that led to bigger audiences and bigger profits.

That "unbiased" newspaper business model carried through into the twentieth century with the two major media innovations adopted by households—radio and television—that were designed to appeal to the largest possible audiences as well. Due to the fact that they were public licenses, TV and radio were required to give equal weight to both political parties. Radio and television shows were created with mass appeal prioritized over individual appeal. *I Love Lucy* and *The Andy Griffith Show* gave way to *M*A*S*H* and *The Cosby Show*, but the goal remained the same: creating a type of entertainment that appealed to everyone, from eight to eighty.

The twentieth century was the golden age of pop culture centrism. You didn't get exactly what you loved the most, but you got what everyone could love at least a little bit; grandma and grandson were both entertained. This shouldn't be shocking, but it may strike you as such given the modern media environment—in order to appeal to everyone, you have to be pretty moderate and reasonable. Which meant that by and large the story of the twentieth century in America was the triumph of reasonableness.

Now let's pause for a moment and think about how astoundingly different the rise of modern American pop culture was. Think about what the average American's life would have been like in 1900 compared to 1965.

In 1900, what pop culture was there? If you traveled to California and you were from New York, something that relatively few people would have even done, what shared interests might you have to discuss with someone from the opposite coast? Food, relationships, children, travel, horses, maybe politics if you read a regular newspaper, which most didn't, but there would have been no shared national discourse in 1900 on television or movies or sports or music. If you were well read maybe you could talk about a popular book, but odds are that other than reading the Bible in church or Shakespeare in school you wouldn't have read that much in common either.

That experience in 1900 wasn't that much different from what might have happened throughout human history. Up until the advent of the printing press, the only way people could easily share stories was orally.

These stories, think the *Iliad* or *Epic of Gilgamesh*, two epic poems you may have claimed to have read in high school or college, were rare and didn't translate across all cultures. Even with the advent of the printing press, literacy was incredibly rare for most of human history. So, for most of human history, popular culture didn't exist. (When it did exist, religion was pretty much the only popular culture.)

Yet by 1965, just sixty-five years later, virtually every kid in America had been exposed to *I Love Lucy* and *Bonanza*. Sports, now integrated and open to everyone, thrived as the national embodiment of our culture; it was the story that united us across our divisions. With the rise of modern technology, sports became a national, not just a regional story.

Suddenly, with the advent of the radio and later television, the most remote holler in West Virginia could be as aware of what was going on in the country as the most urbane New Yorker. Significantly, the entertainment that both consumed would have been very similar too. With a relative paucity of entertainment options available, everyone watched or listened to the same things. Our national discourse became united around first the radio and then the television dial. As a result, all our media was designed to appeal to the largest possible audiences. And the same became true of our sports.

Cable started to change that in the 1980s and early 1990s, but most of the early popular cable channels weren't in the business of creating original content, they just took older popular content and re-aired it. If you're around my age, you could come home and watch TBS after school, but TBS after school was repurposed original pop culture for mass audiences from earlier decades. You could watch *The Brady Bunch* or *The Jetsons* or *The Beverly Hillbillies* or some other popular show that used to air on broadcast television for massive audiences of older generations. Most of cable, in its early years, wasn't about giving us anything new, it was just about giving us older shows in a new format.

All of this conspired to mean that the twentieth century, in retrospect, was about making us all very similar in our interests. More so than any other century, it ended our national balkanization. Television, radio, and newspapers were about connecting massive audiences with shared experiences via limited, but insanely popular, viewing and reading options. When the radio or television came on in the twentieth century, the entire family listened or watched together.

That media environment created a national discourse that even when surrounded by incredibly complex and difficult national issues—Vietnam, the civil rights movement, abortion decisions by the Supreme Court, assassinations of presidents and political leaders like John F. Kennedy, Martin Luther King, and Robert Kennedy—our politics remained middle of the road. Radio, TV, and newspapers— the three primary means of the media making money in this country in the twentieth century—relied upon not antagonizing or alienating large segments of the population, but rather appealing to everyone. The national discourse in media was sober and without flair.

Then came the Internet.

And everything changed.

Because while twentieth-century media was about uniting a divided country under a national popular culture, twenty-first-century media, at least so far, is primarily about balkanizing our country. The reason for that is simple. Massive audiences are declining due to the myriad of entertainment options. Major sporting events are one of the few national apolitical connective tissues we have left in this country. (Unfortunately, in our modern era even awards shows have turned political, thanks to the desire of artists to advocate for political causes like never before. The result? In 2018, both Grammy and Oscar ratings plunged by over 20 percent.)

While sports fans have continued to produce massive audiences, that's become an outlier. Even popular sitcom shows in 2018 aren't that popular. *The Cosby Show* had a 41.3 rating at its apex and brought in tens of millions of viewers for every episode. *Modern Family*, in many ways the contemporary version of *The Cosby Show*, averaged a 2.3 rating with 7 million viewers in 2017. Pop culture, apart from comic-book hero movies and other big-budget Hollywood releases and an occasional show that breaks through like *Game of Thrones* or *The Walking Dead,* has become sort of pop culture.

We all have so many entertainment options now that our interests are spread across the entertainment spectrum. *Mad Men* received tens of thousands of words in media coverage in the *New York Times* during its run on AMC, yet the show averaged only a couple of million viewers. One of my favorite shows, *The Americans,* on FX had an audience of only 700,000 viewers on its live finale in 2018. That's less people than live in North Dakota. Depth of passion replaced depth of viewership as the coin of the media realm. The more passionate your audience, even if it was tiny, the more money you could make.

Initially, ESPN was the beneficiary of this disaggregation, which led to the rise of cable networks. ESPN, by focusing on the targeted niche of sports fans, created the most valuable business in the history of media. Of course, this disaggregation didn't stop with cable, which could still provide substantial audiences in the case of live sports; it moved to the Internet too. But—and this is incredibly key—sports, even as the rest of the world was rapidly changing, still retained the ability to unite us all.

Why?

Because sports weren't political.

In a time and era when everything in the media is about turning us into tribal communities warring with each other in politics, sports stood against the tide, offering an opportunity to unite us. Our local tribes—Ohio State versus Michigan, Alabama versus Auburn, Duke versus North Carolina, Yankees versus Red Sox—meant more to us than our political tribes, and we knew how to put our jerseys back in the dresser when the game was over. Put it this way: Have you ever been celebrating a big win by your favorite team and thought anything about the political beliefs of the person you're high-fiving? Of course not. Sports unite us; they don't divide us.

The new Internet media environment, aided by the rise of social media through Twitter and Facebook, wasn't about having to satisfy every single person; it was only about having to satisfy a small segment of the overall population. You could build a business off appealing to a sliver of the population. That's because the Internet let loose a new business dynamic when it came to media, giving you exactly what you wanted at the moment that you wanted it. The benefits have been incredible for the average media consumer, unleashing a tidal wave of pop culture creativity the likes of which we have never seen before in the history of the world. (Interestingly, that same TV creativity has made our movies pale in comparison. Ask your average person who leaves a two-hour movie whether they would rather have seen the movie they just watched or watched two episodes of their favorite TV show. Chances are most people would pick their favorite TV show.) These shows have even become so popular that many of you reading this right now would probably agree that which shows you favor tells us something about you; that is, we all feel so deeply connected to our favorite TV shows that they reveal something about ourselves to others. But, and this is key, the audiences for all these shows are not very substantial compared to the audiences that pop culture used to produce. Right now, if you're around my age, you probably watched *Saved by the Bell*, *The Fresh Prince of Bel-Air*, and *Growing Pains*. We all, pretty much, watched the same shows in the 1980s and early 1990s. That's no longer the case.

We've unleashed a great deal of creativity when it comes to modern media in the twenty-first century, but we've given up the shared experience of the twentieth century, we've all become our own media islands. Chances are, your tribe, the people in your neighborhood or school or community, are all watching the same shows, but the people different from you aren't watching the same shows anymore.

That might well be fine when it comes to modern movies and TV, but it has been disastrous for our politics. Which leaves us with a big question: If the Internet and social media have been incredibly beneficial to popular culture when it comes to providing a wide variety of entertainment options—that is, the wealth of choices has never been better for viewers and the quality of shows has never been greater either—why has our national discourse on politics collapsed at the same time? Especially when you consider, again, that the divisive issues we're debating right now in this country pale in comparison to the issues that have divided us throughout our national history. Regardless of your politics, I think everyone reading this book would have to agree that whether or not slavery should be legal in the country is a bigger battle than which public bathrooms transgender people use.

So why are we here? Because there's a business in dividing us through political media now, and sports is getting drawn into that national balkanization. Think back to my review of American media history—newspapers, radio, and TV all relied upon massive audiences throughout the twentieth century. Their business models were based upon appealing to everyone. Everyone had to like what you made, or at least not hate it. The result was a very middle-of-the-road, generally inoffensive set of articles, broadcasts, and shows. The same was true of our sports coverage.

Then social media arrived and, I think, big media companies lost their way in figuring out how to respond to it. It's not a coincidence that the Republicans and the Democrats both picked the most hated candidates in the history of our country to represent their parties, Donald Trump and Hillary Clinton. Instead of sharing things that we love on social media, many of us have decided to make decisions that anger others. It used to be the country picked political candidates with a desire to convince others to support those candidates. That was a very twentieth-century way of selecting leaders, pick the candidate that everyone would like. Now political parties don't do that, they pick the candidate that most outrages the other side. Our tribes are perpetually at war with one another.

Sports didn't need to be like politics. Unlike television, where every television show is competing with another television show, there is only one NFL and one NBA and one NHL and one Major League Baseball. There are only a few top college conferences. Sports already appealed to all of us; we didn't need sports to turn into politics.

It was fine, just as it existed.

The problem was ESPN's collapsing business model left the network flailing. It had no idea how to respond to social media, so ESPN chose to overinflate the significance the company placed on it, leading to sports becoming just like politics. When it should have ignored the tribalization on social media and focused on being the uniting force in our country, ESPN, and the sports companies that followed its lead, instead looked for salvation online but instead found damnation. The more time I spend on social media, the more I've come to believe that instead of leading us into a new media age it's taking us back to one that existed in the early days of our republic, when everything was tribal.

What's particularly interesting about ESPN's decision to allow social media to change the way it covered sports is that early in the rise of Twitter ESPN and I were on opposite sides of the social media revolution. In the winter of 2012, I stood outside an ESPN party in Miami before the Notre Dame–Alabama BCS title game speaking with several of their top executives about the rise of Twitter.

By 2012, I had published two books, had a successful local Nashville radio show, and my website, Outkick the Coverage, was beginning to thrive. I'd figured out how to use social media as a promotional vehicle for the content I was creating on my site, and I was very active on Twitter. ESPN was not yet MSESPN. In fact, they were assiduously focused on remaining blandly inoffensive and ensuring that they stuck to sports. The most common social media minefield the company faced in 2012 was the question of what to do about jokes in Bill Simmons's ESPN columns.

It seems quaint now, but the biggest controversy at ESPN back then was whether Bill Simmons could make fun of the WNBA or not.

And that was big, controversial news! ESPN's goal, likely deriving from the Rush Limbaugh contretemps in 2003, was to run from any and all controversy.

While this book takes several shots at ESPN, it's important to note that I have many friends who work at the company as both talent and executives and that far from being contentious, for many years ESPN and I got along well. Indeed, as recently as 2015 the network tried to hire me to come to work for them. Back then we hadn't yet reached the fall of 2017, when one of the top ESPN PR executives would tweet that I'd said the word "boobs" fifty-three times on my radio show in an effort to get me fired. (Seriously, ESPN put its PR team to work to see how many times I said the word "boobs" on my radio show. This was incredible for me to picture. Just some guy in a conference room with a notepad in front of him listening to all three hours of a rival radio network's programming and making a notch every time I said "boobs." And then tweeting out those numbers as if that was going to make me look bad?! Remember when I said I was smarter than all the people in sports PR? Yeah, I'm smarter than all the people in sports PR. To be fair, so are most of you reading this book.)

Back in 2012, those were happier times in our relationship. That day at the ESPN party on South Beach we were debating social media and its impact on ESPN's television programming. In particular, we were discussing the disconnect between how Lou Holtz, the former Notre Dame and South Carolina coach and current college football analyst, and legendary ESPN employee Chris Berman, the man who I'd been thrilled to meet as a child, were received in public versus how they were received on social media. In public, these guys were mobbed, and people loved them. But on Twitter, they got crushed all the time, and most fans claimed to hate them. (Not surprisingly, neither Holtz nor Berman were active on Twitter. Indeed, Berman, the most famous ESPN employee of all time, still does not have a Twitter account.)

Back in 2012 the ESPN executives were asking me a great question:

Do you consider the real-life responses or the Twitter responses to these men in how you value Holtz and Berman on-air at ESPN?

At that point in time the ESPN executives were arguing they needed to take into account the real-life response instead of the online response. Because they felt it was more valid. I was arguing the online response should be their litmus test and was probably more honest. Since that time, I think we've both flipped on our opinions. ESPN has chosen to let social media be their guide and I've learned to value real life.

This is partially because of how much Twitter has changed. Ten times more people use it now, and that has lowered the quality of the average user and the average content. Nowadays, it's fine to use Twitter and social media to get your message out, but worrying about Twitter opinions is the equivalent of obsessing because you look too fat in front of a carnival funhouse mirror.

I've never had someone say a mean thing to me in person despite a public career on sports radio, TV, and social media. Yet just about every single day on Twitter, people say if they ever see me in person they're going to punch me. What happens when those people see me? They end up asking for a picture.

That's because Twitter, and social media in general, isn't real. Everyone on Twitter acts like a WWE wrestler handed the mic at *SmackDown* or *Raw*. They hurl invectives, posture, feign outrage, or threaten violence haphazardly, and generally posture for public acclaim and attention.

But in real life?

They meekly ask for a photo and say how much of a fan they are.

I've learned this reality now, but in 2012, I was still of the opinion that Twitter was real life. It used to be Twitter was where I went to escape real life. Now real life is where I go to escape Twitter.

My Twitter obsession was ridiculed by former FS1 president Jamie Horowitz when he told me reading your mentions was pathetic if you were on TV. Horowitz said I spent too much time on social media— not just me, but everyone like me in sports media—and he said he thought it was dumb. "Why do you read your mentions?" he asked. "You don't walk up to strange people on the street all day asking them what they think of you, so why would you care what strange people online think of you on Twitter? You're the person with the opinion; you're the talent. People talk about their opinions of you and your opinions to other people. You don't talk with them about their opinion of you."

His theory was that Twitter should be a megaphone. Use it to amplify your voice, but don't use it to care what anyone else thinks about your opinion. In many respects I think this is the right way to think about Twitter in the modern era. But it's still a rare opinion.

The overvaluation of Twitter opinions is even more the case when you consider that we now know social media is being constantly manipulated by bots, fake accounts, and foreign countries to inspire angst and weaken powerful institutions. We shouldn't be paying attention to social media reactions, but the ability for people in media to receive constant and immediate feedback is intoxicating. Find me a show where the on-air talent don't finish taping and immediately all rush to their phones to see what people are saying about them, and I'll find you a show filled with liars. Twitter, to the media, is our pond and we're all Narcissus, unable to look away from our own reflection.

Immediate feedback is seductive and exhilarating, particularly in the media industry, where everyone is, at least to some degree, a narcissist. But it's not just the sports media members who are obsessed with social media reaction, it's also their bosses, who have stopped trusting their own gut instincts and become obsessed with what social media thinks of talent, stories, or their sports coverage in general.

This obsession with reactions and opinions isn't new; people in positions of power have always been terrified of the people that put them in that position of power. I'm sure Roman leaders monitored the street graffiti written about them on ancient walls as a clue to how the populace was responding to their leadership. As our media has evolved from newspapers to radio to television to the Internet to, now, instantaneous reaction on social media, it's all too common to find yourself falling into the pond while staring at your own reflection.

Back ages ago, in 2007 or so, college administrators used to spend oodles of time trying to figure out whether sports fan message boards—which they monitored obsessively while claiming they paid no attention to them at all—accurately reflected the overall mindset of a fan base. I can't tell you the number of times I talked to college administrators who would ask me that question: What are the fans thinking? Are message boards or comments online to articles reflective of actual opinions? The answer is no, they aren't reflective of most public opinion. Message boards, like social media, are a stage and everyone is doing whatever they can to draw attention to themselves. This means strong opinions, pro or con, dominate.

The best story I've heard about the false dynamic of message boards came from my buddy Chris Vernon, who talked about how when he first started doing local Memphis radio he went on a Memphis Tiger message board to see what people were saying about his radio show. There was an entire thread that day discussing how Vernon had the worst show in the history of radio. (He's actually very good at radio, but the story is reflective of what many people in media deal with. We all get crushed by anonymous people online no matter how good we are at our jobs.)

Vernon read that thread, and future threads about how bad he was, on the message board, and eventually decided to go to an event where all the guys on the message board met up in person. At the meet-up, the message board crew, previously anonymous under their screen names, all walked around with their screen names on name tags on their shirts. What happened? He recognized many of the guys from their screen names. The same exact guys who had ripped him online came up to him and said how much they loved the show.

Turns out their online opinions were entirely different from their face-to-face opinions.

I've found that to be true everywhere.

Running your life by reacting to what Twitter thinks would be like eating donuts for every meal. Eventually you'd get fat and die an untimely death. The same thing has happened to ESPN. They tried to run a company based on social media junk food. Now they're dying, because, ironically, they'd come to believe that social media was their savior when, in reality, it was a false siren dragging them to a watery grave.

Five years after our Miami conversation before the Alabama and Notre Dame BCS title game, Lou Holtz and Chris Berman were both gone from ESPN, replaced on air by younger, "hipper," and more plugged-in social media talent. ESPN replaced the old white guys who never shared their political opinions with left-wing social justice warriors who were more political on Twitter. Their rationale? ESPN was trying to reflect America. Which America were they reflecting? Not the America actually watching their games; they were trying to reflect the America they saw on social media.

Why were they making this decision? I think it was rooted, to a great degree, in insecurity. By 2017, I was secure in my career, that what I was doing was working and that I had a better idea what my audience wanted than anonymous people on social media did. ESPN was no longer secure in their business. Their ratings were tanking, and their subscribers were abandoning them by the millions. They were looking for a life vest to save them from drowning in social media and instead they found a heavy rock.

Twitter is not, and never has been, real life or an accurate reflection of real life; it's a funhouse mirror that artificially reflects reality.

Desperate to be loved as its business began to crumble, ESPN made the calculated decision to allow Twitter to become their primary sounding board of what sports fans wanted. As multiple stories online made clear every day, ESPN executives and programmers began scanning trending topics to see how fans were reacting online. How do we know this? Because ESPN allowed journalists at Yahoo and *Forbes* access to their planning meetings. Where were their ideas coming from? All of them were coming from social media. That's dangerous because Twitter is an angry and reactionary medium, the hottest of hot takes, frequently dished out without regard for facts at all. The hottest of the hot takes wrapped sports and politics together in perpetual righteous indignation. Everything in the world of Twitter is political.

But that wasn't what ESPN's core audience wanted.

Listening to Twitter backfired in a big way.

Social media isn't saving companies like ESPN; it's killing them.

And it's not just killing ESPN and sports media either; social media—and the resulting mainstream media coverage of social media—has killed stand-up comedy too. Everyone is perpetually offended by jokes, but only offended enough to tweet about them.

How often do you see someone protesting outside an actual comedy club? Almost never, right? And if you did see someone standing outside a comedy club with a sign protesting a joke that had been said inside the comedy club, you'd probably roll your eyes and mutter something about how that person needed to get a life, right?

Yet, to be fair, that protester would be pretty committed to their perspective. They would have taken the time to get a poster board, write out a message, procure transportation to the sidewalk outside the club, and then stand outside on the street corner in the sun, the snow, the sleet, or the rain to make sure you saw their opinion. And you know what 99.9 percent of us would think when we drove by? Man, that person is a fucking loser. If you don't like a comedian's jokes, don't go see him perform. That's your right as a consumer. But only a total loser would stand outside a comedy club and protest.

Furthermore, the vast majority of the time the media wouldn't bother to cover this protest either. At least I've never seen the media cover a protest outside a comedy club as breaking news. However, if that same person retweets a complaint about a comedian's joke while sitting on the couch in their underwear, something that literally takes four seconds to do and doesn't even require pants, it turns into an immediate story. That protester is taken seriously even though that person has put in no effort at all to advance their point of view.

But reporters at so many media outlets now are twenty-six-year-olds writing seven or eight pieces a day. Who has time to get off Twitter and go to an actual protest? Reporters don't even have to leave their desk to turn Twitter outrage into a daily article or series of articles.

If we'd be ridiculing the person who is physically protesting a joke outside a comedy store, shouldn't we also be ridiculing the person who is on social media doing the exact same thing? Yet we don't do that. We treat the offended person on social media's perspective as more valid than the person who would be standing on the street outside the comedy club. If anything, the reverse should be true; we should value the person who is willing to spend their actual time protesting something over the person who is retweeting from their couch in their underwear. (Probably from an anonymous account. And, potentially, from ten or more anonymous accounts to artificially magnify their voice.)

The fact that we give critics of comedy this much attention online has threatened to kill live comedy. The comedy stage is a comedian's live laboratory and sometimes jokes, like experiments if you're a scientist, can go awry. A joke isn't born perfect, yet some comedians have seen their careers come crashing down based on what they've said trying to rehearse an incomplete joke. We've so allowed social media to threaten the ability to tell jokes that many top comedians now require that audiences have their phones collected before the show starts.

Let me share another example with you of another company falling victim to what I call hyperresponsiveness, and then I'm going to tell you about more of the fallout surrounding my CNN statement that I loved the First Amendment and boobs.

You'll recall that in late February of 2018 there was a shooting outside a high school in South Florida. Seventeen people were killed, and social media was in an uproar. The uproar spread so quickly that many companies felt compelled to get involved, even those that had nothing at all to do with the shooting or gun control. One example of that? Delta Airlines.

Delta gave a travel discount to members of the NRA who fly on its airplanes. The most recent discount had been used by thirteen people to travel to the NRA's annual meeting in Texas.

Let's presume that discount, which couldn't have amounted to much, led to Delta taking $200 off the listed airfare for each of these customers. (That's probably too high, but let's presume it cost Delta a grand total of $2,600 off the normal rate.) In the wake of the school shooting, Delta probably fielded a couple of media inquiries about the NRA discount, and it's likely that far-left-wingers on social media and the blogosphere circuit started to speak out about the airline discount and ask why it existed.

Fearful of the stories that might emerge and the existing social media blowback in the wake of the school shooting, Delta panicked and said it would no longer provide any discount to NRA members.

The backlash to Delta's decision was immediate and substantial. Republican politicians in Georgia, Delta's home state, removed a tax subsidy that would have saved the airline $50 million. Fifty million! All because Delta felt compelled to weigh in on a contentious political issue.

If I were a Delta shareholder, I'd be furious.

All Delta had to do was say it provided discounts for individuals from a variety of organizations across the political spectrum. If it wanted to end those discounts for political organizations, it could have easily removed all of them once the shooting story died down. Or, in what would have probably been better business, it could have just left things as they were and not changed anything and maintained that it was being content-neutral in offering discounts to major political organizations from all walks of American life.

Instead, it tried to avoid "bad news" and social media discord and cost itself $50 million.

And what did Delta gain from the decision?

Nothing.

There isn't a single person in America who was going to change their travel plans because Delta gave an NRA discount to members who flew the airline, and there isn't a single person who wasn't flying Delta that is now going to start flying Delta because they ended the NRA discount.

Not one.

I honestly believe that.

Moreover, if you are losing business because some people are changing their airlines over your NRA discounts, are those customers who are going to never fly your airline in the future? Even if there are a tiny, tiny subset of people adjusting their behavior, are they really going to adjust their behavior forever? (Remember that United Airlines saw zero impact on its earnings after it dragged the Asian doctor off the plane, which was probably the worst viral publicity any airline company has dealt with in the social media era.)

I don't believe there is a single person in the country who would choose not to fly Delta or to fly Delta over this issue. This story is completely manufactured outrage with no actual impact.

That's especially the case if Delta offers the cheapest and most convenient route to where you want to travel. In other words, that's especially the case if Delta does its job.

If you fly nonstop to where I'm taking my family, and you offer a cheaper fare, I don't care what political organizations you provide a discount to, I'm taking your airline. Hell, I wouldn't even care if the CEO of Delta had come out and said, "I hate Clay Travis and hope his business fails." I'd still fly Delta if they were cheaper and more direct even if the company hated me.

Further, who in their right mind cares what Delta's corporate stance is on the Second Amendment and, more important, who in their right mind is advising these CEOs that they should worry about what customers think about the company's position on the Second Amendment? (Remember how I told you PR people were idiots.)

Here's what I wish Delta's CEO cared about—ensuring that Delta had the best goddamn Wi-Fi of any airline on the planet.

Instead of worrying about gun rights, how about you make it so the Wi-Fi actually works on your airplanes? Make it so I can write an article on Outkick and know beyond a shadow of a doubt that I can publish that article while I'm flying across the country. Because right now not one airline in America's Wi-Fi is good enough for me to be confident I can pull this off.

My point is: focus on what your business does and leave politics by the wayside.

Sane American consumers do not care what corporations think about contentious political issues. We just don't. We care about whether you deliver the best possible value to us as consumers. I feel like companies everywhere are falling victim to social media activists and media inquiries about nonstories and overvaluing what those people are saying online.

I get it; it can be terrifying if you get a hundred people all making threats to you in the same day on social media. But guess what, that happens to me every single day. It doesn't matter what opinion I've shared. I guarantee I have been told thousands and thousands of times that (insert person here) will never read, watch, or listen to what I say because of (insert opinion here).

Guess what happens?

Those people don't stop reading, watching, or listening to Outkick. (In fact, many of them are reading this book right now. They just paid for the book, making me even richer. Hi!)

What's more, those hundred people might actually be ten people with ten different accounts each trying to manufacture outrage to make you believe it's more substantial than it is.

Much of social media is completely fake.

The truth of the matter is this: as long as you do a good job at your core business, your audience is never going to leave over things that don't involve your core business.

Chick-fil-A is a great example. Do you know how many people changed their behavior at Chick-fil-A over the company's public and evangelical religious stance when it came to gay marriage? ZERO. Do you know why? Because Chick-fil-A's chicken sandwich is so good. (You can also argue Chick-fil-A had no business getting involved in politics either, but when you aren't open on Sundays you're kind of branding yourself as a religious company. Are people really going to be surprised when a religious company has religious political opinions relating to marriage? If anything, this helped Chick-fil-A's overall brand because it served as evidence that they practiced what they preached.) Plus, there are thousands of gay people every single day who eat at Chick-fil-A. Do you know why? Because they love a good chicken sandwich too!

When they began opening locations in New York City, there was a widespread media freakout and confident predictions from writers that they would fail. Surely, no one in woke Manhattan would eat there. As I write this, the line is so long every day at the downtown locations they have a rope line and a bouncer letting diners in a few at a time.

Turns out even people in the wokest parts of our country are just like me with the airline. If the product is good, even if the politics aren't the same as yours, you'll still consume the product.

My advice for every company in America is this: find out what you do and do it better tomorrow than you were doing it today. Then repeat that every day for as long as you can. That's how you go from good to great. If something in America isn't connected to your goal of making your company better at what it does, *don't worry one iota about it and ignore all suggestions that you should care about it.*

My own story of social media outrage ended up being a perfect mirror of our modern era because it exposed an important lesson: you can't respond to social media without angering as many people as you please.

I know this from my own experience.

Back in the fall of 2016, Jack Daniel's, the Tennessee-based whiskey, offered to pay me $3,000 to show up at an event in downtown Nashville and send out a tweet from that event.

Because I like money—and alcohol—I agreed to attend.

But then I got a panicked email from Jack Daniel's. Why? Because I'd said something "controversial." What had I said? That I disagreed with the decision of Vanderbilt University, one of my alma maters, to pay millions of dollars to sandblast the word "Confederate" off a building named Confederate Memorial Hall on their campus.

I could probably write an entire book on the absurdity of our modern-day political correct mores being applied to history, but suffice it to say that as a longtime student of history I find decisions like the one Vanderbilt made to be absurd.

I wrote that on Outkick, and then I got this email from Jack Daniel's.

Hey Clay,

I am reaching out to you to let you know that our client has deemed the attached two tweets from earlier today to be a breach of your agreement with them, and thus has chosen to terminate said agreement.

Just so that we are fully transparent, the section of the contract that you breached was section 6A, Part v, which states:

"the Influencer will not commit any act which brings Jack Daniel's into public disrepute, contempt, scandal, or ridicule, or which insults or offends the general community to which Jack Daniel's advertising and publicity materials are directed, or which might tend to injure the success of Jack Daniel's or any of Jack Daniel's products or services including, without limitation, disparaging Jack Daniel's, its products or services, or its competitors."

Our client believes that these are two acts that brings them into public disrepute and which offends the general community to which Jack Daniel's advertising and publicity materials are directed, so they have asked that you **please do not attend Thursday's event.** [This was actually bolded in their email to me. Seriously.] You can expect to receive a letter from our legal team saying something similar.

Please do not take this action personally—we had no choice but to do this, as the client believes that you went too far with these tweets.

What was my "offensive" tweet?

I tweeted this twice with a link to my Outkick article: "Vanderbilt is paying $1.2 million to sandblast the word Confederate off a building. Unbelievable."

That was offensive?!

Of all the things I've said and written over the years, Jack Daniel's believes this tweet brings them "into public disrepute" and "offends the general community"?

Now leaving aside the fact that the only reason Jack Daniel didn't fight for the Confederacy was because he was too young to fight in the Civil War—all his brothers fought for the South—does Jack Daniel's have no idea who drinks their whiskey? Which side do you think the average whiskey drinker is likely to be on, mine or the left-wingers erasing history?

I did what I do when idiocy like this happens. I published the Jack Daniel's emails on my website and told them they could go to hell.

The PR people looked like idiots. (Remember, PR people are mostly idiots.) They created a story where there was no story to begin with.

What's more, they confirmed a fallacy that far too many companies have come to believe: the illusion that placating social media outrage works. The truth, honestly, is you're damned if you do and damned if you don't. My advice is to stand your ground and wait for the next viral outrage story to emerge.

Unfortunately, most in sports aren't taking that advice. They're picking the left-wing answer, favoring one side of the political equation over the other. That's what we saw in the biggest test of free speech in sports media: the disparate treatment of conservative political speech and liberal political speech at ESPN.

Let's talk about the case of Curt Schilling and Jemele Hill.

5

Curt Schilling versus Jemele Hill

In the space of one year, ESPN had two employees give strong political opinions on social media. One of those people was Curt Schilling, a white man who had played pro baseball, attaining a great measure of fame thanks to his bloody sock in the Boston Red Sox run to their first-ever World Series championship. By 2016, Schilling had become one of the network's most prominent on-air baseball analysts. The other person was Jemele Hill, a black woman who had been at ESPN for several years but attained growing prominence in 2015 when she received her own television show on ESPN2.

Many ESPN employees in private conversations with me came back, again and again, to the difference in how these two employees were treated. This was the moment, to them, that crystallized ESPN's embrace of far-left-wing politics and repudiation of any conservative political thought.

What happened?

Let's start with the case of Curt Schilling.

In the spring of 2016, Schilling went on his private Facebook page and shared a meme that had gone viral online. It showed an old man dressed in women's lingerie wearing a wig and bright red lipstick. And the picture alongside the man said, "Let him in! to the restroom with your daughter or else you're a narrow-minded, judgmental, unloving racist bigot who needs to die!!!"

The meme was connected to the ongoing debate in North Carolina over whether the state could restrict public bathrooms to the sex on an individual's birth certificate. Schilling agreed with the North Carolina legislature's new law, which was passed with Republican support to combat a local ordinance that had been passed by Democrats in Charlotte to permit anyone to use any bathroom they felt comfortable utilizing.

A screenshot of Schilling's private Facebook post was taken to Twitter, where it was shared and immediately went viral. The usual far-left-wing sports media suspects expressed outrage that Schilling could share this opinion and still be employed by ESPN.

That night ESPN fired Curt Schilling, issuing this statement: "ESPN is an inclusive company. Curt Schilling has been advised that his conduct was unacceptable and his employment with ESPN has been terminated."

(Schilling had previously been suspended for sharing another conservative meme, one that equated the number of Nazis with the number of Muslim extremists.)

ESPN's firing of Schilling for his private Facebook post set a scary and censorious precedent for ESPN because the line they had drawn was expansive—the network was saying there were private political opinions its employees could not share and remain employed there. At the time, I disagreed with Schilling on the North Carolina bathroom debate. I think people should do what they've been doing for sixty years: use whichever bathroom they want without getting politics involved. However, I also don't have a problem with him sharing this meme on his own Facebook page outside of work hours.

As a First Amendment absolutist, I believe in more speech over less speech. That's because the heart of free speech is the marketplace of ideas it fosters, where everyone should feel comfortable sharing his or her own political opinions. When the First Amendment's marketplace of ideas flourishes, that allows our nation to debate and decide who has the best solutions. This is the only way a liberal, inclusive democracy can succeed. We've lost that if we are all afraid to share our private political opinions outside of work for fear we will lose our jobs. The best way to put an end to bad ideas isn't to attack the people who have those ideas. It's to attack the facts they use to support those ideas.

It's important to note that a substantial portion of Americans would also agree with Curt Schilling's position here. Many also might not agree, but also would understand that he merely shared a popular meme on Facebook. Schilling may have simply found the meme funny. Just because you share something on Facebook doesn't mean you agree with it completely. Just like many of you, I share things on social media that I agree or disagree with all the time.

Regardless, believing that transgender people should use the restroom on their birth certificate isn't a fringe political belief; there are tens of millions of people who would hold that exact same belief, including the majority of the North Carolina legislature. Many of the people who share the same opinion as Schilling also watch ESPN regularly because they like sports too. Moreover, whether you agreed with Schilling or not, it's important to note that he shared this statement on his private Facebook page outside of work hours. It's not as if he shared his comments on transgender bathroom issues in the middle of *Baseball Tonight*, on ESPN's airwaves.

ESPN, in the spring of an election year when political discussions are at their apex, had made a direct ruling on private political speech by an employee—you could be fired for a political opinion the network didn't approve of. Even if, and I believe this is very significant, you were sharing that opinion on your own time on your own social media account.

ESPN punished Schilling not because he shared his political opinions in his private time, but because he shared a political opinion that ESPN disagreed with. This is a significant point. ESPN didn't object to Schilling's sharing of a political opinion, they objected to Schilling's sharing of a political opinion the company's leaders disagreed with.

In other words, if Schilling had endorsed the rights of transgender people to use the bathroom of their choice, he'd still be employed at ESPN. ESPN's decision wasn't content-neutral. They specifically fired him not because he commented on a political issue in his private time, but because they disagreed with his conservative beliefs on transgender bathroom issues.

That has a chilling effect on ESPN's employees because the message you have sent to conservative employees is straightforward—you have the right to share your political opinions in your private life so long as they are the same as ours.

What's more, as I said before, ESPN's decision wasn't content-neutral—the network regularly allows left-wing political opinions to be shared on its airwaves. That is, far from applying the same standards to all employees, ESPN has regularly allowed left-wing political opinions on air.

Shortly before Schilling's firing, an ESPN employee used network airwaves to make a liberal political statement. Bomani Jones, a far-left-wing social justice warrior who recently received his own television show on the network, wore a Cleveland Caucasians shirt on *Mike & Mike*, a morning radio show simulcast on ESPN2. It was an awkward stunt designed to draw attention to his belief that the Cleveland Indians nickname and logo was racist. Now that's a liberal proposition—not endorsed by most fans—that the Cleveland Indians should be forced to change the name of their mascot and Jones's office had nothing to do with any sports argument he was making that day. It's a direct work act that's being distributed by ESPN. That is, Jones's far-left politics, liberal and fringe in nature, were okay to be distributed by ESPN on their airwaves without censure, but Schilling's nonwork, conservative Facebook post was deemed unacceptable to the company.

This has happened over and over again.

In 2018, ESPN's Max Kellerman said on air that the Notre Dame Fighting Irish mascot needed to be changed because the Fighting Irish moniker was offensive to some Irish people.

Really, he said this live on ESPN.

> How hard is it for you, or anyone, to empathize, simply
> empathize, with a group who is offended—even if it is a minority
> of the group that is offended. . . . Many Irish-Americans are
> not offended, but many are. And should that [the Notre Dame
> Fighting Irish moniker and the leprechaun mascot] also change?
> The answer is yes, unequivocally yes. Pernicious, negative
> stereotypes of marginalized people that offend even some
> among them should be changed. It's not that hard.

Leaving aside the absurd logic here, how can you reconcile this disparate treatment? Two ESPN employees advocate extremely fringe liberal positions on the air with no sports connection to either while they are working and the other employee advocates a mainstream conservative opinion on his personal social media page while not working. If you were going to treat everyone equally, aren't Kellerman and Bomani Jones's political positions more of an issue for ESPN?

It's a stretch to argue these are "sports" opinions from either Jones or Kellerman, but the network's bias was truly exposed when they allowed Rachel Nichols, who hosts her own show on ESPN, to deliver a full-throated endorsement of the NBA's decision to pull its all-star game from Charlotte over the North Carolina transgender bathroom law. That is, ESPN allowed Nichols to endorse the opposite political perspective of Schilling *on ESPN's airwaves*, but wouldn't allow Schilling to share a different opinion on his private Facebook page. This is outrageous.

It's clear that ESPN is making decisions not based on political speech itself, but based on whether it agrees with the content of that political speech. You can advocate for far-left-wing political opinions on the network's airwaves, but you can't advocate for conservative political beliefs in your own private time on your own private social media pages.

That's the very definition of unequal treatment.

If, say, ESPN had a policy that all employees were to refrain from discussing political issues in any public arena, then Schilling could be fired for his political statements.

But ESPN doesn't have that policy.

Read again ESPN's statement when they fired Schilling. I want you to note the scary irony here: "ESPN is an inclusive company. Curt Schilling has been advised that his conduct was unacceptable and his employment with ESPN has been terminated."

Isn't ESPN essentially advocating a political position here? It's taking the opposite perspective of Curt Schilling. It's not just that ESPN has a different standard for conservative and liberal opinions, it's that ESPN itself is espousing far-left political opinions.

If the corporation can have a political opinion, isn't it hard to argue that individual employees can't have their own opinions outside of the time they appear on ESPN's airwaves? Essentially what ESPN is saying is that it's fine if you have a political opinion, but it better be the same as ours.

That's what totalitarian governments do.

Read as such, how scary is this statement?

What ESPN is really saying is: "We're an inclusive company. Unless you disagree with us, in which case we're exclusive. And you're fired."

How amazing is it, in this age of diversity, that companies only want diversity of color, not diversity of opinion? Wouldn't it arguably strengthen Disney and ESPN to have people working for it that advance every opinion under the sun, liberal and conservative, so that they can better reflect the country as a whole? There have been thousands, maybe even tens of thousands, of Disney and ESPN employees who agree with Schilling's opinion. Some of them may have even shared the same meme. How nervous are they? What they've been told is pretty clear: you're welcome to have opinions, but they better be the same as ours.

Hello, George Orwell's 1984, welcome to the People's Republic of ESPN.

The firing of Curt Schilling terrified conservative ESPN employees and effectively put them on notice, don't share your conservative opinions in any public manner, even away from work. This opinion, that ESPN had chosen sides in the culture war and picked far-left-wing politics, was echoed by an ombudsman covering the network who wrote in December of 2016 on ESPN's own website what many ESPN employees were telling me privately.

I'm quoting from this article now:

As it turns out, ESPN is far from immune from the political fever that has afflicted so much of the country over the past year. Internally, there's a feeling among many staffers—both liberal and conservative—that the company's perceived move leftward has had a stifling effect on discourse inside the company and has affected its public-facing products. Consumers have sensed that same leftward movement, alienating some.

For most of its history, ESPN was viewed relatively apolitically. Its core focus was—and remains today, of course—sports. Although the nature of sports meant an occasional detour into politics and culture was inevitable, there wasn't much chatter about an overall perceived political bias. If there was any tension internally, it didn't manifest itself publicly.

That has changed in the past few years, and ESPN staffers cite several factors. One is the rise of social media, which has led to more direct political commentary by ESPN employees, even if not delivered via the network's broadcast or digital pipes. Another is ESPN's increase in debate-themed shows, which encourage strong opinions that are increasingly focusing on the overlap between sports and politics.

Many ESPN employees I talked to—including liberals and conservatives, most of whom preferred to speak on background—worry that the company's politics have become a little too obvious, empowering those who feel as if they're in line with the company's position and driving underground those who don't.

"If you're a Republican or conservative, you feel the need to talk in whispers," one conservative ESPN employee said. "There's even a fear of putting Fox News on a TV [in the office]."

But Jemele Hill, co-host of ESPN2's His & Hers, isn't buying that. "I would challenge those people who say they feel suppressed," she said. "Do you fear backlash, or do you fear right and wrong?"

That article was published eight months after Curt Schilling was fired and one month after the election of Donald Trump.

I want you to read Jemele Hill's quote again, "I would challenge those people who say they feel suppressed. Do you fear backlash, or do you fear right and wrong?"

Wow.

Those who see issues in only right and wrong, and simplify everything into black and white categories, are typically not deep thinkers or supporters of a robust First Amendment. Hill was straightforward, she believed her far-left-wing political views were right, and everyone with different opinions was wrong.

Far from being chastened for her public endorsement of far-left-wing politics at the company and on social media, within two months Hill was promoted, the new host of one of ESPN's most prominent network shows, the 6 p.m. eastern *SportsCenter*, which was immediately rechristened *SC6*.

Hill, along with her cohost, Michael Smith, was trumpeted in ESPN's announcement about *SC6*.

With a format geared to fit Smith and Hill's personalities, along with a specially-designed set and its own music, The Six

will be different from any other SportsCenter produced since
ESPN's first telecast of its signature news and information
program in 1979. Debuting on the day after the Super Bowl, the
premiere episode of the weekday offering will be hailed with an
hour-long simulcast on ESPN, ESPN2 and ESPNEWS. Smith
and Hill, who previously co-hosted ESPN2's His & Hers and
will be the first African-American duo to host SportsCenter
on a regular basis, will combine some of the best elements of
their previous program with SportsCenter for the new show,
including a deliberate and well-paced conversational format in
which they discuss sports topics, news, culture and social issues.
The program will continue SportsCenter's focus on news of the
day and breaking news as warranted.

"I'm most excited for the viewers to see how much freedom
we are going to have," said Smith, who's been with ESPN since
2004.

The show, which debuted on February 6, 2017, would last just
thirteen months before both cohosts were forced out amid publicly
collapsing ratings and a near-universal revolt among viewers against
what I dubbed WokeCenter, a consistent intermixing of sports and
left-wing politics to the exclusion of actual sports news.

While the show was canceled for low ratings—and as soon as Hill
and Smith were replaced ratings surged once more—the biggest flash-
point didn't come on the air. It came off the air in September of 2017
when Jemele Hill took to her Twitter account to share her own far-left-
wing political opinions.

On September 11, 2017, just as halftime neared for an opening-
night *Monday Night Football* doubleheader airing on ESPN to kick off
the NFL season, Hill tweeted an attack on the president of the United
States. Hill, whose Twitter profile picture showed her standing between Barack and Michelle Obama at the White House, tweeted that

Donald Trump was a "white supremacist" who had surrounded himself with other white supremacists in his cabinet. She also tweeted that many of his supporters were white supremacists too.

Multiple followers on Twitter tagged her tweets and sent them to me. As I scrolled through the comments she'd made, I found it to be a crucible moment in the intersection of sports and politics—Hill's tweets about Trump had nothing at all to do with sports. There was zero connection between her opinion on Trump and her job at ESPN. This was a prominent ESPN employee deciding to attack Trump, his staff, and his supporters for being racist. What's more, she offered zero defense for her position, simply stating it to be true.

She didn't believe she was doing anything wrong. She didn't just believe she was right, and everyone who disagreed with her was wrong. She believed Trump and his supporters were white supremacists. (Including, evidently, the millions of Trump supporters who had previously voted for Barack Obama in 2008 and 2012.)

In my mind there was zero difference between what Hill had done and what Curt Schilling had done; she'd taken a far-left-wing opinion that wasn't connected to sports and shared it on her Twitter account just like Schilling had taken a conservative political opinion and shared it on his Facebook account. Hill didn't feel the same standard that applied to Curt Schilling should apply to her. She was fine with sharing political opinions that negative about Donald Trump because she believed the company agreed with her.

For the past year, it had been clear: ESPN's employees didn't like Donald Trump, and they were attacking him as they'd never attacked any president before, with some of the most virulent and personal attacks possible in today's media. Now Hill had taken it to the next level, branding a white man, the leader of the country, a white supremacist. This was what had been brewing for a long time; it was why ESPN's employees donated 270 times as much money to Hillary Clinton as they donated to Donald Trump.

I sat looking at the tweets for several minutes. I considered Hill a talented opinionist whom I'd previously had on my radio shows. I'd even tried to convince her to team up with me and do a morning radio show a couple of years ago. Anyone else, I would have instantly retweeted the comments.

But I liked Hill.

As a firm believer in the First Amendment's marketplace of ideas, I didn't even believe that her opinions should be silenced. Still, I couldn't escape the Schilling precedent ESPN had set. What would have happened if Schilling, or any other ESPN employee, had tweeted Barack Obama was a black supremacist, and so were his supporters and cabinet? He or she would have been fired on the spot.

I knew what Hill was thinking though. As she'd told ESPN, she believed she was right, and everyone else was wrong.

I couldn't escape one thought: Why should Curt Schilling have been fired for his political opinions and Hill rewarded and promoted for hers?

Schilling's sharing of the Facebook meme was done on his own private time and from his own private Facebook account. Yet it was deemed unacceptable. Not because it was political, but because it was a conservative political commentary ESPN disagreed with. If ESPN followed its own precedent set with Curt Schilling, then Jemele Hill would be fired.

I didn't want Jemele Hill to be fired because I considered her to be a friend. Although in the wake of my sharing these tweets, she unfollowed me and even blocked me on Twitter, which kept me from seeing her tweets from my account. Sadly, this is exactly what I've come to expect from many left-wing sports media figures. They don't want to engage in debate. They believe they are right and anyone who disagrees with them is wrong. And evil and racist and sexist too.

I already knew she wouldn't be fired for her comments about Donald Trump even though it clearly violated ESPN's social media policy and was every bit as inflammatory to conservatives as Schilling's comments about transgender bathroom issues had been to liberals.

Why would ESPN treat the employee comments differently?

Because ESPN agreed with Hill's comments about Donald Trump and disagreed with Schilling's comments about transgender bathroom issues. At ESPN you were free to have your own political opinions . . . so long as they were the exact same as the company's.

I retweeted Jemele Hill's comments about the president being a white supremacist.

The media explosion was instantaneous, one of the biggest sports stories of the year, and it had absolutely nothing to do with sports.

Now ESPN had a decision to make: Would it treat liberal speech the same way it had treated conservative speech with Curt Schilling? Or would it give Jemele Hill a pass because the company agreed with her that the president was a white supremacist?

You can probably figure out exactly how this went: ESPN's statement established its left-wing political bias clear as day:

> Jemele has a right to her personal opinions, but not to publicly share them on a platform that implies that she was in any way speaking on behalf of ESPN. She has acknowledged that her tweets crossed that line and has apologized for doing so. We accept her apology.

Curt Schilling was fired for his conservative political opinions and Jemele Hill faced no consequences at all for her liberal political opinions. That's despite the fact that Hill's assertion that Trump, his cabinet, and his supporters were white supremacists is likely supported by a smaller contingent of the American public than Schilling's belief that you should use the bathroom of the sex you were born. In other words, Hill's political opinion was more controversial than Schilling's was and was supported by fewer sports fans nationwide.

Yet having established that she would face no consequences for her political speech, Hill continued to repeat her belief that Trump was a white supremacist far and wide, on TV, on social media, on radio, and on podcasts. She knew that ESPN wouldn't treat her the same way they treated Schilling because she knew ESPN agreed with her far-left-wing, liberal criticisms of Trump.

This should be utterly terrifying to everyone reading this book because of the standard that ESPN has now established when it comes to political speech—you only have freedom of speech if you have the same political opinions as your employer.

What's more, Bob Iger, Disney's CEO who was then planning on running for president as a Democrat, acknowledged that he'd personally made the decision not to penalize Hill. This means Iger, who was incentivized to attack the president if he wanted to run for president, was using his company to make political statements. If he decided to run for president, then the Hill decision would put him in good stead with black voters in the primaries across the country. Here, they would see, was a white man who stood up for a black woman's ability to savagely attack Donald Trump and face no consequences at her job.

How did Iger explain his decision? "I felt that we needed to take context into account," he said. "Context included what was going on in America. What I felt, what we felt, was that there were a lot of people who were outraged, particularly black people. They felt that the promise that was given to them—liberty and justice for all—during the Civil War or Civil Rights movement—were theirs. What they've seen in the last couple of months is the opposite. It's not only disappointing, it's angered them. I've never experienced prejudice, certainly not racism. It's hard for me to understand what it feels like to experience racism. We need to take into account *what Jemele and ESPN were feeling* during this time." Look at his final line—"what Jemele and ESPN were feeling." He's admitting that Jemele's opinion is the same as the company's.

How can you read these quotes and not see them as transparently political and favoring one side over another? (Bob Iger would decide in 2018 not to run for president due to his announced purchase of many 21st Century Fox assets. He told *Vogue* magazine that he had, in fact, been preparing for a run for president prior to that announced merger. I offered Iger an opportunity to comment on his Jemele Hill decision and other political issues at ESPN for the book, but he declined. The only public comment Disney's CEO has made about me was favoriting a tweet about an article criticizing me in September 2017. That was a bit odd because Iger rarely favorites anything on Twitter.)

Regardless, being the CEO of a prominent company like Disney and setting different standards for political speech based on whether that speech is conservative or liberal has a chilling impact on our national discourse.

It's true that Curt Schilling wasn't fired by a governmental entity for his Facebook post and so the First Amendment isn't directly implicated. The First Amendment applies to governmental regulation of speech, not private consequences of that speech. However, that misses the larger issues at play: Isn't Disney as powerful as many of the states in this country?

Put it this way: If power was your goal, would you rather be governor of Wyoming or CEO of Disney?

Does anyone pick Wyoming governor?

Just about everyone has to work for a corporation these days. If corporations start policing social media comments made outside of office hours and firing employees for political opinions the corporations disagree with, shouldn't that be scary to everyone regardless of their political persuasions? Doesn't that ultimately detract from the First Amendment's marketplace of ideas?

If, as I certainly think is the case, many ESPN employees are terrified to share their political opinions on their social media accounts for fear of losing their jobs, how is that making the debate in this country robust and uninhibited?

Very few of us are so rich and so wealthy that we can live without being employed somewhere. Why should only the extremely wealthy have full freedom of speech today?

Especially when many large corporations are more powerful than state governments. These corporations have more power today to constrict speech than many governments do. That's one of many reasons why it's absurd that a company's employees and a company have to agree on everything.

Sure, Disney is a liberal corporation under Bob Iger's leadership, and you may well agree with his inconsistent decisions in the cases of Schilling and Hill. However, what if someone works at Hobby Lobby, a conservative corporation, and posts a strong belief on the right to abortion or birth control on social media? Should Hobby Lobby be able to fire them for that opinion because their opinion differs with Hobby Lobby's?

I don't think so.

Corporations and employees shouldn't have to be allied on the same side of political opinion. Employees shouldn't fear for their jobs if they share opinions online in their private time. Corporations, as we saw with Schilling, have a great deal of power to enforce agreement when it comes to political speech. That's not okay, and it's not right. Regardless of your political persuasion, you should find it alarming that Curt Schilling and Jemele Hill weren't treated the same by Bob Iger and Disney.

Disney's unequal treatment of political speech would continue over Memorial Day weekend in 2018 when the company announced the hiring of Keith Olbermann to work at ESPN. The same Keith Olbermann who hosted a far-left-wing talk show on MSNBC and had published a book entitled *Trump Is F*cking Crazy*. Just in case you thought Olbermann was joking and utilizing hyperbole to sell books he appended the helpful parenthetical *(This is not a joke)* and spent much of the past two years regularly tweeting that the president was a Nazi, white-supremacist racist who needed to be impeached. So in case you were keeping score, calling the president a Nazi? Acceptable. Saying you think people should use the bathrooms on their birth certificates? Unacceptable.

Much to the chagrin of many of my far-left-wing haters in the sports media, who only support free speech when they agree with it, I'm all in on the marketplace of ideas, a First Amendment absolutist. I believe that you should be able to share any opinion in any way that you see fit. It's the only way to figure out which ideas are the best for our country. I also believe that you shouldn't have to worry about losing your job because of your political opinion that is privately expressed outside of work hours.

The far-left-wing sports media has gone so insane of late that many of them argued that Kevin McHale shouldn't be able to work at TNT or coach in the NBA again because he attended a Donald Trump rally in Minnesota. Seriously. He wasn't even on stage. He was just picked out in a crowd photo.

It's only when everyone feels entirely comfortable sharing their opinions that we allow the marketplace to decide which ideas win. Right now we don't have that. We have an artificially circumscribed level of discourse, and I believe that's why there is so much anger in this country today. Many people don't feel they have the freedom to say what they believe and remain employed.

Whether you agree with Schilling's opinion or not, what we're moving toward is an era when robust debate is silenced, and the marketplace of ideas isn't an actual thriving marketplace. That matters because sometimes fringe opinions on the left or right eventually become mainstream ideas. We need to allow all opinions to live freely and employees to share them freely without fear of termination at their jobs. We need to end the era of acceptable and unacceptable opinions in this country. There's a huge difference between saying "I disagree with you and here's why" and "I disagree with you and you should never be able to utter that opinion in public again and remain employed."

Furthermore, let's return anew to the standard being set by Disney, ESPN, and their CEO Bob Iger. Where is Curt Schilling free to share his opinion on transgender bathroom issues? If he can't do it on his private social media accounts because he's employed by Disney, he's silenced there. Can he do it at dinner with his friends and family? What if a waiter secretly records that conversation and posts it online? Disney would be under the same pressure to act as now.

When and where can Schilling share his opinion and keep his job with ESPN? Given the rapid collapse between public and private life in this country, the answer may well be nowhere.

For those of you who say, "Well, he's free to share his opinion, but not be employed by Disney," why should your personal political beliefs dictate where you can work? I just fundamentally reject this idea that we should all choose which companies we work for based on the company's leaders having the same political beliefs that we do. Liberal, conservative, libertarian, totally uninterested in politics, I think everyone should be treated the exact same so long as their behavior is legal. I think companies are stronger for employing people with all different sorts of opinions. The company isn't speaking when employees give their opinions online, individual people are.

Surely we're all smart enough to see this, right?

Ultimately, I decided to share Jemele Hill's tweets even at the expense of our friendship—and my ability to even see her tweets any longer— because I believe ESPN's policy is unfair, flat-out wrong, and setting the wrong precedent for political speech in all of sports media. What Disney and Bob Iger decide, most companies will follow.

I believe all speech, conservative or liberal, should be treated the same. Either ESPN should make a pronouncement that no employees can share public political opinions, a stance I would disagree with, or they should say that on their private Facebook and Twitter pages their employees are free to espouse the political causes they agree with regardless of whether the company agrees with it or not.

As is, we've reached an untenable place with misplaced incentives. In punishing Schilling for conservative politics and allowing Hill to have free rein when it comes to liberal politics, the message ESPN has sent to social media users is unfortunate—let's police political thought for acceptability.

And is that really behavior ESPN, Disney, or any company wants to encourage?

Because I can't get away from the environment ESPN has encouraged—some losers out there were hitting REFRESH on Curt Schilling's personal Facebook page all day long just waiting for him to express a conservative political opinion they disagreed with.

Just so they could try and get a guy fired for having a political opinion they disagreed with.

Have we really reached an era when we care so much what former athletes think about transgender bathroom issues that we insist that multibillion-dollar corporations take action against them if they have a different opinion than we do?

More important: Does it really advance the cause of transgender advocates to demand Curt Schilling be fired for his opinion? I would argue the exact opposite; this makes Schilling a martyr for many people who agree with him and makes sympathetic people in the middle of an issue recoil. I think this polarizes a debate that shouldn't be polarizing.

Somehow we managed to make it through the 1970s, the 1980s, the 1990s, the 2000s, and the early 2010s without needing politics to be involved in what bathrooms you used. Our policy was pretty straightforward—you used the bathroom of the sex you looked like. No one stood outside the bathroom conducting Crocodile Dundee crotch checks to see which gender you were. (Ironically this entire controversy began when the City of Charlotte's liberal city council decided to protect transgender people's access to the bathroom of their choice. This access, of course, wasn't actually being threatened, but the Charlotte politicians were trying to look as liberal as possible. So Charlotte passed a new law for their city and then the State of North Carolina's legislature, which is more conservative, repudiated that regulation and created a new law canceling it out. Which means, sigh, this entire controversy was totally unnecessary. Republican and Democratic politicians just wanted to find something to fight about. The ultimate irony here, by the way, was that Charlotte, which was trying to be uberinclusive, ended up losing the NBA's All-Star Game and the ACC title game in football even though the city had done nothing wrong. This entire case, to be honest, is a perfect example of how the nation, and the sports leagues, have lost their minds.)

ESPN's decision on Schilling created an incentive for fans sitting in front of their computer screens or phones to wait for someone to say or write something they disagreed with just to demand the company take action and punish that speech. If ESPN hadn't fired Curt Schilling, I would have never shared what Jemele Hill said about the president. And I still don't believe either Schilling or Hill should have been fired, I just believe Disney should treat them the same.

Newsflash: if you're trying to silence the political opinions of others— or cause them to lose their jobs—you aren't a social justice warrior, you're a totalitarian foe of free speech.

That should scare all of us, regardless of our political persuasions.

Especially when ESPN's decision on Schilling created the atmosphere for a one-sided lionization of Colin Kaepernick when he took a knee on the sideline.

6

Colin Kaepernick's Protest Made No Sense

On Friday, August 26, 2016, before an otherwise unremarkable pre-season NFL game between the San Francisco 49ers and the Green Bay Packers, Colin Kaepernick, a quarterback entering his sixth season in the NFL, refused to stand for the national anthem. The decision, made just over three months before the 2016 presidential election between Donald Trump and Hillary Clinton, would become a cultural flash-point for the intersection of sports and politics—the single decision, more so than any other, that ended the role of sports as an escape from politics and turned sports into just another avenue for political rancor.

The resulting media coverage of Kaepernick's protest, once and for all, demonstrated that the sports media and the sports television networks had an inherent liberal bias that saw virtually no network or media member willing or able to criticize Kaepernick without receiving substantial censure. There is much to unpack from Kaepernick, but most of it, not surprisingly, has little to do with Kaepernick himself, who while becoming a cultural flashpoint has said little of substantive, coherent, or intelligent political thought.

Before we explain how Kaepernick became such a lightning rod, let's first return to what Kaepernick himself has said to explain the protest that he began in late August of 2016.

After the game, Kaepernick said: "I am not going to stand up to show pride in a flag for a country that oppresses black people and people of color. To me, this is bigger than football, and it would be selfish on my part to look the other way. There are bodies in the street and people getting paid leave and getting away with murder."

These postgame comments represented the totality of Kaepernick's explanation of his protest on that night. This is why, in his sixth season in the NFL, he suddenly decided not to stand for the national anthem. As if that weren't enough, Kaepernick made these postgame comments while wearing a Fidel Castro and Malcolm X t-shirt. Later in the season, before a game against the Miami Dolphins, Armando Salguero, a Dolphins beat writer born in Havana, Cuba, aggressively questioned Kaepernick on his Fidel Castro t-shirt. Kaepernick fell apart when he was asked to explain how he could wear a t-shirt with a picture of Fidel Castro while advocating for minority rights. Since, you know, the Castros have an awful record when it comes to oppressing their people and Cubans have no First Amendment rights. No one in Cuba would be able to disrespect the country's anthem like Kaepernick had done. Pressed on the issue, Kaepernick was unable to make any sense at all:

"One thing Fidel Castro did do is they have the highest literacy rate [note: this isn't true] because they invest more in their education system than they do in their prison system, which we do not do here even though we're fully capable of doing that. . . . We do break up families here. That's what mass incarceration is. That was the foundation of slavery, so our country has been based on that as well as the genocide of Native Americans."

As you can see, Kaepernick, when finally confronted about his outfit and his political beliefs, was nonsensical.

Back in August, however, he addressed his political beliefs more substantially. Spoiler alert: they were mostly nonsensical too. Here was Kaepernick attempting to explain why he wasn't standing for the national anthem: "There's a lot of things that need to change. One specifically is police brutality; there's people being murdered unjustly and not being held accountable. The cops are getting paid leave for killing people. That's not right. That's not right by anyone's standards.

"There is police brutality. People of color have been targeted by police.

So that's a large part of it. And they're government officials. They're put in place by the government, so that's something that this country has to change.

"There's things we can do to hold them more accountable, make those standards higher.

"You have people that practice law and are lawyers and go to school for eight years, but you can become a cop in six months and don't have to have the same amount of training as a cosmetologist.

"That's insane. Someone that's holding a curling iron has more education and more training than people that have a gun and are going out on the street to protect us."

Asked what evidence of this he had, Kaepernick replied: "I've seen videos. I've seen circumstances where men and women that have been in the military have come back and been treated unjustly by the country they fought for and have been murdered by the country they fought for, on our land. That's not right."

This interaction with the media was also telling. Kaepernick wasn't familiar with the phrase "blanket indictment" or aware, at all, that his comments might be seen as indicting all of law enforcement. This is not surprising considering Kaepernick chose to also practice in socks depicting police officers as pigs:

Q: Are you concerned that this is seen as a blanket indictment of law enforcement?

KAEPERNICK: What's that?

Q: It can be seen as a blanket indictment of law enforcement.

KAEPERNICK: As far as what? I don't really understand what you're trying to get at.

Q: You say people are getting murdered by police. You seem to indict all of police.

At least now, hopefully, Kaepernick is familiar with the term "blanket indictment."

Later in the conversation, Kaepernick was asked about his specific political opinions in an election year:

Q: Does the fact that this is an election year have anything to do with the timing?

KAEPERNICK: Once again, it wasn't a timing thing. It wasn't something that was planned. But I think the two presidential candidates that we currently have also represent the issue that we have in this country right now.

Q: Do you want to expound on that?

KAEPERNICK: I mean, you have Hillary who's called black teens or black kids super-predators.

You have Donald Trump who's openly racist.

I mean, we have a presidential candidate [Hillary Clinton] who's deleted emails and done things illegally and is a presidential candidate. That doesn't make sense to me, because if that was any other person, you'd be in prison.

So what is this country really standing for?

Kaepernick, it would later emerge, also had never bothered to vote in his life. It is telling, however, that just about everyone reading this book is hearing for the first time that Colin Kaepernick said Hillary Clinton should be in prison. Isn't it amazing what quotes the left-wing sports media embrace? It seems like a pretty big deal that Kaepernick, amid his nonsensical rambling, said that Hillary Clinton should be in prison. That wasn't covered by the left-wing sports media because it didn't fit their narrative.

Covering these quotes would have also necessitated that the media acknowledge what all of you reading this right now are thinking: Kaepernick's political beliefs are essentially nonsensical. Yet other than these comments, Kaepernick has not spoken publicly for the past two years, preferring to spend his time on social media sharing inflammatory posts and memes. Kaepernick would later tweet that police are modern-day slave catchers and his girlfriend would compare the Baltimore Ravens owner to a plantation owner and call Ray Lewis, the most famous Baltimore Raven of all time, an Uncle Tom.

Kaepernick was unsigned for the entirety of the 2017 football season and subsequently filed a collusion lawsuit against NFL owners, claiming they were unlawfully conspiring not to hire him. As part of that lawsuit, the NFL owners were deposed. What did Kaepernick wear to these depositions? A Kunta Kinte shirt and a "Slave Patrol" t-shirt. Seriously.

Given his outlandish provocations, it's worth noting that Kaepernick is of mixed race; he has a white mother and a black father, and was raised by a white family after his parents gave him up for adoption. Prior to his protest Kaepernick was most well known for taking the San Francisco 49ers to the Super Bowl and losing to the Baltimore Ravens and Joe Flacco. He has made, at publication date, just shy of $44 million in his six seasons as an NFL quarterback, including $14.3 million in the final year he played in the NFL, when Blaine Gabbert beat him out as a starting quarterback and he began his protest. He is 2–16 in his last 18 games as a starting quarterback in the NFL.

Before we diagnose the liberal bias in the fawning media coverage that Kaepernick has received, let's aggressively unpack what Kaepernick has said. First, on the day he began his protest: "I am not going to stand up to show pride in a flag for a country that oppresses black people and people of color. To me, this is bigger than football, and it would be selfish on my part to look the other way. There are bodies in the street and people getting paid leave and getting away with murder."

Even though he hasn't said it concretely, it appears that effectively Colin Kaepernick is protesting oppression against "black people and people of color" and police shootings of minorities. Let's do what the media should have done and hold political figures—it seems clear that's what Kaepernick hopes to be—accountable for what they have said.

First, the federal government is not oppressing black people or other people of color. There are no federal laws presently in place that discriminate against black people in this country. There is a difference between racism, which exists in this country, and oppression under the law based on race, which does not exist. This is not a controversial opinion for anyone with a legal background or a decent education in modern civics.

Even still you can't say there are no discriminatory laws on the books on ESPN. Indeed, ESPN's Paul Finebaum, who hosts a four-hour daily radio show on the SEC Network, went on ESPN and said exactly this about the Colin Kaepernick protests, "This country has issues, but this country is not oppressing black people."

The resulting firestorm from the left unfolded in a now predictable manner. Finebaum, who is a good friend of mine, but didn't want to talk about the issue for this book, went back on television and said: "I could spend the rest of my life trying to talk my way out of it, but I can't. I blew it. I simply did not have a good grasp of the situation. I know better. I've lived in this country, I see what is going on across the country from North to South to East to West, and I have no excuse.

"I can't explain why I articulated the words the way I did, but I did, and there is a public record of it, and there's a natural reaction, and I respect that. All I can say is that I made a terrible mistake in trying to express a feeling that I probably—not probably—I had no right to express. I don't know whether this will mean anything to anyone, but I feel compelled to answer your question that way—that it was a terrible mistake on my part and my eyes are wider-open today than they have ever been as a result."

I want you to think about this for a moment. Paul Finebaum, one of the men with the largest audiences in sports today talking about football, said he had no right to express an actual fact on television if it hurt some people's feelings.

Paul Finebaum was exactly right; there are no federal laws that oppress people of color or blacks based on their race in the country today. That would be flagrantly unconstitutional. There is certainly a history of discrimination in this country based on race, but we have eliminated those laws through rigorous lawyering. (If those laws still exist today—which I don't believe they do—they could be challenged and would be struck down by every court in America.) But it's an alarming sign of where we are as a country, and in sports media in general, that a Jewish white guy like Paul Finebaum, who I know doesn't have a racist bone in his body, feels compelled to apologize for stating a noncontroversial fact on ESPN.

The reaction to Finebaum's comments had a chilling effect. If a white man, even one with a large audience like Paul Finebaum's, can't give his opinion on Kaepernick's protest, and demonstrate its inherent flaws, without being attacked by a far-left-wing mob and forced to apologize, what benefit is there in challenging Kaepernick at all? The shouting down of Paul Finebaum on ESPN had a chilling effect on what could and couldn't be said by mainstream sports media figures. Why risk your job over this issue? The message to anyone who wasn't a far-left liberal was clear, shut your mouth.

Regardless, the first part of this Colin Kaepernick statement, his assertion that minorities are being oppressed by the federal government, simply isn't true. Yet it speaks to the liberalism of the sports media that no one challenged Kaepernick on this opinion at the time he said it and that even if someone like Paul Finebaum challenged Kaepernick on it a few days later, he had to apologize for making a factual statement that made some people uncomfortable.

A rigorous and unbiased sports media should have felt comfortable asking a question like this of Colin Kaepernick: What tangible decisions does the United States government—at the time led by a black man as president and a black woman as head of the justice department—make that oppresses people of color? The answer is, there are none. Which is why the follow-up question for Kaepernick should have been: Can you give me actual governmental actions that legally treat black people differently in a negative fashion that you feel need to be changed? Again, once you demand that your voice be heard in this fashion, you need to explain what you want changed. I don't want banal generalities. I want specific issues that have so troubled you that you feel the need to stop standing for the national anthem for the first time in your six-year NFL career.

Because, here's the deal, when I review federal law in the present day, what I see is the exact opposite of black oppression. Everyone is treated as equally as they possibly can be by the federal government. There is no systemic racism in our federal government. In fact, affirmative action is actually a governmental attempt to treat black people unequally—that is, more favorably than other people—solely because of their race. If anything, the United States government's laws discriminate *in favor of black people based on their skin color.*

I'm open to hearing what systemic oppression Kaepernick believes the United States government is undertaking and what he believes needs to be redressed. However, he has provided none of these specifics so far. If you want me to treat your opinions with respect, you need to provide opinions worthy of respect. Not just insipid generalities.

The first rationale for Kaepernick's protest—stopping the direct oppression of people of color and minorities by the federal government— doesn't exist. He's protesting a nonissue.

Okay, what about police shootings of black people? Well, he's wrong here too. Let me explain.

First, the paid-leave comment is a sign of Kaepernick's painful lack of understanding. Police get paid leave when any shootings occur to allow an investigation to take place into that shooting. That's a union-negotiated part of all police contracts that has nothing to do with the race of who is being shot or whether police are justified or unjustified in the shooting. They aren't being rewarded for shooting someone with a paid vacation; this is a standard practice to ensure that if someone is behaving outside the law, they don't go rogue and continue to shoot people—white, black, brown, or yellow—with impunity. Furthermore, an automatic leave is given whether the shooting is justified or unjustified, questionable or unquestionable, whether the victim is unarmed and not dangerous or in the process of committing serial murder. Kaepernick's commentary on police receiving paid leave in the wake of shootings is unsophisticated, uneducated, and, significantly, went totally unquestioned by anyone in the sports media.

Second, if a police officer is "getting away with murder," it's because one of two things is happening: (1) the police department is covering up for a guilty party or (2) a jury fails to convict a police officer who has been charged with a crime. Let's discuss the second one first. If a police officer is charged with a crime and not convicted of that crime by a jury, it's because that jury didn't find him guilty beyond a reasonable doubt. Juries face difficult decisions and must reach a unanimous verdict to find a police officer defendant guilty or not guilty. Whether you agree or disagree with their decisions, if you're upset with the verdict, your issue is with our juries, not our police.

So that leaves us with only one remaining rationale for Kaepernick's protest—that police are getting away with the murder of black people. Giving Kaepernick the benefit of the doubt, let's say that local police are getting away with murders of innocent black people and their wrongdoing is being covered up by the blue wall of silence.

Okay, if that were the case, what tangible action would you request on behalf of your federal government to ensure that didn't happen? Maybe Kaepernick isn't aware that there is a state and federal system of justice in this country. If you're unhappy with the local or state level investigations, you could bring in the federal government's justice system to investigate as well. Maybe, to be very generous, Kaepernick was protesting to request more federal oversight of police shootings of minorities. Even though he hasn't been able to succinctly elucidate that goal, maybe what he's seeking is that the federal government ensure that local police departments didn't cover up illegal police shootings with biased and unfair investigations that favored the police at the expense of minority victims. You'd also want these investigations to occur in all cases of police shootings, not just those involving white police officers and black citizens, which represent a small percentage of police shootings in general, but Kaepernick hasn't expressed any issue with white people being shot by police, only minorities.

That seems like a reasonable request, right?

Well, guess what? President Barack Obama and Attorney General Loretta Lynch—and before that Attorney General Eric Holder—were already doing exactly that! The federal government, which Colin Kaepernick was protesting, helmed up by a black man as president and a black woman and black man as attorney general and head of the justice department, was already conducting their own federal investigations into questionable police shootings of minorities. That's how we know, for instance, that the Michael Brown case in Missouri, the famous hands-up, don't-shoot case, was a lie, because the federal government, just like the state and local governments, cleared the police officer in that case. The federal government, representing the flag that Colin Kaepernick refused to stand for, was already doing everything it could to protect against citizens, including minorities, being wrongly shot by police.

This means that effectively Colin Kaepernick's entire protest was about demanding an action that was already taking place. Putting it in layman's terms, Kaepernick basically walked into McDonald's and took a knee at 11:01, right when he believed McDonald's switched to serving lunch, demanding that breakfast be served all day long at McDonald's. And then the manager, hearing about the protest, could have walked out and extended his hand to Kaepernick and said, "You can go ahead and stand up. We already serve breakfast all day long here." But no one did that. No manager came out, no one in the media came out and told Kaepernick and the social justice warriors that breakfast was already being served, that what they wanted was already taking place.

I voted for Barack Obama twice and think he was a good president who inherited a disastrous mess from George W. Bush, who I believe was the worst president of my lifetime—I can see many of you rolling your eyes as you read this book. However, if Obama would have simply come out and said, "I respect what Colin Kaepernick's doing and agree with him that far too many people in this country are victims of violence, but we are already conducting investigations to ensure that police officers who commit crimes are charged with crimes. What he's protesting for is already taking place," much of the protest's moral imperative would have faded.

This is where I believe Barack Obama, a liberal sports fan, fell victim to the same blind spot that the sports media, made up of almost completely liberal sports fans, fell victim to as well. They believed in Kaepernick's political stance even if that political stance wasn't justified when you examined the logic behind his decision. They decided to side with feelings instead of facts.

What's more, if you didn't agree with Kaepernick's actions, as likely many sports media did not, they saw what happened to Paul Finebaum when he dared to question the legitimacy of Kaepernick's protest on ESPN. The lesson was clear: don't say anything negative about Kaepernick if you want to keep your job and avoid being publicly branded a racist.

The truth was this: Colin Kaepernick was protesting the federal government, demanding that they undertake an action that they had already undertaken. His protest made no logical sense at all. He was effectively taking a knee during the national anthem because he was opposed to the violent death of black people in America.

Yeah, join the club, bud.

If you're opposed to violent minority deaths, do you know who you should be protesting, by the way? Not the federal government. You should be taking a knee to protest black violence against other black people since that is the real plague on urban neighborhoods today. According to the most recent FBI statistics, over 93 percent of all black murder victims come at the hands of other black people.

Look, I don't think Colin Kaepernick is a bad guy; I think he's just painfully unaware of the fact he was protesting the federal government, demanding that they do something they were already doing. His depth of knowledge comes from Twitter, where inflammatory videos and fake news are the coin of the realm. As my good friend Fox Sports commentator Jason Whitlock likes to say, Colin Kaepernick is Twoke, Twitter woke. Social media is great for making you feel things, but it's not particularly good at making you know what's true and what isn't. And it's certainly not very useful at all for educating anyone on complex facts.

Far from being beneficial to our country, Kaepernick's protest inflamed and encouraged the propagation of a falsehood—namely that unarmed and innocent black people are regularly being murdered by police officers in this country.

This is the biggest lie in twenty-first-century American society.

Let me share the data with you because it's eye-opening and because no one else in sports media will do it. One of the problems with sports—and the larger media society in general—is the failure to explain and share factual evidence if it contradicts our feelings or preconceived political beliefs.

The *Washington Post* has a database that has cataloged all police shootings nationwide over the past several years. Let's look at those of 2016 and 2017. Combining the data from two years of this database, you will find the following stats: In 2017 police shot and killed 987 people and in 2016 they shot and killed 963 people. (Numbers for 2018 are tracking at roughly these same rates as well.) Plainly, everyone reading this book regardless of race, sex, gender, or religious affiliation is opposed to violent deaths of innocent people. But police have violent jobs and sometimes, albeit very rarely, they have to shoot and kill people who are threats to the rest of us.

When police do shoot, do you know whom they typically shoot and kill? White people.

In 2016 and 2017 there were 1,804 people shot and killed by police with their race cataloged in that *Washington Post* database.

Here was that racial breakdown:

923 white, 51% white
456 black, 25% black
339 Hispanic, 19% Hispanic
86 other races, 5% other races
(146, race unknown)

So only one-quarter of all deadly police shootings involved black people in the past several years. Despite what the media may tell you, many of those shootings would have been committed by minority police officers too. Seventy-five percent of all police shooting victims in 2016 and 2017 were white, Hispanic, Asian, or another race.

So when Colin Kaepernick took a knee to protest police shootings of black people, he was actually ignoring the fact that 75 percent of all police shooting victims weren't black.

Now you can certainly argue that black people represent just 12 or 13 percent of the population, so these shootings, given that 25 percent of the victims are black, reflect racial discrimination, but remember, police don't interact violently with the vast, vast majority of us. Young men are typically the perpetrators of violence in America today. And as a percentage of their population the most likely violent felons in the country? Young black men. (Despite representing only 6 percent of the population, young black men, those between the ages of sixteen and forty, commit over half of all murders in this country.)

This isn't racism; these are facts. (Although, interestingly, any fact that makes people uncomfortable is now labeled racist.) And if you take into account rates of violent crime, you find out an interesting detail—black suspects are actually *less likely* to be shot by police when violent criminality data is considered on a per capita basis. (Remember, these are just acts of violent crime. I'm not talking about low-level drug offenses or nonviolent crime. Black people commit well over 25 percent of all violent crimes, including over half of all murders in this country. In other words, violent crime is not committed at the same rate by all races. Black people commit far more acts of violent crime than white, Hispanic, or Asian people do as a percentage of their population. And, again, I'm eliminating nonviolent drug offenses from this data and just using the most recent FBI data on violent crimes.)

Okay, let's dive into the data more.

How about unarmed people shot by police? Well, we have 2016 and 2017 data for that too. Presumably, people who are unarmed are more likely to be innocent of any wrongdoing.

Here are those combined numbers of unarmed deaths for the past two years. (Numbers which are similar to 2018 data at the time of publication as well.)

52 white, 45% white
38 black, 33% black
22 Hispanic, 19% Hispanic
4 other races, 3% other races

Now we are getting somewhere. First, what you'll see is there have only been 116 people shot and killed by police who were unarmed in the past two years. Remember, unarmed doesn't mean without danger. Someone attacking an officer with fists or legs or reaching for an officer's weapon would be unarmed. The same is also true of someone beating up another person. Furthermore, many of these police shooters, despite what the media may show you, would have been minority officers shooting and killing minority offenders. That is, as small as these numbers are, the number of shootings that were white police officers shooting unarmed black victims is even smaller.

Second, this is *incredibly* rare.

How rare?

Bees, wasps, and hornets killed more unarmed people in 2016 and 2017 than the police did. (Bees, wasps, and hornets nabbed 118 of us to 116 killed by the police.) If you don't carry a weapon, you were literally under more danger from insects than you were from police over the past two years.

Putting this into even more context, you were five times as likely to be killed by a train as you were a police officer if you left your house unarmed in the past two years.

Yet this factual data hasn't taken root in the sports community because it's less powerful than social media fear. Worse, the sports media praises athletes who share and further propagate this fear because it reflects the sports media's political viewpoints—that America is an awful, racist place.

In 2016, LeBron James said this about police violence and the Kaepernick protests: "It's a scary-ass situation that if my son calls me and says he's been pulled over, that I'm not that confident that things are going to go well and my son is going to return home."

This is just fundamentally untrue from a statistical basis.

If LeBron had said, "It's a scary-ass situation that if my son leaves the house with all the bees, wasps, and hornets in this country, I'm not that confident that things are going to go well and my son is going to return home," and his son isn't allergic to bees, everyone would have ridiculed him.

Yet he was universally praised for the "wokeness" of his take about police violence by the far-left-wing sports media.

This is unfortunate because sharing unwarranted fears about law enforcement makes police interactions between minorities and police more likely to end with violence. Indeed, here's another stat you won't see any other athlete or member of the liberal sports media share: in 2016 police were 18.5 times as likely to be killed by a black person as they were to kill a black person.

From a statistical basis, if somebody needs to be scared when a police officer pulls over a young black man it isn't minorities. It's the police. Hell, if Colin Kaepernick really wanted to make a difference he should have taken a knee . . . for the police!

Even the *Washington Post*, in an article about its own database of police shootings in 2018, would write that it was now difficult to argue there was any racial bias when it came to police shootings of unarmed people. The fear is real in the black community, but the statistical evidence isn't there to support that fear.

Furthermore, if, as he stated in the protest, Kaepernick cares about "bodies in the street and people . . . getting away with murder," shouldn't he be focusing on all the people shot and killed by police since 75 percent of them are white, Hispanic, or Asian? Isn't it a flaw of his protest that he's focusing on a small minority of police violence victims? And if Kaepernick just wants to focus on minority victims of violence, shouldn't he focus more on the problem of all the people getting away with killing black people in America? Every year thousands of black people are killed in this country. As I stated earlier according to the most recent FBI data, 93 percent of all black murders are committed by black people. So the best way to save minority lives is to focus on unsolved black murders by partnering with police to solve those crimes, not stoking unwarranted black fears of extremely rare police violence.

Kaepernick focused his protest on a tiny, tiny percentage of deaths. It was the equivalent of an obese man who weighs 700 pounds deciding his big toe is too fat. In so doing, Kaepernick ignored over 99 percent of black murders in this country in which race isn't involved to focus on the 1 percent that might, in some small way, involve race.

In so doing, he managed to alienate people who would otherwise agree with him. People of all races, genders, ethnicities, and religions are against the murder of the innocent. Instead of uniting these people Kaepernick politicized sports, the very place most of us go to escape the serious things in life. Especially at this time in our country, when unity is so rare.

All of these facts matter—#FactLivesMatter—and provide substantial context and factual data to the Colin Kaepernick protest, which was motivated by feelings, not facts.

Yet almost no one else in the sports media is writing it or saying any of this.

Why?

Because if they're white, Hispanic, or Asian they're afraid of being called racist, and if they're black they're afraid of being called an Uncle Tom.

Remember, as Paul Finebaum said in his apology on ESPN, he had "no right to express" his factual opinion on the oppression of black people by the federal government when it contradicted someone else's feelings.

Why? Because he was white.

Fear of being called racist is so powerful that Colin Kaepernick's entire protest, which makes zero logical or factual sense when examined in detail, could happen and virtually no one would challenge it.

What's more, this fear of publicly being branded a racist wasn't just prevalent in the sports media, as you'll see in the next chapter; that failure and the fear of challenging Kaepernick's protest also led to the NFL's response being incredibly bungled and for ratings to collapse.

All because the NFL, its commissioner, and its owners, were afraid of sharing all the data I just shared with you. Make no mistake, the NFL blew it when it came to Kaepernick's protest, and the league paid a heavy price.

7

The NFL's Bungled Response to Kaepernick

Whether you agree or disagree with Colin Kaepernick's protest, you probably agree the NFL bungled its response to the protest.

That's because at the time of Kaepernick's protest the NFL had a specific rule in place mandating that players stand for the national anthem. It's not that controversial of a rule either; it's the same one that the NBA has. (In late May of 2018 the NFL implemented a new policy for the anthem, which we will discuss in detail later in this chapter.)

You may feel, as I do, that standing for the national anthem is a strange way to begin a sporting event, particularly one involving for-profit professional businesses. You may also even stand in front of your seats at an NFL game, as I do, and wonder why the United States government is providing planes to fly over stadiums before kickoff. Or even stranger, why people feel compelled to cheer so wildly at the spectacle of a military plane flying over a stadium. The reason the NFL does it isn't complicated: NFL owners have decided that being firmly connected to the military is good for business. And if you're an employee and your boss decides something is good for business, guess what, you do it or you leave.

It turns out that being patriotic was so good for NFL business that the league was actually paid by the different branches of the military for some of those tearful military family reunions you saw at halftimes across the country. You know, when a service member came back home, and the kids and wives or husbands all gathered on the field for a spontaneous celebration that brought tears to our eyes.

Paid. Advertising.

Yes, the NFL got money to bring dads and moms back to their kids from wars overseas and surprise the youngsters.

If that's not cold-blooded accounting, I don't know what is. That's why the NFL isn't a hero or a villain in the Colin Kaepernick story. It's just a big business, and big business wants what's good for big business, which is almost always more money.

I respect the cold, hard logic of a balance sheet. That's what capitalism is, a valuation of a business from a numerical perspective. Whether you're a superstar quarterback or you sell beer at games for minimum wage, everyone can be reduced to a number. You're either worth what you're being paid or more than you're being paid. Otherwise, your job doesn't make sense from a business perspective, and your job might be yanked away at any instant. Trust me, I know, I've been let go twice in the sports media business. It's why I started Outkick seven years ago, to control my own future.

The NFL has long fancied itself as similar to the military. Coaches see themselves as field generals leading players/soldiers to battle for terrain against an evenly matched foe. They seek tangible geographic goals—first downs—while lining up in formations and battling it out on the offensive and defensive lines "in the trenches." Defenses attack the offense via blitzes, long offensive pass plays are called "bombs," and offenses often adopt specific military jargon—the "Air Raid" for instance—to signify their particular method of "attack."

Football, in both language and scope, is intensely militaristic.

That's why it's not suprising that playing the national anthem at sporting events began as a gesture of support for the troops during World War II. During World War II the playing of the anthem was much more than a gesture; over six hundred NFL players would serve during World War II with twenty-one players dying in combat. The NFL's union with patriotism was, at least in World War II and later in Korea, a reflection of the gridiron greats' willingness to put down their pads and take up arms to defend the country. While baseball was a bucolic nation's national pastime, football was our preparation for combat.

By the Vietnam era, that connection between football and military service had dwindled. Partly because only six NFL players served in Vietnam, and partly as a result of the increasing wealth of football players. It's always been a rich man's war and a poor man's fight, and football players have become very rich men since World War II.

While players like Pat Tillman, the Arizona Cardinals safety who gave up the NFL to enlist after 9/11 and died fighting overseas, have received substantial and deserved acclaim for their sacrifice and dedication to the country, the number of actual NFL players who have been under fire serving the country is virtually nonexistent today.

Pro athletes are coddled multimillionaires who, as they rise in life, become increasingly unlikely to risk their lives for the country. In this, they are like most of the rest of the country, the more money you or your family makes, the less likely you are to enter the military and risk your life on behalf of the country.

While the national anthem may well have begun as an ode to the servicemen overseas during World War II, the last "good war" that involved the military draft and soldiers coming from all strata of society, it owes its continuing existence to the fact that most of you reading this book right now have always heard the anthem at sporting events and never really questioned why.

Plus, the military is made up of millions of NFL fans. The military, which is composed of many virile and fearless men (and women) in uniform, and the NFL, which is also composed of many virile and fearless men in uniform, see in each other an uneasy mirroring, a duality of purpose and dedication to teamwork and mutual unit advancement. Even without any real possibility of soldiers taking off their football uniforms and putting on military uniforms, that connection lives on—because it makes the league money.

Personally, I find the playing of the national anthem before American sporting events to be a strange anachronism. Pro sports are for-profit businesses designed to make as much money as possible. Teams and leagues are rapacious corporations hell-bent on extracting the largest possible profits from their enterprises. At its most basic business level, a stadium, which is frequently built with taxpayer money to allow a for-profit team to make more money, is a venue for watching an entertaining event.

If we stand for the national anthem before sporting events inside our stadiums, shouldn't we also stand for the national anthem before movies in movie theaters? If the national anthem came on before the latest Star Wars movie and everyone stood and removed their caps until the anthem was over, wouldn't that seem a bit strange? (At least it would to those of us who are civilians. Members of the military have emailed me to point out that this exact thing happens on their bases. That makes logical sense to me, because standing and removing your caps before the entertainment begins shows respect for the military service that allows us to enjoy entertainment options.)

The reason that behavior inside a movie theater would seem strange to most of us is because we haven't been doing it for our entire lives. (In general, there is much value in life to asking why we do things. This is one of many reasons why kids are so great. Because they are young enough to ask why things happen instead of just doing them because we've always done them.)

My personal belief is that the national anthem shouldn't be played before pro sporting events. (I think it makes more sense at college sporting events since public colleges and universities are governmental institutions.)

I also understand this is a minority opinion.

I once made this argument to my dad, and he was furious with me. To him, and most others like him, the national anthem before sporting events is a sacred moment of shared reflection, a time to acknowledge that but for the sacrifices and service of our military this game wouldn't be possible.

When Colin Kaepernick sat—and subsequently modified his protest to kneeling—during the national anthem, he stepped right into a national fault line. He was exploiting the weak underbelly of the NFL's policy of having players stand for the national anthem. (Begun, as always, for money.) Prior to Kaepernick most players had done what you or I do when the national anthem was played: they'd stood with their hand over their heart or stared off into the distance thinking about whatever they'd like. Some thought about the sacrifice of the military, some thought about their upcoming assignments, some analyzed which cheerleader was the best-looking. Each of us has our own private reveries during the anthem.

In the wake of Colin Kaepernick's protest, both the fans and the media spent an inordinate amount of time debating whether the kneeling was disrespectful of soldiers or not and discussing the history of the national anthem. (By the way, is there anyone less qualified to discuss the history of the national anthem than football players and analysts?) But those were just sideshow distractions.

The larger issue was this: Kaepernick's protest, whether you supported it or disagreed with it, was bad for the NFL's business. Because the cardinal rule of NFL business, and every business, is don't alienate any of the people who pay money for your product.

Reaction to Colin Kaepernick's protest largely broke along political lines. If you were a liberal Democrat, by and large, you supported the protest; if you were a conservative Republican, you did not. (This is a generalization of course, and many differed with the opinion of their chosen political parties.) Many people tried to avoid taking a political position by stating they supported Kaepernick because he had the First Amendment right to protest, but that simply dodged the larger argument and was mostly untrue.

Most people say they support the First Amendment when they support and agree with the underlying speech being made. If you're having trouble visualizing it, think of it this way: What would the reaction have been if Kaepernick had taken a knee to protest gay marriage being legal in the United States? Or what if he'd taken a knee because he believed abortion was murder? There would have been an absolute uproar with either of those stances too, right?

Although, interestingly, then Kaepernick would have been a hero to many on the right in this country and a villain to many on the left. The same left-wingers calling Kaepernick a hero for kneeling to protest police violence would have demanded the San Francisco 49ers release or suspend Kaepernick immediately if he'd kneeled to protest the legalization of gay marriage.

That's because the people who claimed they were supporting Kaepernick's First Amendment right to protest weren't really supporting his First Amendment rights at all; they were supporting the speech that they'd agreed with. If they really believed in the First Amendment, they would have realized that the moment Kaepernick made his opinion known, thanks to the marketplace of ideas in this country, everyone else would have had the right to agree or disagree with his position as well. What many miss, especially on social media, is this: the First Amendment is a two-way street. You have freedom of speech, but you don't have freedom from the consequences of that speech.

I can't tell you the number of people who reacted to my disagreement with Kaepernick's protest by arguing that Colin Kaepernick has the freedom to speak his mind. Of course he does, but so do you and so do I as well.

Which is why I think the example of Colin Kaepernick kneeling to protest gay marriage or abortion is so fascinating. It puts you to the test famously articulated by the French philosopher Voltaire: "I disapprove of what you say, but I will defend to the death your right to say it."

It's easy to believe in free speech when you agree with what the speaker says, the real challenge comes when you disagree with what the speaker is saying. As Larry Flynt, the publisher of *Hustler* magazine, famously said, "Freedom of speech doesn't protect speech you like, it protects speech you don't like."

As I've aged, I've come to believe more and more in the power of the First Amendment and come to see it as the most important right we have in America. (I've also come to believe more and more in the power of boobs, but that sort of goes without saying.) Indeed, the underlying thesis of this entire book is this: if sports fans aren't able to say what they actually think, and if corporations restrict what their employees can say by rewarding or punishing employees for their political beliefs, then the marketplace of ideas is broken. Our country suffers as a result.

It's only with robust, uninhibited debate that we reach a national truth. If people like Paul Finebaum are shamed into retreating from their opinions because those opinions aren't politically correct or favored by large corporations and CEOs like Bob Iger, then we're ignoring legitimate debate to build artificial parameters of discussion constructed to avoid ever hurting anyone's feelings.

Put simply, I don't care about your feelings. I care about facts.

My standing as a First Amendment warrior comes as much of a surprise to me as it does to you. In law school, I didn't buy books for my third-year classes. That was both to save money and because I was cocky enough to believe I could make good grades for the entirety of the year without going to class or reading anything.

One of those classes in my third year, spring semester, was the First Amendment with Thomas McCoy, one of the most prominent First Amendment legal scholars in the country. I skipped the class for the entire semester in favor of working on a novel and going out drinking as often as possible. When I sat for the final—in law school the only grade you receive frequently comes at the end of the year on a final exam—I thought, and still believe, that I did a fantastic job on the exam.

Professor McCoy gave me a D.

When I asked him to justify the grade—the exams are graded blindly and can't be altered by more than one letter grade without justification—he exercised his First Amendment right and claimed he'd lost the final and couldn't show me my graded exam.

I never made lower than a B- in any law school class and McCoy's D, which was the final exam of my entire educational career, was the only D I ever received in any grade in any class at any school. So it was awfully convenient that Professor McCoy couldn't find my exam. (I think he punished me for refusing to come to class the entire semester.)

Several years later, Vanderbilt Law School, without a trace of irony, now aware that like many alums I had achieved some measure of financial success, sent me a heartfelt plea to help endow a scholarship in the name of Thomas McCoy. I immediately exercised my First Amendment right to lose that request for a scholarship endowment in the trash can.

Yet here I am, a First Amendment warrior who, as this book began, was in a battle to preserve his radio show over his simultaneous love of the First Amendment and boobs. While I didn't read any of the cases that year in law school or spend any time in class, I've later reread all of those cases and taught myself First Amendment law on my own.

Most ironic of all, I have ended up with the same opinions as Thomas McCoy and probably become one of the foremost proponents, in public life connected to sports at least, of the marketplace of ideas: the First Amendment idea that all speech should compete for attention in the marketplace and the best ideas will win. It's essentially wedding capitalism and evolution to the First Amendment.

Now back to Colin Kaepernick and my hypothesis on what the reaction would have been if Kaepernick had kneeled to oppose the legalization of gay marriage and abortion by the federal government.

Whether you agree or disagree with gay marriage and abortion being legal, Kaepernick's kneeling during the national anthem would have made sense then, because the federal government—via the Supreme Court—actually legalized, supports, and enforces gay marriage and abortion rights as the law of the land in this country. (At least for the moment! That's a little Supreme Court justice humor for you.)

Unlike Colin Kaepernick's own protest, which requested that the federal government do what they were already doing—which was ensure that local, state, and city police were not getting away with the murder of minorities via conducting independent federal investigations—the federal government, via the Supreme Court, has allowed gay marriage and abortion. If Kaepernick had kneeled during the anthem to protest those court decisions, that would have actually made logical sense. And probably rendered him unemployable, certainly by the San Francisco 49ers.

As a First Amendment and boobs absolutist, I would have supported Kaepernick's First Amendment right to protest no matter what he was protesting, gay marriage or police violence, but I would have also understood why the decision to protest was so controversial and why it threatened the core of the NFL's business.

Because what was happening was truly unheard of. A player in uniform at work, an employee of a specific team, was making a political statement in a manner that was incredibly divisive to the supporters of his team's league and business. It set the precedent that all NFL players, in uniform and at work, could also protest to draw attention to their own political beliefs.

Interestingly, the NBA, which mandates that players, coaches, and trainers are to stand and line up in a dignified posture along the sidelines or on the foul line during the playing of the anthem, had its own controversy in 1996 when Denver Nuggets guard Mahmoud Abdul-Rauf refused to stand for the anthem due to his belief that the United States flag and the anthem was a symbol of oppression. In other words, nearly twenty years prior to Kaepernick the NBA faced the exact same situation as the NFL.

Then NBA commissioner David Stern's response was swift and without leniency. He immediately suspended Abdul-Rauf, fined him one game check, or nearly $32,000, and refused to allow him to play in the league until he stood for the anthem. As a result, Abdul-Rauf's protest ended quickly, lasting just one game. Since that time no NBA player has refused to stand for the anthem and the league has faced no controversy surrounding its policy.

Unlike NBA commissioner David Stern, NFL commissioner Roger Goodell did nothing for two years, hoping the controversy would disappear. When the league finally acted in May of 2018, it did so only as a result of the NFL's TV partners at Fox, CBS, NBC, and ESPN missing their projected budgets by over $600 million due to league television ratings dropping nearly 20 percent in the two years since Kaepernick's protest began. The league, the TV partners, and the owners all believed NFL ratings were down, to a large degree, because of the politicization of football.

Regardless of what your own political beliefs are, losing nearly 20 percent of your viewership in two years is awful for league business. People don't come to NFL games to find out what players think about divisive political issues. Just like people don't go to the movies to see what Iron Man or Batman think about global warming. (Imagine if before the latest Spiderman movie began, Spiderman, in his superhero uniform, came on the screen and told you that a woman deserved the right to choose whether to have a baby or not. People would lose their minds.)

The closest analogy to Kaepernick's protest is clearly Mahmoud Abdul-Rauf's NBA protest twenty years before. A protest that many of you are probably reading about for the first time on the pages of this book. That's because Kaepernick, like Mahmoud Abdul-Rauf, protested in a time of relative peace and didn't have an actionable goal with his protest. That makes both Kaepernick and Abdul-Rauf substantially different from either Muhammad Ali or Tommie Smith and John Carlos at the 1968 Olympics.

While many, notably Kaepernick and his defenders, have sought to link Kaepernick's protest to Muhammad Ali's opposition to the Vietnam War and Tommie Smith and John Carlos's black power salute at the 1968 Olympics, those men's actions were substantially different.

As a boxer, Muhammad Ali was an independent contractor, responsible only for himself, and as Olympic athletes, Smith and Carlos made their gesture one time at the end of their careers as Olympians. Most significantly of all, none of these men were employees of companies or playing in leagues at the time of their political protests.

Further, Ali in particular was protesting a specific action by the federal government and his protest was controversial because of the content of the protest, not because of the method of his protest. Most people don't oppose Kaepernick's stance; they oppose the method by which he made his opinion known.

"I ain't got no quarrel with them Vietcong" was a mission statement; Muhammad Ali wasn't going to allow himself to be used as propaganda justifying the Vietnam War.

What was Kaepernick actually protesting?

As we said earlier, a very generous reading of his political statements would suggest that Kaepernick was protesting the killing of innocent black people by police officers. If so, who is actually opposed to this stance? In other words, who out there in America today thinks police should be killing more innocent people, regardless of their race? What Kaepernick is in favor of is already supported by 99.9999 percent of Americans of all races, creeds, religions, and ethnicities. Most of the negative reaction received by Kaepernick was directed at the method of his protest, refusing to stand for the anthem in uniform on the field, not the actual protest itself.

Unlike Kaepernick, Muhammad Ali had a concrete—and controversial—goal, the end of the war in Vietnam, and his protest eventually ended when the Vietnam War ended, and he returned to box.

Kaepernick? Even he had no idea when his protest would end. Asked that specific question in the aftermath of his protest beginning back in 2016, Kaepernick said as follows: "Yes. I'll continue to sit. I'm going to stand with the people that are being oppressed. To me, this is something that has to change and when there's significant change, and I feel like that flag represents what it's supposed to represent in this country is representing the way that it's supposed to I'll stand."

As you can see, even by reading this strangled series of sentences, Kaepernick's protest had no goal, and he himself said he had no idea when that protest would end. Except, you guessed it, ESPN's Adam Schefter reported Kaepernick was prepared to stand for the anthem if he was signed in 2017. (By 2018 that report was being challenged amid Kaepernick's collusion lawsuit directed at NFL owners for failing to sign him. So Kaepernick's protest may or may not still be going on and may or may not have ended. We don't even know at the time of publication.)

As if that weren't enough, Kaepernick protested the United States flag when Barack Obama and Loretta Lynch, the two most powerful people in the federal government, a black man and a black woman, were already doing exactly what he wanted them to do, but was potentially willing to end his protest after Donald Trump was elected and Jeff Sessions became attorney general? This would have been like Muhammad Ali dropping his opposition to the Vietnam War right as Richard Nixon escalated the war.

It's just flat-out nonsensical.

Especially when you consider that Colin Kaepernick's protest, unlike Ali's, which helped to end the Vietnam War, might have been so inept that he could have swung the election.

Let me explain how: Donald Trump won the states of Michigan, Pennsylvania, and Wisconsin by only 83,161 total votes. That's fewer than watch a single football game in Michigan's Big House, Ohio State's the Shoe, or Penn State's Happy Valley. Is it unreasonable to believe that around 42,000 football fans in these states might have switched their votes from Obama in 2012 to Trump in 2016—as 8 million voters did nationwide—because of Kaepernick's protest and the resulting exhaustive media coverage of that protest? I don't think so. If you believe that 42,000 football fans in the Big Ten states of Michigan, Pennsylvania, and Wisconsin could have changed their votes over this issue—as I do—then it's not a stretch to believe that Colin Kaepernick's protest cost Hillary Clinton the election. (At some point maybe Hillary can add the Kaepernick protest to the approximately twenty-eight different explanations she's already given for why she lost the election.)

Not only was Kaepernick's protest nonsensical and lacking in any coherent strategy, he managed to work against his legitimate goals.

But let's return to the Muhammad Ali comparison and explain why, despite what Kaepernick's defenders would argue, he's nothing like Ali.

In April 1967, Ali refused to register for the draft, stating: "Why should they ask me to put on a uniform and go 10,000 miles from home and drop bombs and bullets on brown people in Vietnam after so-called Negro people in Louisville are treated like dogs and denied simple human rights?"

This was a bit of theatrics since Ali, like all famous Americans, including Joe Louis in World War II, wouldn't have been put on the front lines if he were drafted. He would have been used as a prop to increase soldier morale and entertain the enlisted men. The worst thing that could have happened to the war effort would have been Ali being killed overseas. The military knew that and Ali did too. But he also believed the war was a bad decision, and he was smart enough to point out the inherent hypocrisies that existed in modern American life.

When Ali refused to submit to the draft, he was stripped of his heavyweight titles, fined $10,000, and sentenced to five years in prison. Though Ali never served time in jail, and after three years the Supreme Court overturned his conviction and allowed him to return to boxing, he did become a prominent opponent of the war, using his platform to speak out against the Vietnam War on behalf of all Americans and memorably synthesizing and exposing America's existing racial hypocrisy by remarking "Ain't no Vietcong ever called me nigger."

Ali's decision was a brave one because it directly contradicted the existing precedent set by another black heavyweight champion from the South, Joe Louis, who had enlisted in the segregated armed forces during World War II saying, "Lots of things wrong with America, but Hitler ain't going to fix them."

Interestingly, both Louis and Ali have been proven to be correct in their stances, but Louis's military service receives a fraction of the attention Ali's refusal to serve does. Why? Because most Americans agreed with Louis's stance when it came to fighting against Hitler. But what if Louis had refused to serve in World War II and had said whatever Hitler offered to the world was no worse than America's treatment of minorities? Certainly some would have supported Louis's statement at the time, but I think the verdict of history would have been vastly different.

Regardless, I think you'd agree that the consequences of Ali and Kaepernick's stances are much more different than they are similar. The American government sought out Muhammad Ali to demand that he undertake a specific action, and when he refused to do so, they took away his boxing title, stripped him of his right to make a living, fined him thousands of dollars, and sentenced him to five years in prison.

Kaepernick undertook a voluntary protest, his team supported him, the NFL levied no punishment during the season, and he continued to cash his multimillion-dollar paychecks throughout the rest of the season. What's more, unlike Ali, whom the government wanted to put in jail, the federal government, through President Obama, actually supported Kaepernick's protest. The only possible consequence for Kaepernick has been that no team has been willing to sign him as a backup quarterback since his protest began. But, again, much of that has to do with Kaepernick's own behavior. The Baltimore Ravens were prepared to sign Kaepernick before his girlfriend called the team owner a racist plantation owner and compared Ray Lewis to an Uncle Tom.

The Seattle Seahawks were prepared to sign Kaepernick a year later, but Kaepernick refused to share his plan regarding the national anthem.

Ultimately, however, the biggest difference between the two men is that Ali's protest sought a tangible goal—the end of the Vietnam War on behalf of all people—Kaepernick's protest sought an outcome that was already taking place—ensuring that local police shootings were investigated by the federal government. (I'm making this the goal of Kaepernick's protest because it's the only tangible thing I can see that he protested.)

What's more, and I think this is a massively important distinction to repeat, Ali was not an employee; he was an independent contractor. Just as Floyd Mayweather today can get away with issues of domestic abuse because he's his own boss, Ali didn't have to answer to an employer for his political stances. He wasn't playing for a team in the NFL, the NBA, the NHL, or Major League Baseball. And he wasn't protesting inside the ring before a boxing match.

Anyone out there analogizing Muhammad Ali and Colin Kaepernick is pushing a political agenda with no factual support for that argument whatsoever. Kaepernick's protest, from a historical perspective, is nearly identical to the NBA protest of Mahmoud Abdul-Rauf, a player most of us have long since forgotten.

Now let me put my lawyer hat on and talk about Colin Kaepernick's protest from a legal perspective. To do that, let's leave sports behind for a moment and focus on your own jobs. Most of you reading this right now make a living working for someone or something. (Some of you, like me, are lucky enough to own your own businesses, but even those of us who own our own businesses have to make money somehow. That is, we're responsive to a marketplace of consumers. If we alienate our marketplace of consumers, our revenue declines.)

Many of you reading this book right now will have received this book via mail delivery, either at home or your office, from UPS, FedEx, or the United States Postal Service. If you were home when this book arrived, you might well have opened the door and had this package handed directly to you. If that happened, then you received this package from a man or woman in a uniform, either the brown UPS uniform; the blue, black, red, and white of FedEx; or the multiple blues of the United States Postal Service. Other than potentially commenting on the weather or giving a general greeting, odds are the person delivering this book said nothing to you of any substantial nature.

He or she just did their job.

When he drove away, other than the logo of his company on the side of the vehicle, there was nothing to tell you anything about your delivery man's employer either.

Now imagine your reaction if when he'd passed you this book he'd been wearing a "Make America Great Again" hat or his shirt had been emblazoned by an "I'm With Her" pendant that you found impossible to ignore. If, in addition to these clear political statements, he'd also encouraged you to vote for a Republican or Democrat, and when he'd driven off you'd seen one of their political stickers emblazoned on his work vehicle, you'd have probably found this a bit strange.

Leaving aside what UPS, FedEx, or, even more substantially, the U.S. Postal Service, since it's a government entity, might think about their employee's behavior, I think all of you would agree that it would be bad for the delivery business to endorse one political side or the other. Half of you voted for Trump, half of you voted for Hillary, but the business needs to serve everyone.

Why alienate half of your customers for no reason?

If a FedEx, UPS, or Postal Service employee advocated for a politician on the job, he'd be fired, maybe the first time he did it. And certainly by the second or third time. Every single one of you reading this right now would have understood that decision.

I bet every single one of you, however, would also agree that the FedEx, UPS, or Postal Service employee has the absolute right to put a political sticker on his own private vehicle and drive that to work. And I bet that all of you would agree that outside of his or her own home, that employee could also put up a yard sign supporting a candidate or political party of his or her own choice. In America, we understand that there is a difference between political speech at work and political speech outside of work.

Now let's take my example outside of the delivery business. Let's go inside Walmart or McDonald's, two of the biggest employers in the country. What would you think if you ordered a Big Mac, fries, and a Coke and when your meal came the McDonald's worker told you, "Abortion is murder. I hope you'll support candidates who agree in the next election." (Or the statement was pro-choice; the politics don't matter, just that they're being expressed at work in a uniform.)

Or if when you checked out of Walmart the Walmart employee in uniform said, as he scanned your kid's latest Xbox game, "Gay marriage is an affront to civilized society and God will damn us for allowing it." (Or the opposite side of this political equation; again, the politics don't matter.)

I think all of you reading this right now would agree that the FedEx, UPS, USPS, McDonald's, or Walmart employee would be out of line for sharing his or her political opinion with you while in uniform at work. Regardless of whether you agreed or disagreed with the political opinion, you'd agree it was a bad idea for a company that existed to serve all Americans to pick sides in an evenly divided country.

It's not just private employers either. If a police officer pulled you over and was wearing a "Make America Great Again" hat above his uniform this would go viral in an instant on social media and the officer would be fired or reprimanded within hours. Our own United States military members are not allowed to advocate for political candidates in uniform for this exact reason.

Now, having left the world of sports, let's go back to sports. If you agree with me that all of those employees would be behaving inappropriately by advocating their political opinions while in uniform at work, why should Colin Kaepernick be able to advocate for his political beliefs while in uniform at work?

Put simply, he shouldn't. The NFL had a specific rule that mandated that players stand for the national anthem and a punishment could have swiftly nipped this form of protest in the bud.

What I said at the time, and continue to say, is that the NFL should have immediately fined Kaepernick for refusing to stand for the national anthem and donated all the money to a wounded warriors fund. That way Kaepernick could have made his political statement, but money could have gone directly to members of the military.

I suspect the outrage would have been minimal and the likelihood of the protest continuing beyond a season, or even a few games, would have been low.

If Roger Goodell had been smart, he would have studied the NBA's reaction to Mahmoud Abdul-Rauf's protest and cited it as precedent when he made his own decision.

Furthermore, it's not as if NFL players have unrestricted First Amendment rights on the field anyway. The NFL already suspends, fines, and penalizes players on a regular basis for a variety of on-field acts, be it illegal hits, improper touchdown celebrations, or uniform violations. The idea that players have full freedom of speech on the football field is laughably absurd. The NFL even fines players for inappropriate on-field language, something Colin Kaepernick should know about since he was called for a penalty and fined for using a racial slur on the field during game action in 2014.

Instead of undertaking these actions, the NFL didn't do anything for the entire season about Colin Kaepernick's protest, even as it spread to additional players and even as the league's ratings plummeted by 8 percent in 2016.

The NFL didn't come up with a policy that made sense in the entire 2016 off-season either, even as the Colin Kaepernick free-agency drama occupied months of attention. When Kaepernick wasn't signed, he sued the league for collusion.

Why do I believe Kaepernick wasn't signed? Because Kaepernick's talents weren't good enough to justify the business hit that many NFL teams would take for signing him. His problems exceeded his talents. If Aaron Rodgers, Russell Wilson, Tom Brady, Matt Ryan, Cam Newton, or Drew Brees had knelt to make a political statement, it wouldn't have mattered what cause they had espoused.

Aaron Rodgers could have knelt and expressed sympathy for ISIS and just about every NFL team would have tried to sign him if he were a free agent, but who wants a backup quarterback who alienates at least half of your fan base and is unlikely to start, barring an injury? NFL coaches don't want distractions in the locker room, particularly distractions that aren't good enough to win them games.

In his final 18 games as a starting NFL quarterback, Kaepernick went 2–16 with the San Francisco 49ers. Remember that he'd been beaten out by Blaine Gabbert—Blaine Gabbert!—before his protest began in the late summer of 2016. Maybe Kaepernick will be signed before the 2018 football season, but my guess is his problems will still exceed his talents. At press time that's the case.

Faced with an entire season to come up with a solution to the Kaepernick problem, the NFL did nothing, hoping the issue would just go away. Then 2017 happened, and Donald Trump dove headlong into the controversy that I saw brewing in my own family.

Addressing an Alabama audience on a Friday night before a weekend of football in September of 2017, Trump attacked Colin Kaepernick and the NFL: "Wouldn't you love to see one of these NFL owners, when somebody disrespects our flag, to say, 'Get that son of a bitch off the field right now. Out. He's fired. He's fired!' You know, some owner is going to do that. He's going to say, 'That guy that disrespects our flag, he's fired.' And that owner, they don't know it. They don't know it. They'll be the most popular person, for a week. They'll be the most popular person in this country."

Trump continued, "But you know what's hurting the game more than that? When people like yourselves turn on television, and you see those people taking the knee when they are playing our great national anthem. The only thing you could do better is if you see it, even if it's one player, leave the stadium, I guarantee things will stop. Things will stop. Just pick up and leave. Pick up and leave. Not the same game anymore, anyway."

Trump's base exploded with glee and NFL players, who live in a world where everyone has to be perpetually offended, kneeled in mass protest of Trump's comments. Including, ironically, some NFL players overseas in London who stood for the British national anthem and then kneeled for the American national anthem, evidently having forgotten that we had to go to war with Britain to gain our own independence.

In total, roughly 180 players kneeled the weekend after Trump's comments.

Closer to home, my own Tennessee Titans team, located in a blue city in a deeply red state that Donald Trump won with ease, elected not to take the field for the national anthem before their game against the Seattle Seahawks.

I'm politically moderate, and as I discussed above, not wedded to the idea of playing the national anthem before sporting events—I voted for the libertarian Gary Johnson in the 2016 presidential election—but the decision took away my enjoyment of the beginning of the game. Fans roundly booed the team and in subsequent days one of the Titans top players, tight end Delanie Walker, had this to say: "And the fans that don't want to come to the game? I mean, OK. Bye. I mean, if you feel that's something, we're disrespecting you, don't come to the game. You don't have to. No one's telling you to come to the game. It's your freedom of choice to do that."

Titan cornerback Logan Ryan followed up by saying, "If they don't want to watch, that's their choice. That's perfect."

Are you kidding me?

This is insanity.

Do the players not realize that it's the fans who pay their salaries?

What's more, the NFL players receive 47 percent of all NFL revenues. If you alienate your fan base then eventually your salary goes down. That's why it's unfortunate that the NFL signs multiyear deals with TV partners. Because I guarantee you this protest would have stopped really quickly if every NFL player suddenly started receiving 20 percent less in every paycheck to reflect the declining TV ratings. It's one thing to support Kaepernick in theory, but how many NFL players would support Kaepernick if it cost them 20 percent of their salary? Virtually none, I'd wager.

Comments like these from Tennessee Titans players represented the ultimate disconnect between players and fans and reflected a larger issue, long sublimated by the ability of sports to unite fans despite our political persuasions. How would a league and ownership made up mostly of white Republican voters and owners handle a crisis brought to bear on behalf of a league that was over 70 percent black and democratic?

As if that weren't enough, the NFL was incapable of breaking the political tide. To combat the tanking ratings and overall politicization of the league, NFL owners met in New York City to suggest solutions.

That meeting did not go well.

Houston Texans owner Bob McNair referenced the tenuous state the league found itself in and said, as a result of the protests, "We can't have the inmates running the prison." McNair managed to mangle a popular idiom, "We can't have the inmates running the asylum," and NFL players lost their minds when ESPN reported his quote and then spent multiple days covering the reaction to the quote too.

At no point in ESPN's coverage did they explain that the phrase was a common idiom and not to be taken literally. That's even though, presumably, ESPN employs many people who knew this.

Why temper the racial antagonism in sports when you can inflame it?

Believing not that the Texans owner had messed up a common saying, but that he'd called them all inmates at work in a prison, multiple Texans players left work. The player reaction to McNair's comment then became lead news as well. That's despite the fact that players should be familiar with idioms because they're used in sports *all the time*.

Here are some popular sports idioms: the ball is in your court, that's par for the course, he hit a home run, she is out of her league, we're coming down the home stretch, down for the count, full court press, move the goalpost, keep your eye on the ball, lightweight, saved by the bell, and even the name of my website, outkick the coverage.

And that's just idioms derived from sports.

Our regular-day speech is peppered with idioms, words that don't literally translate to how they're used. Here are a few more: piece of cake, that costs an arm and a leg, hit the nail on the head, you can't judge a book by its cover, there's more than one way to skin a cat, when pigs fly, a penny for your thoughts—the point of these examples is that *none of these are literal statements*.

If I said "Curiosity killed the cat," would any of you wonder why curiosity wasn't being charged with animal cruelty? I mean, any of you who don't play football for the Houston Texans.

The Houston Texans owner should be thanking his lucky stars he didn't say "We can't let the monkeys run the zoo," because if he'd said that he would have been led before a firing squad and publicly executed immediately before the national anthem. *Idioms are hate crimes, y'all!*

It's impossible for the country to get any dumber.

Until next year, when the Houston Texans will probably take a knee to protest the pot calling the kettle black.

Racist!

Of course, player stupidity is one thing—it's probably even too much to expect your average athlete to know idioms exist, much less use them correctly. That's especially the case when we're in an era when Golden State Warriors forward Draymond Green, asked to comment on what the Texans owner said, confidently opined, "You can't use figures of speech in 2017." (Fuck me. And just when I signed a book deal too?! It's going to be awfully hard not to use similes, metaphors, puns, personifications, hyperbole, understatements, paradoxes, and oxymorons in modern-day language anymore. Fun fact for athletes out there: an oxymoron isn't related to a moron and satire isn't a part of a car either.)

Shouldn't we at least expect for sports media members, who are theoretically better educated than athletes and have read a book for fun in their lives, to point out that what Bob McNair said in a private meeting was a common idiomatic phrase? And that he wasn't, in any way, comparing players to inmates or his team to a prison? You might expect that, but you'd be wrong; there was money to be made turning this into racism.

The liberal sports media—led by the usual suspects at MSESPN—went right to work, turning this into a modern-day civil rights issue, laced with racism and inappropriate commentary. The sports media commentary reached laughably absurd heights of stupidity when former NFL player Charles Woodson, appearing on ESPN's pregame show on Sunday before kickoff, said he refused to use the o-word.

Which o-word?

Owner.

Then Randy Moss, the greatest wide receiver in league history, felt compelled to point out that NFL team owners didn't own the players.

Thanks, Randy.

Seriously, this happened on MSESPN in its actual pregame coverage for the NFL. No wonder that show's ratings were down double digits in 2017. Do you know any NFL fans who want to tune in to an NFL pregame show and be told that using the word "owner" is unacceptable or be told that team owners don't actually own the players?

This is the depth of the problem the NFL found itself in during 2017, when suddenly everything was racist and unacceptable.

Houston Texans owner Bob McNair would apologize for the comments in 2017 and then take back the apology in 2018, claiming that he'd been referring to the league's commissioner and executives and their management of the political crisis and not the players. Regardless, proving that what goes viral is often nonsensical and artificially divisive, McNair was so committed to racial healing that he'd quietly paid for every black victim of the Charleston, South Carolina, church shooting's funeral. Remarkably that story received a thousandth of the coverage of his comments in the private NFL meeting.

Even if you thought McNair's idiom was poorly chosen and you wanted to take it literally, the allegation that it was racist didn't make sense.

After all, the Texans are not an entirely black team; there are white players as well. Didn't it require the listener to be racist to infer the Texans owner was calling only his black players inmates in prison? And then to equate the black players with inmates because black people are in jail in substantial numbers in this country? That's especially the case since more than half of the prison inmates in this country are white, meaning this racist connection isn't even accurate. Shouldn't the white players have been even more outraged by the comments since they make up the majority of prison inmates? (According to the most recent Bureau of Prisons data, white people make up 58.4 percent of prisoners and black people make up 37.9 percent of prisoners.)

While McNair apologized for the comments, both immediately upon saying them in the private meeting and later publicly when his quote came out, he shouldn't have. He should have said: "I apologize for using a popular idiom that most people in America today are too dumb to understand. What I should have said was this, so everyone, even the idiots, would understand me perfectly: I believe NFL players kneeling for the national anthem is incredibly bad for the NFL, and I think it's a perfect example of employees ruining a business. So from this point forward, let me be abundantly clear: if you have an issue with the way I run this team, you are welcome to seek employment elsewhere. Because I will not allow the actions of a few idiots to ruin my business in the great state of Texas."

Boom.

He might have gotten elected governor of Texas on the spot.

So what was the final team reaction to McNair's comments?

The Houston Texans protested the national anthem by kneeling because their owner used an idiom they didn't recognize!

What in the world had the national anthem done to deserve disrespect?

Yet in so doing the players actually proved McNair's exact point by executing this protest—that the inmates were running the asylum in the NFL. Worst of all for the NFL, the politicization of the league's sport, now aided by attacks from Donald Trump, was causing fans to abandon the league in massive numbers.

Including in my own family.

My father-in-law is a lifelong woebegone Detroit Lions fan. Every year that I have known him, come Thanksgiving, he's put on the Lions game, and we've watched the team play as a prelude to our Thanksgiving meal. He even bought tickets for my wife and me to attend a Titans-Lions game on Thanksgiving in Detroit back in 2008.

This past year at Thanksgiving I noticed something strange.

My father-in-law didn't have the game on as we prepared for Thanksgiving dinner. I asked him to put the game on because I'd bet money on the Lions. It was a bad bet—go figure. He told me that he'd stopped watching the NFL because he was fed up with turning on football games and seeing protests and having to hear about politics during football.

My father-in-law is an independent voter, having supported Democratic and Republican candidates in the past, but he abandoned the NFL in 2017.

Millions more did the same.

The result? NFL ratings plunged by an additional double-digit decline in 2017. That was after going down 8 percent in 2016. That means league ratings were down nearly 20 percent overall from 2015, in a preprotest NFL. Now many prognosticators have blamed a variety of reasons for the NFL's ratings decline—and ratings remain strong for the league in a vacuum—from cord-cutting to Netflix to poor play to injuries to the presidential race and politics in general sweeping away the nation's attention, but the number-one reason I hear for why fans abandoned the league is because of the overall politicization of the NFL.

During the course of 2017, the NFL became one of the most polarizing brands in America.

The most polarizing brands in 2017 were, as follows: Trump Hotels, CNN, Fox News, NBC News, the *New York Times*, MSNBC, and the NFL. The NFL had become the seventh-most-polarizing brand in America in the wake of Colin Kaepernick's protest and Donald Trump's comments on NFL players kneeling.

That's incredible.

After doing nothing for two years, the NFL finally implemented a new policy for the anthem in May of 2018. Players were to stand for the anthem if they were on the field, but they could also remain in the locker room if they didn't want to stand for the anthem. Teams, not players, would be fined for players failing to stand for the anthem.

With this new policy, the NFL believed it had enacted a perfect compromise. The reality was something different, players were furious and the controversy exploded anew. This happened despite the fact that the NFL anthem policy was even more lenient than the NBA's policy for the anthem.

As the Philadelphia Eagles prepared to visit the White House to celebrate their Super Bowl win, a brand-new controversy erupted over that visit and President Trump canceled the celebration when he alleged players were planning to not show up for the event. Recognizing that his base of Republican supporters believed the players should stand, Trump repeatedly attacked the NFL for its new policy and demanded that all players stand for the anthem.

The far-left-wing sports media praised the Eagles players for their courageous stand, which was, of course, the exact opposite stance the sports media had adopted in 2012 when Boston Bruins goalie Tim Thomas elected not to attend the White House celebration over his disagreement with Obama's politics. Back in 2012, ESPN, *Sports Illustrated*, Bleacher Report, the Huffington Post, and *Newsweek* had all featured front-page articles crushing Thomas for his decision to put politics in front of his team's celebration. The reaction in 2018? Every one of these sites ran articles praising the Eagles for their courage, bravery, and commitment to political activism.

I'd like to say I was surprised, but it was exactly what I expected. The sports media didn't apply the same logic to Tim Thomas as they had to the Eagles; they praised the Eagles and crushed Thomas. The only difference? Which political party the athletes supported.

Whether you agree or disagree with Trump on the anthem issue, the politics here are clear, Trump wins. Bigly. Why? Because unlike the NFL, Trump doesn't have to please the entire country, he just needs 270 electoral votes. The NFL has fans with a variety of opinions on the national anthem, Trump's fans have just one—stand.

The NFL's failure to act on Kaepernick's protest has allowed Donald Trump to seize control of a divisive cultural battle. By politicizing the anthem, Kaepernick's protest created an equal and potentially more fervent reaction. And Donald Trump was capitalizing on the NFL's mess.

To make his anthem point abundantly clear Trump arrived at the college football national title game between Alabama and Georgia and strode onto the field, where he proceeded to put his hand on his heart for the national anthem before the game.

The move stunned organizers of the game, who were told only a few minutes prior to the anthem that Trump would be doing this.

Trump, an innate showman with a gift for playing to his base in these divided times, knew exactly what he was doing.

For the next several months the profile picture on his Twitter page was him standing with his hand on his heart for the national anthem. The message was clear: the NFL better fix its problem or Trump would exploit this controversy in the coming election cycles.

The apolitical world of football, thanks to Kaepernick's kneeling, the NFL's bungled response, and Trump's exploitation of the issue, had become as hot a flashpoint as any in the world of politics.

And as a result, the NFL had lost tens of millions of viewers, including my own father-in-law. At the time of publication this controversy showed no signs of ending, but the final result was clear, Donald Trump had dunked all over Colin Kaepernick and the NFL.

8

The Left-Wing Sports Media Desperately Wants America to Be an Awful Place

At 6:44 a.m. Pacific time on May 31, 2017, the day before the NBA Finals were set to begin, a phone call was made to the Los Angeles Police Department reporting a crime. It was a bright, sunny morning in the City of Angels, and the address given where the crime had occurred was a famous one, the west Los Angeles Brentwood-area mansion of LeBron James.

LeBron was not home, and neither was his family. James was in San Francisco preparing for game one of the NBA Finals against the Golden State Warriors.

Los Angeles police arrived at LeBron James's $21 million mansion within ten minutes of the phone call. What they were told there was interesting; someone had scrawled a racial slur on the gate of LeBron's mansion. But by the time the police arrived, LeBron's employees had already repainted the gate and the only evidence the slur happened was a photo taken by LeBron's associates and provided to the police. (That photo has never been released to the public.)

Later that day TMZ broke the story of the racist graffiti outside LeBron's L.A. mansion, and the media frenzy was unleashed. LeBron's comparison of himself to civil rights martyr Emmett Till was universally praised, and the left-wingers in the sports media took the opportunity to laud James for his response to this awful atrocity.

My response was different. I couldn't get past the fact that by the time the police arrived at LeBron's house the racial slur on his gate had already been painted over. Who cleans up a hate crime scene if they want to catch the perpetrator of a crime? Wasn't that a bit odd?

Instead of falling all over LeBron and praising him for being a victim, I did what media are supposed to do, I investigated the crime itself. What happened, where did it happen, and who did it? When I asked those questions, I ran into some very interesting details. Did you know that over a year after the alleged racial incident happened that the Los Angeles police still have zero independent evidence that a racial crime happened outside LeBron's Brentwood home? I bet you didn't.

Do you know why you didn't know that?

Because today's liberal sports media doesn't fairly and impartially cover the news; they pick the news that justifies their worldview and cover that instead.

This chapter is about the failures of the far-left-wing, liberal sports media. It's about how the far-left-wing, liberal sports media only covers stories that confirm their existing worldview and rejects all stories that challenge that narrative. There are countless examples of stories like these, but we'll start our tour with the racist graffiti outside LeBron James's home, and then we'll move into the fake racism allegations of Seattle Seahawk Michael Bennett. Then we'll touch on Ryan Lochte at the Olympics in Brazil. These stories have appeared in the past few years, and along with the Missouri fake protest we started the book with, they'll demonstrate unquestioned media bias. By the time we finish examining all these stories, I hope that you'll all be more skeptical when you see the mainstream left-wing sports media rush to cover a story in a way that justifies their existing biases. That you'll all have taken the red pill.

So was there ever a racial slur outside LeBron James's mansion?

Let's return once more to the gate outside LeBron James's $21 million mansion at 6:44 a.m. on the day the crime was reported.

When police arrived, the racial slur had already been painted over. This is what initially surprised me when I read the police report. How many of you, arriving at a crime scene, would immediately clean it up before police came to your house to investigate?

Let's use an extreme example: if you walked into the front yard of your home, saw the door busted open, and found a dead man there, would you clean up the mess around him before you called the police? Or would you leave everything exactly as it was and call the police?

I bet there isn't a single person reading this book right now who would clean up the murder scene.

Okay, you might be thinking, but this was just a slur on a gate; it wasn't a murder. That's fair. Let's use the exact same situation if you had a slur or curse word painted on the side of your house: Would you paint over it before you called the police to tell them about it? Or would you leave the slur or curse word there to be viewed by the police and then paint over it after they had conducted whatever investigation they needed to conduct?

The first question about the alleged racial slur at LeBron's Los Angeles mansion, and it's an important one that has never been answered, is why did someone paint over the slur on the gate? If you were reporting a crime, wouldn't you leave the crime scene untouched? Isn't that the most basic of crime scene knowledge? Isn't the type of spray paint important here when it comes to catching the perpetrator(s)? If you were worried about what the neighbors would think of the slur, couldn't you either cover the slur up with a bedsheet or, even simpler, open the gate since the gate slides open so as to be entirely invisible from the street?

Furthermore, the people at LeBron's house already had the paint to repaint the gate at the house? And there was someone there to repaint it that early in the morning with the exact right color of paint and with that little amount of time passing between the call to police and the police arriving? Have you driven in L.A. traffic before? Unless LeBron employs a full-time painter who lives at the home, that seems just about impossible. And all of that happened before the police got to the house ten minutes after the call? Doesn't that seem incredibly unlikely?

Here's another point: LeBron's gate is easily visible from the street and sidewalk to anyone in the neighborhood. It rests directly on a major street with many driving by all day. There wasn't a single person out in Brentwood driving past, jogging, or walking their dogs early in the morning before police were called or this gate was repainted? Remember, police weren't called until 6:44 a.m. That's over an hour of daylight that would have passed before police were called. (Presumably the vandalism would have happened overnight, since if it happened during the daylight, it's even more implausible that someone wouldn't have taken photos.) Toss in an additional half hour presunrise when it's bright enough to see the gate clearly from the street, and we're talking about a couple hours when this racist graffiti would have been exposed to the entire neighborhood. Yet no one in the entire neighborhood took a photo or video during this time?

If you lived in Brentwood and went driving or jogging past LeBron's house—everyone in that neighborhood would have known it was LeBron's house—and there was a racial slur on the gate, are you really telling me nobody would have put that on Twitter, Facebook, Instagram, Snapchat, or at least sent the photo to TMZ?

Instead, the LAPD spokesperson said that the police had been provided a photo of the graffiti. You read that right, the only evidence in this entire case is a photo that the police didn't even take themselves and that no one else has ever seen in public. If that's all the evidence there is, could you even prosecute someone here and get a conviction? No way.

No defense attorney worth his salt is going to allow a photo like this to be entered into evidence without independent verification it existed.

Remember, LeBron's people called the police and then leaked this story so we would know it happened. If LeBron didn't want the distraction or the media attention, he could have just painted over it and never given attention to the story. LeBron's crew wanted it to be public, but they didn't want to preserve the evidence? That doesn't make any sense at all.

Unless, and this is one of the thoughts I had as I began to unpack this story, being a victim of racism was the best thing that could have happened to LeBron's brand. Indeed, if you were scripting a Hollywood movie about LeBron, wouldn't him being the victim of a racist attack the day before one of the biggest moments in his career, the rubber match NBA Finals against the heavily favored Golden State Warriors, be just about perfect for your story? What's more, if your entire brand at the time is about fighting for equality as the modern-day Muhammad Ali, is there anything better for LeBron's brand than being a victim of racism? Social justice warriors dream of being victims all day long. But direct racism is so rare in the country today that they spend most of their time now focusing on systemic racism and issues of amorphous white privilege.

The left-wing sports media loves an innocent victim of racism. Hell, you get praised so much for being a victim today that there are hundreds of fake racist attacks happening all over the country every year.

So it's strange to have cleaned up this racial slur.

It gets even weirder from here. The gate with the alleged racial slur outside of LeBron James's home has a surveillance camera pointed at the gate. This isn't a surprise since most $21 million mansions have pretty high-tech security. Particularly when the home isn't even occupied full-time, as was the case with LeBron's. Only, guess what? When the Los Angeles police requested the surveillance video showing the gate, in an effort to identify and catch the perpetrator, they were told something fascinating: the surveillance video wasn't working that night.

Oh.

Well, isn't that convenient?

So you've got a gate on a public street that has a surveillance camera visible to anyone who walks up to the gate. And someone, who would have seen that surveillance camera right there, still paints a racial slur on the gate? Boy, they were really lucky that the camera wasn't turned on that night, weren't they? No one in the entire neighborhood, not someone up walking their dog, going for a walk or a jog or driving to work early in the morning, sees the racial slur or someone repainting the gate, despite the fact that it would have been visible for nearly two hours, and provides independent verification that it ever happened? And when the police arrive the slur has already been painted over, and there is no independent evidence it ever happened?

And a year later the Los Angeles police still have nothing to go on and no suspects.

This entire story of a racial slur on LeBron's gate is a house of cards when you start to ask any questions at all.

Yet everyone in the sports media believes it's 100 percent true and, even crazier, automatically assumes not just that it's true, but that the perpetrator is a racist white person. All this even though there is zero independent evidence that this incident ever occurred.

Could a racist white person have written a racial slur on LeBron's gate? Sure. Could it just as easily have been someone trying to draw attention to racism, who may well have been black or Hispanic or Asian? Definitely. Hell, could it have even been one of LeBron's employees trying to draw attention to himself? That seems even more likely to me, not that LeBron was personally involved in making up a fake racism story, but that someone in LeBron's employ might see it as a way to increase LeBron's necessity for keeping him employed. What better way to prove how necessary you are to LeBron than to make him think his family might be in danger in Los Angeles?

Regardless, I think all of you reading this right now would agree that this story doesn't make sense. Essentially, it just doesn't add up. This is even more the case now that LeBron has joined the Lakers in Los Angeles. If LeBron really thought a racist threatening his family was on the loose, would he move them to the very city where this "crime" is still unresolved?

Now I want you to think about this for a moment, why am I the only person in all of sports media even asking these questions? Why is this the first time that most of you have seen these questions asked? Isn't that the primary job of journalists in this country, to investigate stories and determine whether they are true or not? Why am I the only person you've seen asking these questions?

Partly it might be my legal training. My criminal law professor told us there were only three things that mattered in any case: the facts, the facts, and the facts. With every story I cover, I try to come in with an open mind. I don't look for a case to confirm my existing worldview; I look at every case focusing entirely on the facts. You would have thought the sports media would have learned this lesson from the Duke lacrosse case. But they didn't.

Partly it's also because just about everyone else in sports media is terrified they will be called racist if they question whether a particular act of racism could be true or not. Racism is awful and shouldn't exist, but believing a particular act of racism happened because racism exists is horribly flawed logic.

And it's also because the left-wing sports media wants this story to be true because it confirms their existing worldview, that America is an awful, racist place. The kind of place where Donald Trump could get elected president. Remember, as I told you earlier in the book, over 96 percent of sports media didn't vote for Donald Trump. Over 96 percent! Do you think groupthink might be an issue in this industry?

If the LeBron story just stood on its own as a glaring flaw in the left-wing sports media's worldview, it might be an interesting anecdote, nothing more, but this is evidence of a more systemic failure. The fake racism allegations of Michael Bennett are perfect evidence of yet another massive sports media failure.

In the late summer of 2017 then Seattle Seahawk defensive end Michael Bennett traveled to Las Vegas for the Conor McGregor–Floyd

Mayweather boxing match. After the fight Bennett went out on the town and, according to him, during that night he became the victim of police racism.

Bennett's police racism allegation exploded on the national scene in September of 2017 when Bennett took his accusation directly to Twitter, posting a personal message accusing the Las Vegas police of racially profiling him under the tagline "Equality." Immediately the accusation raced through the country, receiving 400,000 favorites and hundreds of thousands of retweets.

Bennett's explosive allegations, that he'd been racially profiled and threatened with death by racist Las Vegas police officers because he was a black man, became the lead story on television for ESPN, FOX, CBS, and NBC and it surged to the top of every major sports website in America.

Bennett asserted that when Las Vegas police responded to a report of an active shooter in a casino, they decided to tackle him for no reason other than his race.

I was skeptical of Bennett's claims when I read them online. Not because I didn't believe racism existed in the country, but because the story didn't make sense. Why would police decide to handcuff an innocent black man while they were investigating a potential live shooter at a casino? (This was before the actual shooter in the Las Vegas casino killed over fifty people at a country music concert.) Surely, I thought, there had to be something more to this story.

Evidently, I was the only person to think this because the sports media spent the rest of the day lionizing Bennett for his bravery in the face of racist police officers. MSESPN, FOX, CBS, NBC, just about every radio station and newspaper in the country—all of them praised Bennett for being a victim. No one but me suggested, "Maybe we should wait to see what the Las Vegas police have to say about this incident."

If you said anything other than Michael Bennett was a hero and the police were awful human beings, you were a racist.

The NFL even sent out a statement praising Bennett and castigating the Las Vegas police for their treatment of him.

Then Bennett's story started to fall apart.

First, TMZ released a video of the Michael Bennett handcuffing and it looked downright normal. There were no screaming threats from the officers to "blow his fucking head off" or, at least in this video, a gun placed anywhere near his head. If Bennett, as he alleged, was threatened that his head was going to be blown off, you certainly can't hear it. If the officer handcuffing him held a gun to his head, you certainly can't see that in this video either. Indeed, given the fact that we can hear almost the entirety of the arrest interaction, it seems pretty damn unlikely that there were any threats uttered at all.

Later that day the Las Vegas Police Department held a press conference and released a five-minute video from inside the casino that night. The video showed how chaotic the casino had been, and it also revealed that officers entered the casino with weapons drawn and sought to protect the largely black audience exiting the casino.

It always bears repeating: our police officers run toward violence while everyone else runs away from it. As you watch the men and women of the Las Vegas Police Department courageously walking through the casino looking for a shooter or shooters, it's hard not to admire their bravery.

Most important, for purposes of Bennett's allegation, you can also see that the entire casino is full of black people. If police wanted to arrest black people, there were hundreds of them exiting the casino and receiving no molestation at all. Why was Bennett, a black man among hundreds of black people, singled out because of his race? How did that make any sense at all?

Indeed, once you watch this video, Bennett's allegation that he was picked out because he's black is downright laughable. In fact, it's so laughable that Bennett's own attorney has acknowledged race had absolutely nothing to do with his treatment from the police.

Near the end of the video you can see Michael Bennett, crouching behind a slot machine inside the casino, appearing to hide from police. When the police approached him because he appeared suspicious hiding there, he jumped up and ran away from them, refusing commands to stop, leaping a wall, and attempting to escape from them before being caught and detained.

Shortly after releasing this video Las Vegas police explained the evening in question and released a letter demanding the NFL investigate Michael Bennett for telling lies:

> As our uniformed officers entered the casino, they observed Bennett hiding behind a slot machine. When officers turned toward Bennett, he bolted out of the casino, leaped over a four-foot barrier wall, and hid from officers as he crouched close to the wall on the sidewalk.

The letter continues,

> I am sure that your attorney will tell you, our officers had reasonable suspicion, which is the constitutional standard, to detain Bennett until they could determine whether he was involved in the shooting. Our officers, who are both minorities, had the legal right and obligation, to detain Bennett based upon the nature of the call and Bennett's unusual and suspicious actions. Our officers did not detain Bennett because he was "a black man in the wrong place at the wrong time."
> Michael Bennett's claim that our officers are racist is false and offensive to the men and women of law enforcement. We hope you will take appropriate action against Michael Bennett.

Of course, the NFL did nothing to Bennett. (Bennett would, however, be charged with a crime in Houston: for allegedly shoving a sixty-six-year-old paraplegic black woman—and others—en route to the field after Super Bowl LI.)

As these details emerged to cast doubts on Bennett's initial claim, something interesting happened: the same sports media that had feverishly covered Bennett's initial racism allegations went strangely quiet. Gone were the front-page stories about Bennett's encounter with the racist Las Vegas police; gone were the endorsements of his behavior and the condemnation of the police.

The story just . . . vanished.

By the end of September, the Las Vegas Police Department had conducted a full investigation into Bennett's allegations. After reviewing 193 different videos of that night—remember casinos are covered in cameras and the police officers had cameras on them that night as well—the Las Vegas police released a two-minute video that proved their officers didn't racially profile Bennett, didn't use excessive force, and treated Bennett with respect throughout their interaction.

As anyone could see watching the videos, Michael Bennett looks incredibly suspicious, crouching and running when the police are looking for an active shooter.

Police had a reasonable suspicion to stop and detain him.

Remember, the police are responding to reports of an active shooter. What would a shooter likely do? Hide from police and then run from them and refuse their demands to stop when he saw them approach him. Which is exactly what Bennett did in the videos.

Far from being racist, it turns out that the Las Vegas police officers interacting with Bennett were minorities—two Hispanic officers, and one black officer.

As if that weren't enough, when these minority police officers detained Bennett, they were recorded on video politely explaining this entire scenario to him. Bennett even says he understands how his behavior would have looked to the officers. They then take his cuffs off—the entire time in the police car was seven minutes according to Vegas police—and are prepared to let him go. This is, notably, all before the police have any idea Bennett's a famous football player. That is, contrary to Bennett's allegations of racism, the police are treating him with respect and consideration long before they know that he's a multimillionaire pro athlete.

They explain exactly why they detained him, explain why they were suspicious of his behavior, and then—and this is maybe the most amazing part of this entire story—*they let him go after he identifies himself as an NFL player even though he has no ID on him.*

"No, man, my name is Michael Bennett, Seattle Seahawks, look it up," Bennett says when asked for ID by the police officers.

He told the cops to look him up on their phones!

And the cops looked him up on Google images and let him go based on that ID.

Talk about privilege!

Bennett is out in Las Vegas without an ID—how is that even possible? It's not like he's a girl in a cocktail dress and heels—he can't carry a driver's license with him in his jeans pocket?! He gets released from police custody by telling the police—after running from them and refusing to listen to their commands—that he plays in the NFL and to look him up on their phones.

Racism?

Get out of here.

Michael Bennett is a huge beneficiary of NFL athlete privilege.

How many people do you think get let go by police, when they don't have an ID and have been stopped for suspicious behavior, after telling the police to look them up on Google?

Here's the kicker: Bennett then shook hands with police and told them he understood exactly what they had done.

He shook hands with them!

Two weeks later Bennett lied and called these same cops racists in a story that immediately went viral.

When all this factual evidence refuting everything Michael Bennett said comes out, do you know what happens in the sports media?

Crickets.

The story just disappears.

Indeed, it doesn't just disappear. Bennett is, and I can't believe I'm writing this, nominated for the NFL Man of the Year Award and the left-wing sports media continues its coverage praising his bravery and never asking him about his lies for the rest of the season. Bennett even sits for interviews with ESPN and NBC. Those interviews air on national television and the sports media members interviewing him never even ask about the Las Vegas police incident.

It's amazing to see happen, but I've seen it happen again and again over the past several years. A story appears to advance a left-wing agenda, is exposed as an untruth, and then vanishes from all media outlets.

This is incredibly unfair because in covering Bennett's initial racism allegations and then not covering the fact that they were lies, the media does a disservice to the public and serves to further foment racial animosity between police and minorities.

As I said before, I could use countless examples of this unfair and unequal treatment from the sports media to show liberal bias, but I'll only use one more here. It's another massive story that featured a superstar athlete and alleged police misconduct.

For this story, we'll travel to the 2016 Olympics in Brazil.

In the summer of 2016, Ryan Lochte and his American swimming teammates went out drinking after their Olympics ended and ended up stopping late at night at a Brazilian gas station to use the bathroom. While they were there to go to the bathroom, they were all robbed.

Lochte later shared the story about the robbery with his mother, who shared it with a member of the American news media, and from there it blew up into a major international story. Eventually, Lochte went on the *Today* show and shared his version of the story. That story, succinctly told, was this: Lochte and three swimming buddies went out drinking. On the way home to the Brazilian Olympic Village, they stopped to go to the bathroom. The bathroom door was locked, so the four swimmers peed in the grass outside the gas station. One of the American swimmers also bumped into a sandwich poster board hanging on the side of the gas station, leaving behind a scratch on the sign. At this point, two Brazilian gas station security guards arrived, pointed their guns at the American swimmers, and demanded money while screaming at them in Portuguese. Under gunpoint the American swimmers gave the security guards the money in their pockets.

The swimmers were then allowed to leave the gas station.

Several days later, angry over all the media attention the incident was receiving, the Brazilian government then seized the passports of the three American swimmers still in the country—pulling two of them off the airplane as they attempted to return to America. One of the American swimmers was forced to pay nearly $11,000 in extortion money in order to leave Brazil, and all the swimmers were charged with making false statements to authorities.

It would take over a year for the Brazilian courts to eventually resolve the issue, but in the summer of 2017, the Brazilian courts cleared the American swimmers of all wrongdoing. It turned out that their story had been correct all along—they'd been robbed on their way home from a night out drinking.

Yet before all was said and done, the story was such a sports media feeding frenzy that Lochte would lose all his endorsement money and be suspended from competitive swimming for over a year.

And for what?

Getting robbed in Brazil.

As if that weren't enough, somehow Ryan Lochte had, in becoming the victim of a crime, also become a poster child for "white privilege."

Over the past several years the phrase "white privilege" has emerged as a collective phrase designed to summarize the supposed privileged treatment that white athletes receive compared to minority athletes. Lochte and all three of his teammates were white and, as the media story went, they were receiving preferential treatment based on their race. (Lochte is actually half-Cuban, but that didn't matter for this story. He was white because that made the left-wing sports media's views more readily apparent.)

This charge was led by, who else, ESPN, which, and I'm not making this up, featured a front-page, heavily promoted website opinion piece arguing that Ryan Lochte was a perfect example of white privilege. The rest of the sports media followed the lead of this piece, ripping Lochte to shreds in the press, even though they were relying on indefensible logical fallacies and inaccuracies predicated on their preexisting narratives.

I'm going to deconstruct this story because I think it's a great example of the journalistic flaws you regularly find in the sports media today. Even though Lochte and his teammates have been cleared of all wrongdoing, you can still find tons of articles about how the men personified white privilege from virtually every mainstream media outlet in the country. Just Google it for yourself if you wish.

ESPN's article on the subject was the most transparently absurd, beginning, as it did, as an open letter to white people.

The article, written by a white man, literally begins:

Dear Fellow White People:
    White privilege is a thing. And Rio was the perfect example.

Oh, wow, this is absolute perfection. An open letter from a white guy in the media to other white people about white privilege.

The ESPN article begins with a rallying cry:

I've just been working in the media for a long time, and this [white privilege] has become an issue that pisses me off to no end. The social tightrope that black athletes have to walk to avoid criticism is absurd, and at the same time, we can't help but always give white athletes the benefit of doubt. What unfolded in Rio is a great example of how far we still have to go.

This is an important jumping-off point because it elucidates the way many white people in sports media feel. White men in the media—and white women—are far more likely to rip white athletes than black athletes because even the allegation of racism is mortifying to them. For many white people in sports media, the worst thing you can say about them is to call them a racist.

When white men misbehave, every white person in the media wants to line up and grab their pound of flesh. This way when a black guy gets in trouble and white media are forced to talk about it, the white media can point to the way they treated Ryan Lochte and say, "Nuh-uh, we're not racist, look at what we wrote and said about Ryan Lochte."

Now that the facts of Ryan Lochte and the American swimmers are public, and we know they've done nothing wrong, this story joins a long litany of supposed white male wrongdoing that has been much ballyhooed and then disproved: Duke lacrosse, the made-up gang rape at a University of Virginia frat house, Peyton Manning's mooning of a woman at the age of nineteen covered as a sex crime nearly twenty years later, and the Lochte case all have something in common—the American media decided that privileged white men were to blame and railroaded them even though the facts didn't support their opinions.

It's important before we go even further to make this point very clear: most in the American media wanted Ryan Lochte to be in the wrong here because Lochte being in the wrong allows white people to beat up on white athletes.

This, by the way, is not unique to American sports media. Fans do it too. Who are the most hated college basketball players year after year? White guys who play for Duke. Why do mostly white fans direct so much hate at white Duke players? Because if you hate a black college player you might be accused of racism, but if you hate a white college player, that's just good fun.

While I'm focusing on Lochte here, the perfect example of this is Duke men's basketball player Grayson Allen. With the way the sports media covered Grayson Allen's occasional tripping of another basketball player, you would have thought he was Jeffrey Dahmer. There was more negative commentary about Allen tripping a basketball player than there was about most star athletes being arrested for felonies.

Most white people in this country fear being called racist more than they fear any other thing in American public life.

If you rip Lochte and you're a white man or woman in the sports media, you can't be racist.

Voilà, the perfect cocktail for media failure has been brewed.

It's the same with this author of the ESPN article on Lochte. As I've demonstrated to you via the data, most sportswriters are liberal, even if their readers aren't. They allow their worldview to cloud their judgment of the facts in an individual case.

Let's continue in the article:

NBC even let its own version of white privilege, Billy Bush, defend his bro repeatedly, leaving the normally good-humored weather anchor Al Roker as the one man left willing to hold the line and practice anything resembling journalism.

"He's not the kind that can weave a brilliant tale," Bush said. "That he told this story so mellifluously makes me think he could not have invented the whole thing."

The *Today Show* host Matt Lauer also couldn't resist giving Lochte an initial pass. It wasn't until the story completely unraveled that NBC scrambled its jets and changed tactics.

"I don't think the details of the story have changed all that much," Lauer said, even as the details of Lochte's escapade were rapidly falling apart. "There are a couple of details that have changed. But the basics of the story have remained the same."

Here's what's remarkable about this article's criticism of Billy Bush and Matt Lauer at NBC—*what they said was true.*

Bush, who would lose his job over the Donald Trump *Access Hollywood* tape going public, said, "he could not have invented the whole thing."

"I don't think the details of the story have changed all that much," Lauer, who would later lose his job as part of the #MeToo fallout, said. "There are a couple of details that have changed. But the basics of the story have remained the same."

This is 100 percent true too! Every detail in Lochte's story wasn't perfect—news flash, no witness story is ever perfect—but "the basics of the story have remained the same" since Lochte started telling them.

Again, this isn't evidence of white privilege; this is evidence of NBC's hosts' opinions being correct.

If you want to criticize Matt Lauer's coverage of this story, it should be for calling Ryan Lochte and the swimmers being held under gunpoint and forced to pay money a "negotiated settlement."

A negotiated settlement?

Since when has money that you pay at gunpoint ever been anything other than a robbery?

Yet that's the tone Lauer later took after he'd been getting ripped online for exhibiting white privilege.

That was the most absurd part of Lauer's coverage by far, when he decided he'd better rip Lochte to make sure he wasn't called racist.

Remarkably, listening to white privilege critics online made Lauer a worse journalist.

The ESPN article continues:

"Try to imagine, just for a second, what the world's reaction would be if a black athlete got drunk, urinated in public, destroyed some property, then concocted a story in which he bravely stood up to someone with a gun who was attempting to rob him and his friends."

Ah, yes, the *A Time to Kill* moment much favored by liberal sports-writers who love to make the change-the-color argument at every opportunity.

"Now close your eyes. What if he was white?" The perfect John Grisham mic drop trial summation.

Free Carl Lee!

First, Lochte didn't "concoct a story." Lochte and his friends were robbed after peeing outside and scratching a cheap advertisement on a wall. If four NBA players had done this exact same thing, Black Lives Matter would have lost their minds over the Brazilian security guards drawing guns on the players and demanding payment. What would have been among their first arguments? They would have flipped the race too!

"If four white swimmers had done these exact same things, do you think the police would have drawn their guns and robbed them? Of course not. This is racism! Black lives matter!"

And guess what, every white media member in Rio would have written about the "ugly racism" descending on the Olympic games. That would have been the number-one story of the Olympics: black athletes unsafe to go anywhere in the world, the "fact" that black lives don't matter anywhere in the world.

Since, thankfully, no black athletes were robbed in Rio, we don't have a perfect analogy to white swimmers and NBA players. However, we can compare two Olympians who were in the news in 2016: black NBA player Draymond Green with white swimmer Ryan Lochte.

Just before he left for Rio, Draymond Green was arrested and booked for assault for attacking a current basketball player at Michigan State, his alma mater. Just before the Olympic games started, Green then Snapchatted a picture of his erect penis to everyone who followed him on social media. Oh, and he also spent the entire 2016 NBA playoffs kicking players in the groin and was suspended for calling the best basketball player in the world a bitch, a trash-talking move that might well have cost his team an NBA championship and saw the Cleveland Cavaliers and LeBron James storm back from a 3–1 deficit to bring Cleveland a title.

For all that, how many endorsement dollars did Draymond Green lose?

Zero, not one dollar.

Compare that with Lochte.

After peeing outside, being robbed, and scratching an advertisement sign on the side of a gas station, Ryan Lochte has been publicly ridiculed in a way few American athletes ever have for nonfelonious behavior; he has lost $1 million in endorsement income due to his four sponsors publicly canceling his contracts, and three American swimmers were held hostage in Brazil after their passports were seized. As if that weren't enough, Lochte also received a one-year suspension from competitive swimming with many media members arguing Lochte deserved a lifetime ban.

Boy, when you compare these two stories, it sure seems like Draymond Green has some serious black privilege, doesn't it?

The ESPN article wasn't even done ripping Lochte yet:

> As has been mentioned, Lochte is the same age as Carmelo Anthony, Team USA gold-medal winner. But Lochte is a year older than basketball great LeBron James. Try to imagine NBC's personalities twisting themselves into a pretzel in defense of James and referring to him as a kid. The definition of privilege, in this era of Trayvon Martin, Tamir Rice and Eric Garner weren't given a scrap of the benefit of doubt, is Lochte and his USA swimming teammates knowing they could buy their way out of trouble in the middle of the night and still cast themselves as both victims and heroes.

Whoa, whoa, whoa.

Lochte peed on the side of a gas station at the Olympics, and you're comparing him to Trayvon Martin, Tamir Rice, and Eric Garner?

Give me a fucking break.

Can you try harder to mix sports and real life?

What's more "Lochte and his USA swimming teammates kn[ew] they could buy their way out of trouble," writes the "author."

They were robbed!

You don't buy your way out of trouble when you are robbed at gunpoint; someone points a gun at you and commits a felony. Buying your way out of trouble is what Kobe Bryant did when he was charged with rape. You remember Kobe, right? The guy who got not one but two jerseys retired in 2018 and also won an Oscar at the #MeToo Oscars in 2018 despite having paid off a woman to avoid going on trial for rape. (His accuser refused to testify after Kobe settled her civil claims for an undisclosed sum.)

Then, amazingly, in an article about white privilege and Lochte, the ESPN author pivots to talk about a black gymnast, Gabby Douglas, and some criticism she'd received about her body language at the Olympics. These things have nothing in common, honestly, but it doesn't stop a liberal hatchet job from happening.

"Douglas was so shaken by the criticism that she felt compelled to apologize, proof that black athletes constantly have to prove, and then re-prove, their patriotism lest they be subjected to an inquisition on the internet."

An "inquisition on the internet."

This is a loaded phrase that sounds substantial but boils down to a few trolls having said mean things on Twitter.

There was one negative article in the *L.A. Times* about Olympic gymnast Gabby Douglas's body language. That's pretty much the entirety of the media scrum. There were also a few mean tweets. From this, the liberal media has constructed a mountain of racism to support their worldview and contrast it with Lochte.

The truth is this—there has never been more opinion in American history. You can find an opinion on anything. The question isn't whether anyone thinks negative things about Gabby Douglas in the world—of course some people do—it's whether or not it was a common opinion.

There were a thousand times as many articles defending Gabby Douglas as there ever were attacks on her.

This is a perfect example of liberal, left-wing sports media cherry-picking facts to allow them to make the case that they want to make.

Now it's time for the stirring conclusion from ESPN's white-privileged mascot: "I cannot undo some of the horrible things done by people who share my name or my DNA, but that doesn't mean I can't acknowledge that it happened, and attempt to understand how the ripples of those acts still reach this day. Even in sports."

Holy shit.

Did you really write an entire column about Ryan Lochte peeing outside a gas station in Brazil and tie it to your white guilt over four hundred years of American history?

Yes, yes you did.

But that's not all:

> This time around, I got to watch the games with my two beautiful daughters, whom I suspect will never want for much. They had the time of their lives dancing and jumping and twirling in our living room pretending to be Simone Biles, and it filled me with more joy than I can ever explain to see them fall so hard for Biles.
>
> Telling them all about their beloved Simone wasn't the easiest conversation to have with a six-year-old and four-year-old, but I wanted them to know her story: that she was born into poverty, that her birth mother had to put her in foster care, and that her grandparents adopted her and became her parents. Biles still grew up to be the best gymnast in the room and one of their childhood heroes. This is a hopeful thing, and I hope they will remember it forever.

Message: I am not racist, and neither are my children, who like a black athlete.

What the hell does this even mean: "it filled me with more joy than I can ever explain to see them fall so hard for Biles."

Did you doubt that your six- and four-year-old girls could like a person who wasn't white? That's the only way this sentence makes sense.

In what world would you assume that your six- and four-year-old daughters wouldn't like all the American gymnasts, regardless of their color? Are you raising them racist? Should I be writing an entire book jumping with liberal joy because Titans running back Derrick Henry is my seven-year-old's favorite player?

Evidently.

My god, this column conclusion is literally the Olympic equivalent of arguing you aren't racist because you have a black friend.

Honestly, that's exactly what it's designed to do.

The coverage of Ryan Lochte wasn't about journalism or truth; it was about using whatever happens to justify your existing worldview. This open letter to white America was a boldfaced attempt to lecture the world about racism and white privilege. Even if, as was clearly the case when the facts came out, neither of these issues made sense at all given what happened to Lochte.

This is particularly the case when you consider who the left-wing sports media made the heroes of the Lochte case: two Brazilian security guards. The same media in America that didn't trust the Las Vegas police in the Michael Bennett case believed two Brazilian security guards over four American swimmers?

It's completely nonsensical unless you realize what's happening here: the sports media isn't trying to bring you the truth; they are just sharing their political beliefs with you over and over again and disguising it as objective sports stories.

Sadly, just when America needs to be more like sports, America is trying to make sports more like America.

9

America Needs to Be
More Like Sports

One of the primary reasons I'm upset by the politicization of sports is because I believe America should look more like sports and that sports shouldn't look more like America. The best man (or woman) should win regardless of what he or she looks like, and sports should continue to be the ultimate meritocracy.

Now let me explain what I mean.

In sports, all that matters is how good you are at the sport. Where you were born, who your dad or mom is, how much money you have, where you went to school, all of it is stripped away, and we get fair and equal competition. The best man (or woman) wins.

That's why many of you love sports so much.

The most popular sports that we watch don't necessarily approximate the American population. And that's okay! Everything we do in America doesn't have to perfectly reflect the American population. Take football, for example. Black men represent 6 percent of the overall American population, yet they make up 70 percent of NFL players. White men are 26 percent of the NFL, and the other 4 percent are Asian, many of them Samoan, or other races. How about the NBA? The NBA is over 80 percent black with the remaining 20 percent of the players white or other races. The best, and highest-paid, players in the NBA are skewed even more black, with the only white All-Stars in 2018 being Kevin Love and Kristaps Porzingis.

Now if you look at these numbers in the NFL and NBA, there is probably not a high-paying profession in the country that is less diverse than the NFL and the NBA. We have black men, who represent 6 percent of the United States population, dominating the available jobs in the NFL and the NBA, collectively taking up 75 percent of the highest-paying pro athlete jobs in this country.

Yet I never hear anyone suggest that we need greater on-field or on-court diversity in the NFL or the NBA.

Why is that?

Because there's a belief in the meritocracy when it comes to sports.

I don't think there are many people out there reading this book who believe that white, Asian, and Hispanic players aren't getting fair shots at these jobs. The black players are just better and, as a result, they get the jobs.

Now imagine for a moment that a new owner bought an NFL or NBA team and announced he wanted his team to be more inclusive and diverse. In fact, imagine that this far-left-wing, liberal owner announced that he was sick of his team not giving everyone in America someone to look up to, and he (or she, we can't be sexist here!) was going to field a team that perfectly reflected American diversity.

According to the most recent census estimates, 61.3 percent of the country is white, 17.8 percent is Hispanic, 12.7 percent is black, 5 percent is Asian, and the remaining 3.2 percent are mixed race or other ethnicities. Okay, imagine if that NFL or NBA owner set about implementing a brand-new roster. This would mean that either 32 or 33 players on his 53-man NFL team would be white, 9 would be Hispanic, 6 or 7 would be black, and a couple would be other races. That means a bunch of black guys would get fired because of their race and a bunch of white, Asian, and Hispanic guys would get hired in the NFL because of their race.

An NBA roster of 15 players would go from an average of 12 black guys and 3 people of other races to 9 white guys, 2 Hispanic guys, 2 black guys, 1 Asian guy, and one of another ethnicity. So that means a bunch of black players would lose their jobs and a bunch of whites, Hispanics, and Asians would get jobs.

Presumably, these NFL and NBA teams would perform much worse on the field and court because the hiring goal wouldn't have been based on a meritocracy, it would have been based on ensuring that diversity and inclusion led to a roster that reflected what America looked like.

But even this might not be diverse or inclusive enough to satisfy the liberals obsessed with cosmetic diversity—are you noticing something? We don't have any women. To be as diverse and inclusive as possible 51 percent of our NFL and NBA rosters would have to be made up of women. It's fair to say that an NFL or NBA team that perfectly mirrored America in both race and gender would never win a game.

But they would be incredibly inclusive and diverse!

Regardless of your politics, most of you will agree with me that American sports leagues do a pretty good job of finding the best man or woman and getting them on the field or court. And that race, religion, sexual preference, or ethnicity has absolutely nothing to do with success or failure in pro sports. Sports should be our model for what America looks like when it comes to equal opportunity and fairness. They are the ultimate meritocracy.

In other words, if New England Patriots coach Bill Belichick believed a transgender dwarf lesbian could be the next Tom Brady, he'd play him. (And probably even deflate the footballs a bit for his/her tiny hands.)

We believe all this despite the fact that from a business perspective, winning and losing in the NFL or the NBA doesn't really matter that much to the bottom line. That's because relegation doesn't exist. Even if you run a crappy franchise—hello, Cleveland Browns!—you still make oodles of money off the existing NFL business. That is, unlike in modern American business, no pro sports team in the NFL or the NBA has ever gone bankrupt and ceased to exist because of business failures.

Which brings me to a larger question: If we believe that American sports leagues find the best people for their line of work even though the competitive pressures aren't that high, why do we believe that companies in highly competitive fields where bankruptcy is a threat don't do that?

Lately, Google, Facebook, and other tech companies are under siege because their companies don't look like America. These companies are overpopulated with white and Asian men. But the NFL and the NBA are overpopulated with black men, and no one says anything about that. Why can't it be possible that some jobs are overpopulated by race and ethnicity not because bias is at play, but just because the meritocracy of talent is not evenly distributed across all races?

Do you know how many starting NFL cornerbacks over the past twenty years have been white, Asian, or Hispanic?

Zero. (Jason Sehorn was the last white cornerback to start and that was over twenty years ago.)

Do you know how many starting white cornerbacks there have been in the past twenty-five years in the SEC, the nation's best football conference?

Zero.

That's an awful lot of top cornerback positions to end up black. The odds of this happening by random chance are virtually zero as well. One of my buddies is a math professor. I had him calculate the odds that 12 percent of the American population—i.e., black people—would end up getting all sixty-four starting NFL corner jobs for twenty years straight. Here is his email to me:

> For your question I assumed that the jobs get reset every year, meaning that for 64 different jobs, 20 years in a row, we're looking at 1280 total starting spots in the NFL at cornerback. The odds that each one of those corners turns out to be from a group comprising 12% of the population is astronomically

small, 0.12[some sort of squiggly line]1280. Or 2 times ten to the 10000th power. Even if you make black people 80% of the population the odds of all 64 corners being black in one year is still preposterously small, .0000063%.

Those numbers are truly mind-boggling. From a statistical perspective, it's impossible to say this is just chance.

What's also interesting about this is that there isn't a dearth of white, Asian, or Hispanic cornerbacks playing lower-level football. In other words, it's not like there is an access problem here. Go to any flag football league or high school, and you'll see many nonblack players at cornerback. Yet by the time scholarships are doled out, almost all cornerbacks at major colleges and universities are black.

Other sports have athletes made up predominately of one race or another—swimming, tennis, golf, and hockey, for instance, are mostly white—but those sports have clear access and cost issues. That is, every young athlete in the country isn't necessarily able to afford to swim or play golf, tennis, or hockey or have access to the locations where these sports are taught and played. We don't know whether those athletes that grow up to play those sports professionally truly represent the best in those sports. They're more likely to just be the best athletes with access to pools, golf courses, ice rinks, or tennis courts. Could the best swimmer in the world have never swum or the best ice hockey, tennis, or golf player have never picked up a hockey stick, a racket, or a golf club? That's certainly possible. Whereas I think it's much more likely that no one in the world is, for instance, faster than Usain Bolt, because most kids run at some point in their life. We don't have that access and cost issue, at least not as much, in football, soccer, or basketball, where most kids of a variety of races and socioeconomic groups are exposed to the sports and able to play.

Will swimming, ice hockey, tennis, and golf always be dominated by white people and will football and basketball always be dominated by black people? No one knows! That's what's so great about sports.

Now, if you thought this predominance of black cornerbacks represented a flawed market and bias was at play, then an NFL coach could win Super Bowls, or a college coach could win national titles, by exploiting an existing bias in favor of black cornerbacks. After all, an all-white or all-Asian or all-Hispanic secondary would be insanely affordable in the NFL or easy to sign to scholarships in college considering none of these races have produced a starting NFL cornerback in twenty years. (There are occasional white safeties.) But no one is doing that.

Presumably because the talent is not there. (You could also make an argument that white, Asian, and Hispanic players don't work as hard or desire these jobs as much as black players do, but that argument seems difficult to support. I don't think it's a matter of work ethic deficiency; I think it's a matter of talent deficiency.)

I would argue, interestingly, that Bill Belichick has exploited an inefficiency in the football marketplace at the wide receiver position by signing white wide receivers, who were not as highly sought after as their black counterparts. Wes Welker, Danny Amendola, Julian Edelman, and Chris Hogan are all white wide receivers who have excelled for the New England Patriots and done so at affordable salaries. Why were these players available? Potentially because the market valued them less than they did black wide receivers of the same skill level. In other words, the white players were subject to bias based on their race and Belichick saw this bias wasn't justified and his team was rewarded because he was proven correct and exploited a market inefficiency.

Maybe we'll one day see Bill Belichick bring in a ton of white, Asian, or Hispanic players in the secondary. Or maybe we'll see a college coach with the gumption to spend scholarships on white corners. Until we do, we have a perfect example of a profession open to everyone being dominated by a tiny percentage of the overall population.

I'll bet this is the first place that any of you have seen this racial anomaly pointed out. I'll also bet that none of you really doubt that the black corners who have started in the NFL are the best. That's because you believe in the meritocracy of sports.

So why is it totally believable that one racial minority could dominate a highly specialized and highly lucrative field—cornerbacks in the NFL—and other groups couldn't similarly dominate in highly specialized and highly lucrative fields in other industries? For example, isn't computer coding at Facebook and Google also a highly specialized and highly lucrative field? So if white men and Asian men dominate at these jobs, is that really an issue that demands more inclusion and diversity? (The primary difference with computer coding, of course, is that we may also have an issue with access. In other words, white and Asian kids may be more likely to have access to computers and teachers than Hispanic and black kids. I don't doubt that's the case. But the way to remedy that issue isn't by giving people jobs they aren't qualified for as adults just because of their race or gender; it's by pouring money into exposing young children to computer coding and giving them the skills to one day get jobs based on those skills. Put another way, if you looked at the situation with black cornerbacks and decided the position needed to be more diverse, it wouldn't make sense to give less skilled white people those corner jobs just to make the position cosmetically diverse, right? Every sports fan would consider that absurd. It would be to ensure that all kids were receiving training at the cornerback position so they were able to compete for top jobs as adults. So why isn't the same logic applied at Google and Facebook with computer coding? Shouldn't the meritocracy govern there too? Shouldn't we want the best person, regardless of race, to get those jobs as well?)

If we don't demand that our highly skilled and highly trained athletic teams reflect the cosmetic diversity of American life, why should we demand that companies do so? And, just as Bill Belichick did with white wide receivers, if there is a structural inefficiency in the marketplace, wouldn't a new company come along and hire all of these other women and minorities being left on the computer coding sideline and use them to their competitive advantage, besting the discriminating companies?

Remember, unlike NFL and NBA teams, tech companies are born and die with amazing rapidity. It's literally impossible for an NFL or NBA team to go bankrupt, yet look at all the tech companies that go bankrupt every year. Why do we assume the NFL and NBA teams are hiring the best available talent and assume that the tech companies, which operate in much more competitive fields with their future existence at stake every day, don't?

In theory, if companies consistently hire less desirable candidates to fulfill a mandate of cosmetic diversity, then with every hire the companies are becoming weaker. And, interestingly, if it's true that these companies can hire anyone of any background and any skill level and plug them into the company's top jobs, I believe that's evidence they have monopolies. If the skill of your hires doesn't matter when it comes to the success of your company, then your business is a monopoly.

I raise all of these issues for this reason: instead of trying to make sports look more like the country, I think we should try and make the country look more like sports.

The free market, if it's truly a competitive and even playing field, works!

If you think about the history of sports, competition begets inclusion via meritocracy. Why did the SEC start offering black kids scholarships to play football? Because those black kids were better, making SEC teams more likely to win titles. Why did black opportunities flourish in pro sports leagues? Because black athletes outperformed their counterparts of other races.

America's own competitive dynamism, fueled through our sports meritocracy, should be what we aspire to. Instead of making sports more political, we should be making politics—and our country—more like sports.

Sports also provide the best possible route to eliminating racism in the country.

Unfortunately, we are perpetually stuck in the 1960s in the ways we talk about race. This book will be released in 2018 and America has never been more diverse. Yet the sports media drags us back again and again to the 1960s. We keep living the same debates over and over. We are forevermore in the midst of the civil rights movement.

I know America has a legacy of racism, and I know some people still judge others based on the color of their skin, but I believe those people are a tiny minority of the overall American population. Plus, racists in this country aren't all white, and they aren't all racist against black people either. I have a crazy idea that will blow your mind: I think racism in 2018 is evenly distributed across all racial groups. There are white, black, Asian, and Hispanic racists. Yet the media continues to only cover racism as white to black because our story angles are perpetually stuck in 1968.

So how can you be a social crusader in sports in a time when people on your side aren't always good, and the people on the other side are rarely bad? You can't get on your high horse if you live in a time when everyone has pretty similar-sized horses. Anyone spoiling for a big, important fight over race or gender in America usually has to conjure one from thin air.

Fifteen years ago, the Duke lacrosse men, all white, were charged with sexually assaulting black strippers. The story ended up being a complete lie. As one of the Duke lacrosse moms said, there had been a *Newsweek* cover that read "Sex, Lies, and Duke," and the only true word of the three was "Duke."

That story was accepted as truth because so many in the liberal and left-wing sports media wanted it to be true. They wanted rich, privileged white athletes at Duke to rape poor, impoverished black strippers because it fit their preconceived notions of what the world was like. That's troublesome because the job of the sports media isn't to project their worldview onto the nation, it's to cover and analyze sports news from an objective basis.

Yet time after time I see the Duke lacrosse story line playing out in the national media.

It happened again this past March, only this time instead of a men's lacrosse team at Duke it was a women's lacrosse team at Virginia Tech. Instead of being accused of rape, the women's lacrosse team at Virginia Tech was charged with a much less serious transgression. They sang along to a popular rap song.

After winning a game in late March 2018, the Virginia Tech women's lacrosse team celebrated the win by singing songs together on their team bus. Among those songs was a rap song called "Freaky Friday," by a rapper named Lil Dicky and featuring Chris Brown. (I have never felt older than while writing that last sentence.) I wasn't familiar with the song because I'm a dad of three with an early-morning radio show and my late nights out at the bar are few and far between now.

The conceit of the song is that a white rapper, Lil Dicky, changes places with a black singer, hence the title of the song, "Freaky Friday," like the movie by the same name. Lil Dicky wakes up one morning and finds himself inside Chris Brown's body, and Chris Brown finds himself inside Lil Dicky's body.

The song mocks our modern-day decision to define racism by the use of the word "nigga." (The friendly version of nigger. Or, as I should have written it since I'm a white guy to avoid triggering anyone, *the n-word*.)

The lyrics of the rap include the lines I'm producing below:

I woke up Chris Breezy, oh my god I'm the man (oh shit)
I'm so fly and I can dance (whoa, whoa shit)
Wonder if I can say the n-word (wait for real?)
Wait, can I really say the n-word?

What up, my nigga? (woo) What up, my nigga?
'Cause I'm that nigga, nigga, nigga, nigga

Lil Dicky explores the absurdity of our modern-day racial classifications by switching places with a black man, Chris Brown, to comedic result. The video is fantastic and funny even if many of you reading these lyrics right now may be rolling your eyes.

The song is incredibly catchy, such that soon after I learned the song existed, everywhere I went on the beach during 2018 spring break—I was there with my kids, don't worry—the high school and college kids were playing this song.

If you're not responsible for any of the hundreds of millions of views it has on YouTube, you're officially old.

Not surprisingly it's also very popular on college campuses with kids of all races, including the Virginia Tech women's lacrosse team. One of the members of the team posted a video on Snapchat of the entire team, all white girls, singing along to the lyrics after their team's win, and from there it blew up into a major controversy.

In particular, Deadspin, which is where I first saw the video, posted an article with the following headline: "Video Shows Virginia Tech Women's Lacrosse Team Chanting the N-Word; Coach Calls It Teachable Moment."

Only the girls weren't chanting the n-word, they were singing along to an incredibly popular rap song. The song wittily spoofs the idea that there are different rules for who can use certain words based on what color skin they have. Many kids today growing up in a very diverse America are ridiculing what they see as an antiquated notion, that we can define racism based on words and not actions.

The uproar was predictable, featuring the usual suspects. The coach of the Virginia Tech women's lacrosse team is an Asian man named John Sung, and he told the *Roanoke Times*: "This is a teachable moment. It's not something that we're proud of. The team is very apologetic and sorry. There's nobody of any color that should say it [the n-word]. Period. There's nobody that should say it. There was no malice involved. They just thought that they were singing along to a song. They had just won. They're singing songs. The first couple songs were Disney songs. . . . They were celebrating and they were dancing and they were excited. They're good kids that made a bad decision."

Sung also dropped one of the all-time great lines when he said, by way of further explanation, "People forget, I'm a minority."

The Virginia Tech NAACP shared their "disgust and disappointment" in a multipage letter outlining a demand that the players be suspended and that the university take action against them. "We, as a body that dedicates our effort to the fight for equality of all people, disavow not only the actions of said team but the inactions of faculty, staff and most notably, the administration of this university."

As if this weren't enough, within a week of this controversy over the use of the word "nigga" in a rap song, the most outstanding player in the college basketball national title game, Villanova guard Donte DiVincenzo, a white guard who scored 31 points and took over the game down the stretch, had his tweets scoured in the wake of his sudden rise to celebrity. However, his tweets weren't examined in the past year, or even since he had signed with Villanova, left-wing activists on social media, looking to be perpetually outraged, went all the way back to when DiVincenzo was fourteen years old—*fourteen!*—seven years ago, to find that way back then DiVincenzo had been "racially insensitive" when he tweeted out this rap lyric from the popular rapper Meek Mill:

"Ballin on these niggas like I'm derrick rose!"

The headline in *USA Today*, the nation's third-largest newspaper? "An Offensive Tweet from Donte DiVincenzo's Account in 2011 Surfaces."

How did that article open? "At the time of the tweet, DiVincenzo was 14 and living in Wilmington, Delaware, but a white kid using that racially charged word is always a problem."

Always a problem?!

He was fourteen years old and quoting an insanely popular rap song! DiVincenzo's being criticized here is even more ridiculous than the Virginia Tech women's lacrosse team being criticized because he didn't even speak it, he just wrote it. Which is, you know, the same thing *USA Today* did in their article.

Stories like these in the mainstream sports media, of course, are utterly disappointing and perfect evidence of why our national conversation on race is so stilted and stuck in past decades. The sports media aggressively polices words more than actions. We've reached the point where there are essentially three opinions with the word "nigga" or "nigger" and the mainstream media only adopts one of them.

Those three positions can be synthesized thus: (1) white people can never, ever use the word because it's always racist, but black people can use it as much as they want because they have reclaimed the word from racists; (2) context matters—that is, when and where the word is used and which version of the word is used makes all the difference; (3) no one should use the word, white, black, Asian, or Hispanic.

My position is that context matters. The far-left-wing, liberal sports media's position is that context never matters and white people can never use it.

Yet if the word were always racist, wouldn't repeating it in a news article, especially one written by a white man as was the case here, be just as racist as repeating the lyrics either in spoken or written form? In other words, how is *USA Today* repeating the Meek Mill lyric in a story about DiVincenzo using the Meek Mill lyric in a tweet somehow not offensive if a white person uses it when, in both cases, a white person is writing the word? That's exactly what happened here.

Well, *USA Today*'s editors would likely argue they are using the word in a story about the use, not using it themselves. Oh, gotcha. That means *USA Today*'s own coverage of the use of the word in a tweet, in a story written by a white man, is acknowledging that the context in which the word is used matters!

USA Today is also saying they can use the word in a story about a white kid repeating the rap lyrics in a tweet, but a white kid can't repeat the lyrics in a tweet because that's racist. Is your mind twisted into a logic pretzel yet?

Furthermore, the fact that DiVincenzo's tweet when he was fourteen years old is worthy of being investigated and written about by one of the largest newspapers in the country, seven years after he sent the tweet, is evidence of how far-left-wing the national sports media is. You talk about thirsty for left-wing sports media content. Good Lord, are we really setting the news media standard that a white kid quoting a rap lyric when he or she is fourteen years old is a national news story if he or she later becomes famous?

Surely that can't be the standard for public news for the third-largest newspaper in the country, right? There can't be anyone out there, especially not anyone with kids, that believes everything an eighth- or ninth-grader tweets is worthy of being written about when that person becomes an adult.

Regardless, the outcome was predictable. DiVincenzo deleted his Twitter account and claimed he'd been hacked. That's unfortunate because I wish DiVincenzo, whose nickname in high school was "The Michael Jordan of Delaware" had simply said, "Yeah, when I was fourteen, I was a big fan of Meek Mill, so I quoted a popular lyric from his rap that spoke to me at that point in time. I wanted to be as good handling the basketball as Derrick Rose was."

For good measure he could have then added, "I don't think there are very many white guys who play college or pro basketball who are racist. But you are welcome to ask all my teammates if I'm racist for liking that rap lyric, I guess. But I think it's kind of weird that grown adults like you are writing articles about tweets from ninth-graders. But you do you."

(Yet another teenage Twitter controversy emerged in May of 2018 featuring Wyoming quarterback Josh Allen, who would be drafted seventh overall by the Buffalo Bills, when it was determined he'd also tweeted the word "nigga" as a teenager. Allen apologized, but the lesson here seems pretty straightforward given the media's fixation on childhood tweets. Delete everything you ever tweeted when you were a teenager.)

All of you reading this can readily determine the different uses of the same word based on the context in which it is used. So can the vast majority of people in America today; we all know that the context of our word usage matters. That's the entire point of language itself. There's a difference between former Philadelphia Eagles wide receiver Riley Cooper screaming, in anger, at a black security guard that he's a "fucking nigger" at a Kenny Chesney concert and the Virginia Tech women's lacrosse team singing along to a popular rap song or a fourteen-year-old kid tweeting a popular rap lyric.

The Virginia Tech women's lacrosse team wasn't insulting black people; they were paying homage to hip-hop culture by doing what people do when they love songs, by singing along to the lyrics of those songs, which were created by a white and black duo.

The "Freaky Friday" rap song wasn't using a racial slur to denigrate others based on their race; it was exposing the ludicrous rules of race language in this country. The song is, in fact, a perfect example of the American melting pot. You remember the idea of a melting pot, right? The concept that America takes what everyone from a variety of different races, ethnicities, religions, and sexes creates and makes it better and more popular for everyone.

There's a cultural war right now between people who believe in the melting pot, aka people like me, and far-left-wingers who are primarily active on the Internet and in sports media who believe in something called "cultural appropriation." That's what the NAACP was attempting to assert in their letter, and it's what happened this spring when a white girl wore a Chinese dress to a prom, and Twitter lost its mind over the cultural appropriation of the act. (Even though Chinese people in

China—you know, the people from whom the culture actually derived—thought it was fantastic.)

What people who allege cultural appropriation really want is for the races to be separate and for the days of Jim Crow to return, when everyone only consumed content created by people like them, and everyone was isolated into their respective worlds divided by race. Much of our modern conversation about race isn't about making the country better; it's about scoring political points.

I fundamentally reject the idea that cultural appropriation is in any way negative because it is leading us backward, not forward. Also because the concept of cultural appropriation as a negative is absolute bullshit. The Greeks and Romans created our foundations of democracy. Should we not be able to borrow from them to create American democracy? Coffee came from either Africa or the Middle East depending on which origination story you believe—should the rest of us in the world not be able to drink it? Hell, the printing press is from Europe and was created by white men. Should only white men be able to publish books? How about the Internet? It was also created by white men. Should only white men be able to write online and get on the Internet?

Plainly, this is ridiculous. All human creations, regardless of who creates them, belong to all humans. Yet it's where the logical arguments for cultural appropriation lead us: not to inclusion and the embrace of the best ideas from a huge and diverse world population, but to exclusion and segregation. The entire purpose of a capitalistic democracy—and America in general—is to take the best products or ideas and bring them to the most people possible.

The argument that white college girls can't sing a rap song or fourteen-year-old white kids can't share their favorite rap lyrics without being accused of racism is, frankly, the absolute end of racism allegations. We have moved from counting slaves as ⅗ of human beings in this country and excluding all but white men who owned land as voters, to now arguing that white girls can't sing a rap song and white teenagers can't share rap lyrics on social media without being racist. We've reached the backward and ironic point where allegations of racism now have more in common with segregationist arguments espoused by racist white people early in the twentieth century than they do with the modern-day civil rights movement in the 1950s and 1960s.

Imagine the reaction if you went back to Selma and told those marchers, "You may think you're making a difference and that it was a big deal to elect a black president in 2008 and 2012, but we've got a major problem brewing in 2018 that I'm not sure our country will survive—white girls are singing black music too much. They absolutely love it. How do we make it stop to ensure that racism doesn't triumph?"

Those marchers would have looked at you like you were crazy. They would have considered the election of a black president to be a revelation and the acceptance of black culture by Southern white girls to be a great thing. Because what civil rights marchers wanted was integration, the very foundation of inclusion. They wanted a seat at the table of American democracy. That's what they were demonstrating for.

In fact, if we could go back in time to the civil rights era, who do you think would have more issues with Southern white girls singing along to black music in 2018, the civil rights protesters or the white racists?

It's the white racists!

This would have been what white racists feared the most and what the black civil rights protesters hoped would one day happen—that black entertainers would be so embedded in white culture that Southern white women would embrace their creations.

It speaks to how backward we've become on issues of race in 2018 that the modern-day NAACP is now arguing for the exact same thing that the white opponents of the civil rights protesters wanted: a separate world with different rules for different people depending on their race.

Where do you even end this logical absurdity being advocated by the NAACP and their liberal white allies? Should black artists release music for black people and then an edited version that only white people are allowed to buy to ensure that white people aren't racist? We've tried and rejected that separation of the races—it's called separate but equal, and the Supreme Court ruled it unconstitutional.

Worse, how far does the logic espoused by the far-left-wingers extend? Can men sing along to songs by women if the word "bitch" is being used? Isn't that sexism by the same logic? Can Katy Perry even sing the song "I kissed a girl and I liked it," or is that culturally appropriating lesbianism? All of this is a large circle jerk of masturbatory absurdity, which makes it perfect for the left-wing sports media that now often features white people lecturing other white people online about what is and what is not racist.

The purpose of art, in its most basic sense, is to allow the consumer of art to see, hopefully a bit more clearly, our common humanity through the eyes of the artist. Whether it's literature, film, TV, music, paintings, or sculpture, art ennobles and expands the mind by challenging our preconceived notions and making us see the world around us in a way we have not seen it before.

We're now in a strange era when the far-left-wing liberals in this country want to argue that art is only made or intended for people who look like the artist. That's not progressive; it's regressive—the exact same arguments that would have been made to exclude minorities from the larger global marketplace in past centuries. The exact same arguments made by the racist white people in the civil rights era.

Newsflash: songs exist to be sung by people who like them. Double newsflash: it's a good sign that young people in America today don't like just the music of people who look exactly like them. That's called progress, a sign that despite the retrogressive far left, the melting pot continues to be the predominant way most Americans experience popular culture today.

We sample everything from people from all walks of life and pick the ones we like the best. Eventually, the most successful art changes the world, typically for the better. As many of you would acknowledge. How many of your opinions on life changed after you read *To*

Kill a Mockingbird, watched *The Godfather*, or listened to Kendrick Lamar's latest album?

What's scary about our modern-day politics of race, exemplified through sports media stories like these, is the degree to which the far left wing of America believes that grown college kids have to be protected from bad words. You know what's truly racist? The belief that black people can't tell the difference between someone singing or tweeting a rap lyric and calling them a nigger. Even worse than that is the idea that black people are incapable of controlling their own behavior when confronted by racist words.

That's insulting.

We can't bubble-wrap our kids. That's why sports are so important. Sports teach us to win and lose, strive and fail, to accept defeat but never surrender our quest to become better.

The Virginia Tech women's lacrosse team did nothing wrong.

After all, if words are too powerful and offensive to be spoken aloud by all people in this country, how can any segment of the population be allowed to make money off them? Especially if—and this is likely the case given who owns most record companies—the people making the most money from them are white? What Lil Dicky and Chris Brown did was to brilliantly satirize our modern racial politics. Then the Virginia Tech women's lacrosse team embraced that satire.

Only their satire of racial politics collided with adults in the real world, the same people still lost forever in the 1960s civil rights era. The biggest irony of all is that the marchers and the white racists have switched places in 2018; the NAACP has become what they used to hate.

So has the left-wing sports media.

Yet stories like these happen again and again and again.

At the end of this year's NBA season the television announcer for the Oklahoma City Thunder, Brian Davis, said that Oklahoma City point guard Russell Westbrook was playing "out of his cotton-picking mind." Davis was using the phrase "cotton-picking" as it has been used by older Southern men, both black and white, for generations, as a substitute for a curse word. Immediately social media lost its mind, and the Oklahoma City Thunder suspended Davis for a game—because "cotton-picking" sounds like slavery and this phrase, which was used in the context as a compliment, was problematic and unacceptable. (He was later removed from his job when the season ended.) However, it doesn't seem to date back that far, and the oldest use we can find of it was from Bugs Bunny. You can Google it.

The dust-up led to this absurd apology from Davis: "It is with great remorse and humility that I accept this suspension for the insensitive words I used during Wednesday's broadcast. While unintentional, I understand and acknowledge the gravity of the situation. I offer my sincere apology and realize that, while I committed a lapse in judgment, such mistakes come with consequences. This is an appropriate consequence for my actions."

Are you kidding me?!

He did absolutely nothing wrong.

This entire statement makes me want to pick up my laptop and hurl it out the window. This is Paul Finebaum and Rush Limbaugh all over again. The lesson being sent here is: shut up, white men, don't say anything at all. (Which is, interestingly, exactly what ESPN commentator Michelle Beadle said on *SportsNation* recently. If she'd said this about any other race or sex she would have been fired on the spot.)

I don't believe you solve this country's issues by shutting down speech. At some point, I'm sure people will come after me again for something I write or say. Maybe it will even be for something I write in this book.

If that happens, do you know what I'm going to tell the people I've upset?

Deal with it, you pussies. Also, maybe for good measure, my life's mantra in an acronym, which is DBAP (don't be a pussy).

Maybe at this point you're wondering if we are doomed for politics and sports to be forever intertwined. I don't necessarily think so.

I think there's one man who can save us if we just follow his lead. That man? Michael Jeffrey Jordan.

10

Michael Jordan versus LeBron James

As a child of the 1980s and early 1990s, I had three posters on my bedroom walls. I had Michael Jordan dunking from the free throw line during the 1988 slam-dunk contest against Dominique Wilkins. (Jordan took off from just inside the free throw line, but let's not allow the myth to be shattered by reality.) I had an iconic black and white poster of Bo Jackson wearing football shoulder pads with a baseball bat resting on his shoulders. And I had Eric Davis, the star outfielder for the Cincinnati Reds, chasing a flyball in the outfield. (I liked this one better than the picture of Eric Davis in a full suit posing beside a massive gun with baseballs as bullets and the tagline "44 Magnum.")

If you're around my age, you remember the poster craze we all went through. Athlete posters were everywhere in the 1980s, and you could travel to your local mall and flip through the athlete posters at the back of a store like Spencer's Gifts. You'd flip through, maybe a bit slowly because you were tantalized by the girls in their scanty bikinis, but you hadn't really hit puberty yet, so your real gaze of longing would come to rest on awesome athlete posters. Such as the "Bash Brothers." My god, that poster was glorious. There were Jose Canseco and Mark McGwire before we all knew they'd been using steroids, sitting on a police cruiser in the Oakland A's infield, wearing dark suits, yellow shirts, and green ties, holding gigantic baseball bats and wearing awkward porkpie hats. The photo made no sense at all, but we would all stand, jaw agape, and gush to our friends, "This is so cool!"

I mean, those 1980s posters were unbelievable. They had Christian Okoye, my favorite running back on Tecmo Super Bowl—the greatest sports video game of all time and I will accept no arguments to the contrary—wearing a Kansas City Chiefs jersey with a Freddy Krueger glove beneath the tagline "The Nigerian Nightmare." Behind him was a bed with random football players attempting to sleep in full uniforms, clutching the covers up to their chins in terror. There was "The Land of Boz," which featured, for some reason, Seattle Seahawks linebacker Brian Bosworth in a tank top on a golden brick road alongside a woman dressed like Dorothy and other strange assortments of *Wizard of Oz*–related paraphernalia. Utah Jazz forward Karl Malone, dressed as the sexiest mailman of all time, delivering the mail in a mailman's uniform that was, for some reason, ripped to reveal his bulging muscles. We had the "Rocket" Randall Cunningham wearing his full Eagles uniform and standing, without needing a spacesuit, on the surface of the moon. Which looked somehow even less ridiculous when you considered that Wade Boggs was posing in his Red Sox uniform in front of the earth, like a gigantic baseball player come to swat earth into another dimension, under the tagline "Out of This World." Hell, Chicago Cubs legend Andre Dawson was posing in front of Wrigley Field with a bat on his shoulder. Okay, that sounds normal. Except, there was a gigantic hawk resting on Dawson's bat, and the hawk had its wings extended like it was about to take flight and attack all of us. The Cubs, perhaps terrified that Dawson would be harmed by the hawk, refused to allow their logo to be used, meaning Dawson was wearing a white uniform with blue pinstripes and no team logo. We didn't care, it was "The Hawk, baby!" If you thought that was wild, Kirk Gibson posed as an African big-game hunter, in full khaki outfit, replete with hat, and, wait for it, a bamboo prison enclosure behind him (crammed with two imprisoned pitchers wearing their uniforms!) with a hand-scrawled sign that said "Don't feed the pitchers." The inexplicable tagline at the bottom of the poster: "Big Game Hunter."

One of my favorites was Green Bay Packers quarterback Don Majkowski, aka the guy Brett Favre would replace, who had dubbed himself "The Majik Man," and posed on Lambeau Field wearing a Vegas-style magician's costume mixed with a football uniform. The "Majik Man" posed with a magic wand in his right hand, causing the football to levitate in front of him. On the scoreboard behind him the board said "It's Majik time," and the Packers had just 14 points with 32 seconds left in the game, which was, to be fair, an accurate reprisal of the Majkowski era's lack of actual magic.

All of this has left me wondering why I'm writing a book at all. Hell, I should just found a company and sign up athletes to redo these 1980s-era posters and make a billion dollars selling these things everywhere.

The era of sports posters was unequivocally egalitarian, every major sports star of our childhood, white or black—we only really had white stars or black stars or Fernando Valenzuela in 1980s America—was treated the exact same way. For the first time in American history, it wasn't uncommon at all for white kids like me to have posters of black athletes all over their bedrooms.

That was because in 1980s America sports had become our unifying principle. The color of your skin mattered a whole lot less than the color of your jersey. In fact, race, at least in my experience, was virtually a nonissue to 1980s American sports fans.

Look back at all of those athletes mentioned from the ridiculously awesome 1980s-era sports posters—can you remember any of them having any political opinions at all? I can't.

In fact, when I look back over my entire childhood as a sports fan, I can't even remember a legitimate racial or political controversy in the world of sports aside from Rush Limbaugh's tempest at ESPN in 2003. (That's leaving aside the O. J. Simpson murder trial, which was an extreme racial controversy but wasn't directly related to sports; it just involved a sports figure.) Maybe I was just blind to the stories, or maybe the media covered them differently, but my childhood sports memories are just about sports being about, wait for it, sports.

Now I'm not saying that sports and politics haven't intersected before. We talked about Muhammad Ali in this book, and we all know the significant impact that integrating sports made on society at large. However, I wasn't born in an era of segregated schools, and much of the racial maelstrom of the American South predated my own life. From the time I entered integrated public schools in the fall of 1984 at Goodlettsville Elementary until I graduated from Martin Luther King Magnet High School in 1997, I don't remember a major racial controversy in sports.

Sports was where we all went to escape the serious issues in life. (By "serious issues in life," I mean trying to find a girl who would be willing to sleep with us.)

I'm not saying race was invisible in sports, but sports had, much like popular culture as a whole, sought to inculcate the belief that all of us were all pretty much the same.

The Cosby Show was the quintessential 1980s television show espousing this worldview. Yes, the Cosbys were black, but Cosby made the conscious decision to make his character a doctor and his wife a lawyer and to put his family in an upper-middle-class household. While race occasionally played a substantial role in the plot, the more likely story lines were related to family hijinks, the dad who was still a child, the exasperated mom who tried to make sense of the family mess, the cute children who made mistakes but tried to be good. The result? We all gathered around and watched each night, and regardless of our backgrounds, the universality of the Cosby appeal connected with all of us. If you were black, were there things in the Cosby show that specifically spoke to your culture in a way it didn't to others? Sure, the black art hanging on the walls, the popularity of jazz, the occasional struggles rooted in racial dynamics, but the underlying message was this—we all have a lot more in common than we have differences. Everyone loved *The Cosby Show*. (Except, you know, the women Bill Cosby raped.)

It wasn't just on *The Cosby Show* either; the rise of black superstardom in a post–civil rights era was taking place in sports, music, and Hollywood movies too. Within the space of my generation, from 1980 to 2000, we saw Oprah Winfrey become the most wealthy and powerful daily talk-show host, Michael Jackson become the most popular and wealthy musical artist of his generation—I still remember my seventh-grade science teacher at Martin Luther King Magnet, Mr. Bass, playing Michael Jackson's "Black or White" music video in class to teach us a lesson about equality regardless of race—Will Smith conquer music and acting on his way to becoming one of the highest-paid actors in America, Michael Jordan become our first sports billionaire, and, ultimately, Barack Obama, in 2008, be elected our first black president.

I would argue that these black superstars are inextricably intertwined. They represented the championship of talent over race, the meritocracy of American life finally presenting opportunity to all regardless of racial background. None of these stars, not Bill Cosby, Michael Jackson, Oprah Winfrey, Will Smith, Michael Jordan, or Barack Obama, made race an explicit part of their appeal.

Barack Obama, a very talented politician who understood the power that his race reflected, also simultaneously understood that everyone knew he was black already. He didn't need to make a big deal of the fact that he was black because it was self-evident. "I'm not the president of black America," he famously stated. On other occasions, Obama expressed displeasure with politicians like Al Sharpton and Jesse Jackson, whom he saw as "professionally black." That is, politicians whose careers only existed so long as they appealed to that limited share of the electorate. Obama understood that he couldn't be elected president if he was just the president of black America, he had to appeal to all races and creeds to put together an electoral coalition. In so doing he was following the path trod by Bill Cosby, Oprah, Michael Jackson, Michael Jordan, and Will Smith.

Black people, even in 2018, are only 12 percent of the population. They aren't even the largest minority group in this country. Hispanics are. To win an election, or win talk television, or sell movie tickets, or become the first sports billionaire, you have to broaden your appeal beyond your race. You have to appeal to everyone.

This was the story of my youth, the rise of superstars of all races, the posterization of all athletes, regardless of color, the globalization of sports appeal to all of us, regardless of our race, our gender, our ethnicity, or our religion.

And in sports, one man was more responsible for this rise than anyone else—Michael Jordan

Everyone loved Michael Jordan, we all unironically wanted to be like Mike.

I had Air Jordan shoes. I ate Big Macs and drank Gatorade and practiced fadeaway jumpshots in my backyard and played basketball with my tongue wagging as I counted down the clock before I would rise up—hanging in the air like Jordan over Cleveland Cavaliers guard Craig Ehlo—and drain the winning jumper.

I was furious when Jordan lost the Eastern Conference Finals to the Detroit Pistons. When Jordan won the title and cried after his dad had been murdered, I cried too.

Bill Cosby helped to make Michael Jordan possible and Michael Jordan helped to make Barack Obama possible. They were, all of them, inextricably connected—the rise of the black meritocracy.

Jordan's ascension to billionaire status was highly calculated; it wasn't an accident. Jordan realized early in his career that the key to being universally beloved was to dominate in his sport and, significantly, just stick to sports. Stand above the haters, no matter what they might hate him for. Of course, in our modern social media era, the cry "stick to sports" is much derided in left-wing sports media circles, but that's exactly what Michael Jordan did. He played basketball better than anyone else in the world. He stuck to (dominating) sports throughout his career, and as a result the NBA achieved levels of ratings dominance it has never since equaled.

The television ratings for the final three Chicago Bulls titles are still unequaled in NBA history, and 35.9 million people watched game 6 of the 1998 NBA Finals. No other NBA game in league history, and certainly none in the past twenty years, not game 7 of the Warriors and Cavaliers in 2016, not game 7 of Lakers and Celtics in 2010, not any other game ever, has even come remotely close to that number of viewers. That's despite the population surging from 276 million to 327 million since 1998. There are over 50 million more Americans in LeBron's era than in Jordan's era, and even with that 50+ million fewer people in 1998 Jordan still had more viewers.

No basketball player has ever captivated a bigger audience than Michael Jordan.

The truth of the matter is this: sticking to sports was incredibly good for Michael Jordan and for the NBA.

Jordan stuck to sports despite the fact that others tried to pressure him to be political in his career and that he received criticism from media elites for his studied neutrality. Jordan didn't see his role as a sports figure necessitating that he also speak out on political issues.

The biggest example of the political world trying to use Jordan's brand to advance their cause came before Jordan had even won an NBA title.

In 1990 the state of North Carolina found itself embroiled in a bitter political contest surrounding a United States Senate election between the Republican, a white man with ties to the state's segregationist past, Jesse Helms, and the Democrat, a black man named Harvey Gantt, a former mayor of Charlotte who was seeking to become the only black person in the Senate. The election would ultimately go down to the wire, with Helms triumphing by a 53–47 margin.

The campaign included a controversial ad, called "Hands," which featured a white man's hand crumpling up a job rejection notice letting him know that the job he had interviewed for had gone to a "less qualified minority candidate."

In 1996, Helms and Gantt faced off in another high-profile battle wrought with racial tempest, and Helms triumphed once again, this time by a 54–46 margin.

Most of you won't have remembered this Senate race from nearly three decades past, but you might well have heard a quote that came out of the first race in 1990—"Republicans buy shoes, too."

The quote originates from a 1995 book about Michael Jordan's return to basketball. That book, *Second Coming*, by Sam Smith, features a discussion about Jordan's aversion to politics. Here's the relevant paragraph: "[Jordan] was approached by U.S. Senate hopeful Harvey Gantt, a black politician who was running against Jesse Helms in North Carolina, Jordan's home state. Gantt had hoped that Jordan's name would help him defeat Helms, widely regarded as a virulent racist. But Jordan declined. He wasn't into politics, he explained, didn't really know the issues. And, as he later told a friend, 'Republicans buy shoes, too.'"

In recent years Jordan has denied saying this—although Smith has stuck to his reporting and the word "shoes" has often been replaced with "sneakers" as we did for the title of this book—but it speaks to our modern era of mixing sports and politics that this is now considered to be a negative quote. Isn't this just smart branding? In a fifty-fifty country, why would it make sense, if your goal is to appeal to everyone, to pick a side in something that has nothing to do with your profession or business?

Jordan's involvement in the North Carolina Senate campaign was unlikely to have made any difference at all—LeBron James campaigned for Hillary Clinton all over Ohio in 2016 and Donald Trump crushed her in the state anyway—but it's a way for left-wingers to attack Jordan for his focus on his profession over politics.

For not being, in essence, professionally black.

It's an attack that Jordan experienced during his playing days as well, but it's one that is magnified now in an era when sports and politics are intertwined thanks to the far-left-wing sports media fixation on mixing the two.

In a 1992 *Chicago Tribune* piece, Jordan was taken to task by community activist and sports legend Jim Brown for his silence in the wake of the Rodney King beating and the resulting riots in Los Angeles. Jordan responded: "Naturally when things like [the riot] happen and I'm asked to comment on it, people tend to expect me to do more, be more opinionated, more vocal. The cry now from Jim Brown is to be more vocal. But they make it sound like Magic Johnson and myself are the only wealthy black people in America. Where are the Eddie Murphys? Where are the Arsenio Halls? Where are the Bill Cosbys, these type of people?"

In 2015 fellow basketball legend Kareem Abdul-Jabbar took aim at Jordan over his desire to avoid politics and appeal to all Americans, stating: "You can't be afraid of losing shoe sales if you're worried about your civil and human rights. He took commerce over conscience. It's unfortunate for him, but he's gotta live with it."

Much of this criticism is, I believe, rooted in jealousy. Michael Jordan still sells more tennis shoes than any active NBA player—the Jordan brand by itself is almost as big as the nation's second-largest shoe company, Adidas—and Jordan pocketed over $110 million from Nike in 2016, over triple what LeBron James makes. Even without Jordan having won an NBA title in twenty years Nike sells nearly $3 billion a year in Air Jordan–related brand products.

Indeed, according to *Forbes* magazine, in 2016 Jordan made more money off his shoes than current NBA stars LeBron James, Kevin Durant, Kobe Bryant, Steph Curry, James Harden, Carmelo Anthony, Dwyane Wade, Russell Westbrook, and Kyrie Irving did combined.

That would suggest that maybe, just maybe, staying out of politics is good for sports business.

Having said that, in his retirement years Jordan has dipped his toe into politics, donating to Barack Obama's Senate campaign in Illinois in 2004, a donation that led Obama to joke that he didn't know whether to cash the check or frame it. In 2012, Jordan hosted a $3 million fundraiser for Barack Obama's presidential reelection. In 2016, Jordan spoke out about police and community relations for minorities, donating $1 million to the NAACP and $1 million to an organization designed to foster better minority and police relations.

But these are relatively muted political stances, and even the $1 million donations were vintage Jordan, donating to the NAACP and an organization designed to create better minority and police relations. It was a stance designed to appeal to everyone.

The truth of the matter is this: mixing sports and politics is bad for business. It isn't that helpful for politics either. LeBron James aggressively campaigned for Hillary Clinton in his home state of Ohio, yet Trump won 80 of the state's 88 counties, the most dominant performance in the state for a Republican since Ronald Reagan won 82 in his 1984 landslide. Trump won the state by nearly 446,841 votes, a virtual landslide in what was supposed to be a tossup state. This suggests, wait for it, that no one cares what LeBron James thinks about politics, even in a state where he is wildly popular and even in a year when he brought a title back to Cleveland.

As you can see by the data on shoe sales, Jordan's legacy as a brand has only continued to grow despite his career ending.

This is a rarity.

Indeed, there has never been a player whose brand has had the shelf life of Jordan's. The lesson I would take here is that Jordan's transcendent fame and brand value has much to do with Jordan's willingness to inspire positive nostalgic feelings among his fans while retaining cogent power over younger players. Why does that happen? I think it's because everyone loved Jordan. Why did everyone love Jordan? I'd suggest it's because he assiduously avoided politics throughout most of his career and focused on dominating on the basketball court.

Republicans really do buy sneakers too.

Yet modern-day basketball players haven't followed Jordan's path; they've felt the need to interject politics into sports obsessively. None more so than LeBron James, who is perpetually compared with Michael Jordan both on and off the basketball court.

As his career nears an end on the basketball court, LeBron James is taking the opposite approach, electing to regularly speak out on political issues. I believe this is a calculated decision by James, an attempt to shift the conversation from Jordan versus LeBron on the court, a debate I think LeBron is unlikely to win, to make LeBron the modern-day Muhammad Ali, an outspoken political activist, as opposed to an inferior Jordan.

In recent months LeBron has said Donald Trump is a "moron" and that his views are "laughable," "scary," and "racist." After LeBron criticized the president in February of 2018, Fox News host Laura Ingraham told James to "shut up and dribble." That clip went viral, and James responded, "I am more than an athlete," with the hashtag #wewillnotshutupanddribble.

What's fascinating about the resulting sports media coverage of the controversy was how positive it all was. The left-wing sports media falls all over itself to praise James with hardly a word of disagreement. Based on the breathless and hyperventilating left-wing media coverage of his commentary, you would think James is Mahatma Gandhi in sneakers, a modern-day Nelson Mandela on the hardwood. But what has James actually said? He's endorsed less violence, less racism, and more equality in the country. Is there anyone who disagrees with any of these positions?

Has James elevated our national discourse in any way? Of course not. His political commentary is mostly riddled with banal clichés and has the depth of a Twitter or Instagram post. While Ingraham was called racist for her comments, her point was well taken—if you want to talk politics, shouldn't you have to demonstrate you have a cogent political philosophy to be taken seriously? If LeBron James wants me to take him seriously as a political prognosticator, I'm certainly open to that idea, but I at least need to see him talk for a half hour in a sit-down interview with a non–sports figure grilling him on particulars before I decide if he has any substance to his positions.

My bet is any interview like this would end up looking like Katie Couric's sit-down with Sarah Palin, then the vice presidential nominee for president. All that would be left of LeBron would be blood and guts if he was aggressively questioned about his political beliefs. Why? Because LeBron plays basketball for a living. He's not spending that much time paying attention to complex political issues and developing nuanced analysis and plans for societal advancement. He's the equivalent of a millionaire actor or actress who wins an award and goes up on stage to spend their Oscars acceptance speech telling us to save the whales, or that racism is bad, and we shouldn't do it.

Most of us roll our eyes and move on when we see this at awards shows because actors and actresses have been making comments like these for so long. Yet the sports media loses its mind praising the athletes for the most basic, trite, and clichéd political comments imaginable.

So why won't we get a Katie Couric with Sarah Palin–style of interview in sports media? It's because athletes don't need sports media much anymore and sports media knows this. So most sports media has become obsessed with ensuring that they don't lose the only thing that makes them different from the average fan—their access. Most sports media members aren't that interesting and aren't producing that much original content. And if they don't have access to the athletes, they don't have a job. So most people in the sports media bend over backward to avoid offending any athlete, lest their access be restricted.

Add in the fact that most left-wing sports media agree with LeBron James about Donald Trump and you realize that the left-wing sports media doesn't want LeBron James to be exposed for the lack of depth of knowledge he has in politics. They want to use LeBron as a proxy to argue political opinions that they already have, only can't voice themselves. LeBron is the megaphone by which left-wing sports members can espouse the beliefs they hold while pretending they aren't getting political at all. LeBron James is the vehicle they use to politicize sports when most fans don't care at all.

How do you expect us to stick to sports, these sports media members and networks can argue, when the athletes we cover aren't sticking to sports? Of course, this is a logical fallacy; the media chooses which stories become headlines. ESPN could easily say, "Okay, we aren't going to make coach or athlete political opinions headlines anymore."

That would be one way of addressing athlete and coach political opinions.

Another way would be to aggressively question anything political that an athlete says, but that doesn't happen either. Instead, the left-wing sports media heaps praise upon athletes who share left-wing political opinions and doesn't require the athletes to demonstrate their depth of knowledge. Let me give you two recent examples from James's political bent. One involves shoes, the other involves the historical legacies of racism. Both speak to the failure of the left-wing sports media to speak truth to power.

In the spring of 2018, James played games in sneakers with "equality" sewn into the heels, *equa* on the left shoe heel and *lity* on the right shoe heel. The shoes, black sneakers with gold lettering, were designed to advance a bold political pronouncement: we should all be treated equally. This was the second straight year James had done so, representing his ongoing quest to help market social justice warriordom on behalf of Nike.

God bless LeBron James on behalf of Nike, which is buying and paying for his social activism, to have the testicular fortitude to come out in favor of equality. We've all been waiting for so, so long for someone to have the bravery to stand up against all those people arguing for inequality and tell them why they are full of shit.

Hell, maybe if we're lucky a brave female athlete might even argue in favor of women earning the right to vote and wear pants.

But we'll have to wait for Nike to find a way to monetize that.

In the meantime, a cynic might point out that James is just doing a subtle variation of what Kareem Abdul-Jabbar accused Michael Jordan of doing: instead of avoiding politics to sell (many) sneakers James is using politics to sell (fewer) sneakers. Essentially, James is just a worse businessman appealing to a smaller audience with a less appealing pitch. Let's contemplate this evolution in the sneaker business here, James is trying to become a political shoe salesman to take advantage of a marketplace dynamic he believes exists—America wants its modern-day sports hero to be a political shoe salesman advocating left-wing politics.

Sure, the data suggests this is not true, but the left-wing sports media not surprisingly reacted with rave reviews to James's (brought to you by Nike) brave equality stance on behalf of a $120 billion–market cap company that makes its living paying near slave wage compensation to the employees in Asia who make LeBron James's shoes. The irony of a near-billionaire athlete making tens of millions a year to pitch equality on behalf of a company that produces its product with overseas slave labor is mind-boggling.

But no one else in sports media is even willing to point it out.

Do you have any idea what it costs Nike to make a pair of LeBron's shoes? Reports are that the latest Air Jordans' total cost is around $16.25—$10.75 for materials, $2.43 for labor, overhead is $2.10, and the overseas factory profit is $0.97. The most recent LeBron shoe costs $175 on Foot Locker's website. Assuming costs are roughly the same for those shoes, this means the potential profit built into one of these shoes, profit that goes to Nike and the eventual retailers, is nearly $160.

How can Nike make that much money on a pair of shoes?

By making the shoes overseas and paying workers an average of $3 a day.

Yep, $3 a day!

It would take the average worker making LeBron's shoes two months of work to be able to afford to buy a single pair of the "Equality" Nike shoes they are making at American prices.

This means LeBron James is wearing an "Equality" shoe stitched together by an Indonesian factory worker making $3 a day. And no one is asking him about the absurd irony here.

Now, I'm a capitalist who believes in making as much money as you possibly can, so I don't begrudge Nike for taking advantage of virtual slave-labor wages to produce its shoes overseas. That's even though the average Indonesian Nike worker makes 1/76 of what an American factory worker would make doing the same job. But don't you think it's a bit hypocritical for Nike's equality tagline to be "If we can be equals in sport, we can be equals everywhere" while treating the people who make your products so unequally?

Here are some of the other banal and clichéd taglines that Nike pays LeBron James tens of millions of dollars to endorse:

"Opportunity should not discriminate."

"The ball should bounce the same for everyone."

"Worth should outshine color."

LeBron James says: "We can be equals everywhere."

The recent Nike ad designed to sell his shoes ends with this tagline on the screen: "Equality has no boundaries." (And there's no footnoted exception noting that this is true except for Indonesian factory workers making $3 a day.)

The important thing is these taglines are indisputably true already in athletics. Sports is the ultimate meritocracy, nothing matters but your ability to play well. Everyone reading this would agree. Race, gender, sexual interest, religion, none of it matters. If a lesbian atheist who advocated for anarchy could play quarterback as well as Aaron Rodgers, she'd be starting in the NFL. If a gay, transgender Muslim could score goals like Lionel Messi, he'd/she'd be playing soccer for $50 million a year.

Teams and fans don't care what you believe if you can average a triple-double, put up a perfect passer rating, score goals in soccer or the NHL, or hit forty-five home runs a year in baseball. All that matters is your production. That's an incredibly conservative position: sports are the ultimate meritocracy; the primacy of an individual's talent outweighs everything else. (Look at the career of Barry Bonds. Absolutely nobody likes the guy, but teams put up with him until he got caught cheating, and his knees turned to ramen noodles.)

That's what Nike used to sell back when sports were apolitical—sporting excellence.

"Be like Mike" wasn't any truer of an ad slogan—I couldn't jump higher in my Air Jordans that my dad and mom saved up to buy me, but the message that Air Jordan was selling to me was less cynical. They were selling aspiration, the hope that one day we might all be the next Jordan.

Now Nike, via their paid-for pitchman LeBron James, is advocating for a situation that already exists in American sports—we are all already equal between the lines. The best man, or woman, wins. And by wins I mean makes millions of dollars and gets to star in a television commercial about equality even though your talents are not equal with anyone else's, which is why you're rich and in a sports commercial and everyone else is not.

But if Nike truly believes that "Equality should have no boundaries," shouldn't overseas virtual slave labor not exist in Nike factories? Or, better yet, shouldn't Nike make its product in America and treat American factory workers, the same people it's asking to pay $175 for new LeBron shoes for their kids, equally under American law?

But the left-wing sports media won't ask these questions; they'll just mindlessly share and praise LeBron James and Nike for coming out in favor of equality. And the more interesting question is this: Isn't it the height of hypocrisy for Nike, a company that treats its foreign workers unequally compared to its American employees, to try and make even more billions off American consumers by selling equality in America when it doesn't live up to that standard itself?

Nike made a business decision that virtue signaling equality through LeBron James will sell more of its shoes. That's a strategic business decision and it might well be right, but shouldn't the same social justice warriors who are praising Nike for embracing equality actually demand that the company do what it's asking everyone else to do?

Of course they should. But that requires intelligence and using your brain and thinking beyond the LIKE and FAVORITE button on Facebook and Twitter, something that Nike and LeBron James are gambling none of its SJW fans will be willing to do.

So Nike has moved from making billions selling the apolitical Michael Jordan to making millions selling the political LeBron James. It's brilliant corporate strategy, but it's really the exact same thing. Now to LeBron's credit, Jordan also benefited from a less skeptical news media. Jordan sold an everyman, apolitical false version of himself too. Jordan was a late-night gambler who slept with many women all over the country and lost his marriage as a result. It's altogether possible that Jordan would have been Tiger Woods'd if he'd been playing in the modern era and seen his off-court lifestyle exposed to the masses.

LeBron, so far, has avoided virtually any hint of personal scandal. Which is all the more impressive when you consider that LeBron has been in the public eye since he was sixteen or seventeen years old. But, and this is key, LeBron James and his camp, via Nike and all his other business partners, have decided that what will sell in the modern era is social justice and left-wing political activism mixed with sports. Which is the exact opposite of the decision that Jordan and his camp made.

So far, at least if you look at the data, this isn't true. Jordan's appeal, based on sticking to sports, dwarfs LeBron's appeal based on social justice warriordom mixed with sports.

LeBron's advisers are trying to turn LeBron into a modern-day Muhammad Ali so that twenty years from now he remains as relevant as Jordan is twenty years after his career. Even if, unlike Ali, LeBron has never taken a controversial political stance. Believing in equality and calling the president a moron is nowhere near the same thing as being sentenced to prison for refusing to go to Vietnam.

Now let's consider a second major political moment in LeBron's career—the alleged racial slur that was scrawled on the gate outside of LeBron's Los Angeles–area mansion just before the NBA Finals began in 2017. This was, of course, the third consecutive year that LeBron's Cavs would be taking on the Golden State Warriors—now featuring Kevin Durant—and the sports world had turned its attention to this series. (LeBron would be swept by these same Warriors in the 2018 NBA Finals as well.)

Mere days before the 2017 finals began came a blockbuster report that we discussed in a prior chapter—a racial slur had been scrawled on the gate outside LeBron James's $21 million L.A. mansion. Addressing a packed media contingent, LeBron was asked what the incident reminded him of and he compared the racial slur on his gate to the murder of Emmett Till in pre–civil rights America: "And I think back to Emmett Till's mom, actually," LeBron said. "That's one of the first things I thought of. The reason she had an open casket was that she wanted to show the world what her son went through as far as a hate crime, and being black in America."

For those of you who may not be familiar with the history, Emmett Till was a fourteen-year-old black kid who traveled from Chicago to Mississippi in 1955 and was lynched for allegedly whistling at a white woman. The two white men tried for his murder were acquitted of the crime by an all-white jury. No one was ever brought to justice for the murder of this innocent fourteen-year-old.

It's one of the ugliest stories in American history.

Yet one of the first things LeBron thought of when he heard that someone allegedly wrote a racial slur on the gate of his $21 million second or third mansion was Emmett Till's open casket?

And no one else in the sports media thought this was a patently absurd analogy to make?

I feel like I'm taking crazy pills here.

There is absolutely no comparison between these two crimes.

The easiest difference to point out is that the Los Angeles police initiated a full-scale investigation into who wrote a racial slur on LeBron's gate in an effort to catch the perpetrator. Anyone who was caught for this crime would probably go to jail for years. Unlike in Mississippi where the justice system failed Till, the entire justice system was arrayed to ensure that LeBron James and his family got their full measure of justice following this incident. Leaving aside the extreme differences in the crimes, and the fact that the "crime" in LeBron's case might not have even happened, the justice system is not even remotely comparable in these two situations.

Second, LeBron didn't leave the racial slur up on his gate. In the event he wants to follow the Till logic, isn't that the closest he can come to having an open casket? If LeBron wants to shock the nation with the brutality of modern-day racism, instead of immediately painting over the racial slur before police even arrived to conduct their investigation—which is a strange decision regardless—shouldn't he have left it alone to aid the investigation? Shouldn't LeBron have left it up on the gate outside his house? It's not like his family or kids were staying there at the time of the incident.

Comparing your situation to the lynching of an innocent child and then also talking about the open casket was a totally absurd analogy to draw in the first place, but the only similar decision LeBron could have made in any respect was to leave the racial slur up on the property for others to see. If he immediately thought of Emmett Till, shouldn't that idea have occurred to him? Yet he didn't even do that.

Third, there's an incredibly important distinction to draw here: Emmett Till was murdered because of his race, whereas people like LeBron *more* when he's the victim of racism. Think about that for a moment. This racist act, if it actually happened, helps LeBron's brand. He engenders sympathy from the American public for this act. That in itself proves how much the country has changed in nearly seventy years.

Fourth, how did no one suggest to LeBron before he spoke to the public that maybe comparing a racial slur spray-painted on the gate of his $21 million mansion in 2017 to an infamous historic lynching isn't the best analogy to draw. LeBron's situation in 2017 is nothing like what happened in Mississippi in 1955, and it will only serve to inflame the rhetoric here.

Yet LeBron was universally praised by the liberal sports media for his bravery and the only person in all of sports media who pointed out the absurdity of this historical analogy in a written article was me.

That wasn't all LeBron said either, he also said this at the same press conference: "No matter how much money you have, no matter how famous you are, no matter how many people admire you, being black in America is tough. We've got a long way to go, for us as a society and for us as African Americans, until we feel equal in America."

I want you to look at this quote for a minute and think again about what LeBron is selling to the public through his "Equality" sneakers and his Nike millions. LeBron is selling the idea that things are bad and he's trying to overcome them. That's the only way his social-justice-warriordom "Equality" shoes make any sense at all. To be the modern-day Muhammad Ali, LeBron needs for things to be bad in this country. He needs for unfairness and inequality to exist. He doesn't have the Vietnam War or the civil rights movement like Muhammad Ali had, so he has to create his own racial obstacles for what he's selling to have cogency and legitimacy.

This is an important detail that most haven't realized about the brand direction LeBron has chosen—he needs bad things to happen to him or America for his quest to make America equal to have any legitimacy whatsoever. You can't be a superhero if there's no crime.

So let's return to LeBron's quote above with this in mind. And let's begin here—do you think LeBron James's life is tough? Because I don't. I think the vast majority of people of all races reading this book right now have a tougher life than LeBron James does. In fact, is there any white, Asian, or Hispanic man reading this book right now who wouldn't trade places with LeBron James in a heartbeat? I bet there isn't.

I'd also like you to note that LeBron James says "We've got a long way to go . . . for us as African Americans until we feel equal in America." The key word here is "feel." Why do we care whether someone *feels* equal? Shouldn't we care instead about whether someone *is* equal?

Feelings aren't rooted in facts; they're rooted in emotions. And rightly or wrongly many people take their lead from LeBron's comments. LeBron's feelings aren't rooted in accurate facts. My personal belief is we need to spend less time on feelings in this country and more time on facts. LeBron's entire marketing campaign is predicated on feelings, not facts.

Well, how about on an individual level then? Does LeBron feel that he has been treated unfairly because he is black? If so, in what ways? He's going to become a billionaire because he's good at basketball. Would a white, Hispanic, or Asian person with the same exact talents and work ethic as LeBron have made more money playing basketball than he has? That seems unlikely. But if it were true, that could be evidence of discrimination. So is LeBron alleging that he's been discriminated against during his NBA or basketball career based on his race? I don't think so.

In fact, instead of being treated unfairly, LeBron has been able, thanks to the opportunities available to him as a basketball player, to make so much money that he can buy a $21 million mansion in Los Angeles that he uses as a *second* or *third* home. Good for him, that's the fruits of his labor, the benefit to him of being born in a capitalistic society like America that allows extreme talent to lead to extreme wealth. But LeBron himself is actually the perfect example of the American meritocracy: he was born into poverty and became a billionaire because of his talents. Nothing else mattered but his ability on the basketball court. In fact, LeBron is paid so well precisely because his talents are so unequal to everyone else in his generation.

History is an important teacher, and LeBron chose to use it to try and make a point to the larger world. But you have to be careful what historical analogies you use. Because if you use the wrong historical analogy instead of looking to the future, you can anchor yourself in the past.

And I think LeBron's financial future as a left-wing social justice warrior is, significantly, tied directly to selling the idea that things are worse in this country than they actually are. As I said above, you can't be a left-wing social justice warrior without there being things worth fighting in this country. Spiderman and Batman need a villain to be superheroes, and LeBron needs a Vietnam to happen for him to be relevant historically off the court.

Unfortunately, that necessity of bad things happening leads LeBron to seek to tie his name and situation to awful things that have happened in the past instead of pointing out how much difference there is between now and the past.

Imagine if LeBron had used a different historical analogy and said this instead when he was asked about the alleged and unproven racial slur on the gate of his mansion:

"I don't know who is responsible for the racial slur on the gates of my home, but the most important thing is my family is okay and that I could use this situation as a teaching moment for my kids. The second most important thing is this—and I told my kids this too—I'm not going to allow the racial slur on the gate of my home to distract me from the progress we're making every day in this country. Did you know that a black man couldn't even make a living playing sports in this country until Jackie Robinson broke the color barrier in 1947? Now I'm going to become a billionaire because I'm good at putting a ball in a basket.

"How amazing is that?

"That's only been seventy years, but the trajectory is clear, every year things get better in this country when it comes to opportunities for all Americans—white, black, Asian, Hispanic, male and female. So when I look down at my kids, I think, what will this country be like in another seventy years, or another hundred years? My kids and your kids all have unbelievable futures. Futures that are better than any that have ever existed in the history of this world.

"Will there still be racists of all colors in a hundred years? Probably. In a hundred years, will there still be kids growing up in Akron, Ohio, like I did without the same advantages that my own kids will have? Definitely. But you know what all those kids should do? They should look up to me and know that in this country anything is possible. I'm living proof.

"So instead of focusing on the actions of one crazy, loser racist lunatic and allowing him or her to take me back onto the distant shores of past racial conflict and division, what I'm talking about to you today is how far we've come. And how far we're all going to go together.

"It won't be perfect, and we're not to Martin Luther King's promised land yet, but it's gonna be amazing here in this country one day for everyone, and I wish I could live forever to see it. But in the meantime, I'm just trying to make this country and this world better when I leave it than it was when I got here.

Now if you'll excuse me, I gotta go prepare to kick the Warriors' ass."

That would have been eloquent, inspiring, and forward-gazing. But that was Michael Jordan's brand, not LeBron's. Instead of leading us to a beautiful future, LeBron compared himself to Emmett Till. And instead of bravely leading us into the beautiful future, he dragged us back into the ugly past.

LeBron, and many liberal social justice warriors like him, need America to be an unfair and unequal place. The fact that most in the sports media praised LeBron James for what he said about this alleged racial slur and for his "Equality" sneakers doesn't show how eloquent LeBron was; it shows us how low the standard is for athletes speaking out on social issues. And that's a true shame, because low standards don't make champions.

LeBron's words did not befit a king.

And they would have never been uttered by Michael Jordan.

In the space of twenty years, Nike has moved from the aspirational, apolitical, everyman appeal of Air Jordan to the backward-looking, banal cliché-driven politicization of LeBron James. America has voted over and over again that they prefer what Jordan is selling much more than what LeBron is selling but—and this is significant, and what we will address in the next chapter—the left-wing sports media prefers what LeBron James is selling, an unequal, unfair, racist, inegalitarian America.

Today, most in the sports media would say Michael Jordan asserting that "Republicans buy sneakers, too" is just about the worst thing a corporate pitchman could ever say when he was asked for his political opinion.

But if you look at revenue, ratings, and generational appeal, sticking to sports is good business, and the smartest possible decision Michael Jordan could have made for his brand.

Twenty years after his last title, more kids—and adults—still want to be Michael Jordan than want to be LeBron James. That's because it's always more powerful to be the champion of your own story than it is to be the victim of your own story.

11

How to Make Sports Great Again

As a white man with brown hair and green eyes, I believe sports is our national connective tissue.

Go back and read that opening sentence once more, staring at my descriptor. Did you need me to tell you that I was a white man with brown hair and green eyes before I got to my opinion? Of course not. It was totally unnecessary. You either agreed with me or didn't agree with me the moment you read the second part of the sentence.

We've entered into a strange, retrogressive place in an American society ostensibly committed to total equality where what you look like gives legitimacy to your opinion. And we've even taken the next step where what you look like is openly stated: "As a Hispanic transgender woman who was raised in the projects, I believe . . ." Hold up. Why are these signifiers in place at all? I can see what you look like already and that shouldn't have any impact on whether I agree or disagree with you, right?

Choosing to believe or disbelieve someone because of the color of their skin is the very definition of racism. Choosing to believe or disbelieve someone because of their sex is the very definition of sexism.

Yet we've reached a new era in equality—your race or gender is supposed to make you more equal. This era has antecedents in olden-day gentry. Remember when kings and queens and members of the aristocracy would pepper their speech with a long and flowing introduction?

For instance, it's rarely uttered now, but did you know that Prince William's full regal title is His Royal Highness the Duke of Cambridge, Earl of Strathearn, and Baron Carrickfergus.

None of these titles mean anything to most of us today—I'm sure there are still old fuddy-duddies in Great Britain who obsess over them—but they were the very definition of identity politics in olden times. Your official title was a big deal, and it carried substantial authority when you conveyed your opinion. And anytime you gave your opinion, you rattled off that title beforehand to stamp down doubters.

The same thing is happening in America today, a country, ironically, which was founded to do away with rewarding individuals with titles for things they didn't control. No one controls their race. (Although, interestingly, liberals would argue we do control our genders. If you want to make a liberal's mind spin out of control, ask them to justify why it's incredibly offensive to question an individual's gender decision, but also, conversely, incredibly offensive for someone to choose their race. If you can be transgender, why can't you be transracial? Shouldn't the logic be the same? Just as some people feel as if they were born in the wrong gender, couldn't others feel as if they were born in the wrong race? At least there's a blood test that says definitively what sex you are. Race is too complex even for that, as anyone who has done DNA testing can tell you.)

Regardless, identity politics has swept across our country, and I want you to keep track of how often you hear people preface their opinions by telling you what you can already see. That is, how often do people identify their race and gender as in some way justifying their political belief. And every time you see someone do that, I want you to pretend that I started every opinion in this book by saying, "As a white man with brown hair and green eyes, I believe . . ." Because doing so will show you how patently absurd this identity politics era is. And, unfortunately, how it has also come to infiltrate sports.

Frequently, just as it does in modern life, identity politics in sports leads to absurd results, as happened in the fall of 2017 with ESPN. How left-wing and politically correct has the sports media become? This story seems as if it were written in the *Onion*, but it's all true.

In the wake of the Charlottesville, Virginia, protests surrounding the statue of Robert E. Lee there, ESPN panicked about an upcoming game they were airing to kick off the college football season. The University of Virginia was hosting William & Mary in an opening game that would have limited appeal outside the state of Virginia. ESPN had already assigned their announcing team to the game, and the play-by-play voice was a man named Robert Lee.

Which is where our story on the absurdity of identity politics in sports media begins.

I was tipped off by multiple sources inside ESPN via Outkick fans who work at the company that a man named Robert Lee had been moved to another game because he had the same name as the long-dead Confederate general.

This would seem to be substantial overreach since, you know, Robert E. Lee the Confederate general died in 1870 and no one presently living fought in the Civil War. Most people watching the game would have been able to realize that two people can have the same name and not be the same person.

So when I looked into this tip, one of the first things I did was Google "Robert Lee ESPN" because I wasn't sure who he was.

And my jaw dropped.

Robert Lee is Asian.

Immediately, I reached back out to my sources. "You didn't tell me he was Asian!" I texted them.

It turns out ESPN was worried that an Asian announcer with the same name as a dead Confederate general might trigger some of their viewers and lead them to become offended, so they'd removed him from the game.

Shortly after confirming the story, I published it on Outkick and immediately it blew up, becoming a modern-day metaphor for the absurd lengths people and companies will go to when it comes to political correctness.

ESPN, caught flat-footed by my story, issued this statement acknowledging that my story was accurate: "We collectively made the decision with Robert to switch games as the tragic events in Charlottesville were unfolding, simply because of the coincidence of his name. In that moment it felt right to all parties. It's a shame that this is even a topic of conversation and we regret that who calls play by play for a football game has become an issue."

The story to me is a perfect encapsulation of the failures of identity politics and the pursuit of cosmetic diversity over intellectual diversity. Far too often in America today, companies of all stripes, but particularly in sports media, want people who look different but think the same.

ESPN has cultivated that exact kind of groupthink.

Frankly, most media entities in sports have too.

That's how no one raised their hand at a corporate meeting discussing Robert Lee and said, "Guys, maybe I'm totally out of line here, but do you really think any of our viewers are going to conflate a dead white Confederate general and a living Asian man? And even if they do, what's the worst thing that could happen here? Someone might make a joke on Twitter and say something like, 'Looks like Robert E. Lee is doing whatever he can to sneak back into Charlottesville and show a picture of Robert Lee calling the game.' So I've got a suggestion: we open with both men in the booth, and have them identify themselves, and then we don't show them on the screen again. We don't put their names under them when we see them talking in the booth so no one can screenshot it and make fun of his name. But if someone makes a joke on Twitter about this, it's going to last about fifteen minutes and then be gone. On the other hand, if we pull this guy off the game and word gets out that we did it—and we should assume word will always get out on stories like these—what do we lose then by looking way too sensitive to an issue like this?"

ESPN didn't have a single person who said that.

Why?

Because all of ESPN's employees look different but think alike on issues such as these. They're all left-wingers whose audience is predominantly, especially in college football, voting Republican. That disconnect is incredibly problematic because it leads to decisions like these.

Here's an important point that is rarely stated: the people who are most zealously advocating for diversity in the workplace—and by diversity they mean different colors, not different ideas—aren't doing it because it benefits society; they're doing it because it benefits them directly.

In the opening of this book I talked about the Missouri protest as my red pill moment; that was the story that propelled me to examine my surroundings in a new light. I've written about the difference in treatment for liberal political views as opposed to conservative political views in sports. Jemele Hill was protected when she called Donald Trump a white supremacist and Curt Schilling was fired when he supported a transgender bathroom bill in North Carolina, but I've also seen the difference in my media career.

Many times I've been asked why, given the fact that I have a thriving radio show, a dominant online platform, and a huge audience daily on Periscope and Facebook Live, I don't have a daily television show.

The answer is: because I was told I'm too conservative for sports television.

Really.

Let me explain.

In the spring of 2015 Jamie Horowitz, the president of FS1, offered up the morning TV slot on FS1 to me. The proposed three-hour morning show on Fox Sports would feature a former athlete and me, would air nationwide on Fox Sports Radio, and would also be simulcast on

FS1. Horowitz agreed the show could air from Nashville. (I haven't wanted to move my family from Nashville because we have a great life here.) It seemed like a perfect fit.

The only catch was I couldn't do the show alone; we needed to have a former athlete on with me as a cohost.

And that cohost had to be black.

Horowitz's viewer data led him to believe that the show we'd be going up against, *Mike & Mike* on ESPN, skewed white, and the opportunity for ratings and growth required that the show going up against them feature black talent.

Coincidentally, I had been talking about doing a radio show with Eddie George for a while. That had nothing to do with Eddie's race. I believed that his football background—Heisman trophy, NFL and Big Ten bonafides—would play well in the middle part of the country with my SEC fandom and lack of athletic talent. Plus, Eddie lived in Nashville, and loved the idea of doing the show. So Eddie and I traveled out to Los Angeles and did a guest show together live on FS1.

After that broadcast, Horowitz and his crew didn't believe that Eddie and I would be contentious enough for a TV show—that is, we didn't embrace debate enough—so he tabled that idea and said we needed to find another black guy to cohost with me. For anyone who has ever done daily radio, chemistry with your cohost is important, and I wasn't willing to agree to appear with a guy I didn't know well.

At that point, I told them thanks but no thanks on the TV and radio show simulcast and I decided to start doing my daily Periscope and Facebook Live shows instead. Now you can say that decision was crazy—who passes up TV and radio for an unproven medium like Periscope and Facebook Live?—but Pete Vlastelica, my then boss at Fox Sports Digital, was extremely enthusiastic about the idea, and along with a crew in digital, we designed the first-ever daily sports show airing on multiple mediums.

That show, which costs virtually nothing to produce, has thrived.

So much so that when I spoke at the University of Tennessee recently and asked the hundreds of kids in the crowd there how many of them had watched the show on their phones, every hand went up. When I asked the same group how many of them had a cable or satellite subscription of their own, not one hand went up.

Look out, cable.

To their credit, my bosses at Fox Sports Radio, Don Martin and Scott Shapiro, didn't care what race I was. They just wanted me on the air. In September 2016, we debuted the radio show nationwide with me as a solo host, and it has since dominated in its time slot, becoming the most successful morning show in the history of their network.

With our surging ratings and rapid affiliate additions and podcast downloads unlike anything FSR had seen in the morning time slot, the Fox Sports TV crew took note. At the 2017 Super Bowl, Jamie Horowitz and I went to lunch, and he offered me my own TV show on FS1. The offer came with new stipulations. I needed to give up talking and tweeting about politics and pop culture. From Donald Trump to *Game of Thrones*, give it all up. All Horowitz wanted me to do was talk about sports. He offered up Skip Bayless as the perfect example of who my TV role model should be. He said he'd taken Skip from making $150K a year to $6 million a year and he could do the same for me because I was every bit as talented as Skip and much younger.

I asked him why I couldn't talk about politics and sports when I saw other people on FS1 and ESPN regularly talking about politics and sports. He told me that was different because they were talking about politics from a liberal perspective and that was okay, but advertisers didn't like when you talked about sports and politics from a conservative perspective. As a Southern white conservative—his description of me, not my own—I didn't have the same freedom to mix sports and politics as a liberal would. This was, in many ways, the lesson learned from Rush Limbaugh's analysis of the way the media covered Donovan McNabb. No one, at least not yet in sports, has ever lost his or her job for being too liberal.

I'm not opposed to talking about politics in sports, as all of you reading this book can tell. I'm opposed to talking about politics and sports
if it's done from only one side, and with no integrity or intelligence.
If someone wants to argue Colin Kaepernick is a hero, that's fine, but
someone else should also be able to argue he's a fraud. Right now that
doesn't happen in most sports media. We're confronted with an artificial debate question—how heroic is Colin Kaepernick?—that artificially stifles the marketplace of ideas, creating the exact opposite of a
robust debate. By the way, the fact that I, a two-time Obama voter who
has never voted Republican, worked for the Al Gore presidential campaign, worked on multiple Democratic congressional campaigns, and
is pro-choice and anti–death penalty and fine with gay marriage, am
considered "too conservative" is perfect evidence of how far left-wing
sports media has gone.

When Horowitz made his offer to me and asked that I give up talking
about anything but sports, I specifically asked him what he'd have me
tell my audience, which loved the fact that I talked sports, politics, and
pop culture. "I'd tell them," he said, "thank you for getting me here, but
I don't need you anymore."

Now it's important to note that I respect Jamie's TV ability and talents. Indeed, it wouldn't shock me if somewhere down the road we end
up working together. In fact, the two of us are very similar; we both
have tremendous faith in our instincts and the courage of our convic-
tions. I don't blame Jamie for trusting his instincts instead of mine. After all, he knew Skip Bayless–style TV worked. He'd turned Skip into a
superstar and made tens of millions of dollars for ESPN off a show built
around someone like Skip. It makes sense that he'd want a younger
Skip for the next generation.

But for better or worse I trust my instincts too. You don't go from
an online readership of zero in 2004 to a thriving multimedia business
in 2018 by doing what other people tell you to do. If I'd listened to everyone else, I never would have left a secure job practicing law to write
a book about SEC football. And when you have two people who both

trust their instincts—and those instincts tell them different things—it can be hard to get a deal worked out.

I talked over the offer with my wife, my agent, with lots of talented people at Fox Sports whom I respect immensely, with sports media people outside the company, and ultimately decided to turn down the TV offer. I never said a word publicly about either of these TV offers until nearly a year later when the New York *Daily News* reported the news in the wake of Jamie Horowitz leaving FS1.

But when all this happened, I took another red pill. I was explicitly told that my political opinions weren't allowed in sports, but that liberal sports opinions were allowed. In other words, exactly what conservatives allege: that much of the "mainstream" media conspires against any opinions being shared that aren't left-wing.

It's not a conspiracy theory; it's an economic reality.

Furthermore, people of color are far from being discriminated against; many companies are actively trying their hardest to recruit people for jobs based on the color of their skin. I have been in countless meetings for both writing and TV where executives have begged for suggestions of young black guys or girls to put on television based solely on their race.

That seems crazy to me.

Shouldn't sports of all places pick the best person for the job regardless of their race, politics, gender, sexual preferences, or ethnic background? Television and radio, to me, are just like sports. Either you have the talent to perform at a high level or you don't.

Every morning I sit down in front of a mic and talk to a massive audience without any safety net for three hours of live radio. There isn't a single line scripted or a single prepared comment. Just like sports, what I do is intensely competitive and you can either do it or you can't.

What I look like has nothing to do with whether or not I can do it well.

It's a meritocracy.

Which is exactly as it should be.

I hope I'll do television again one day—right now I believe I hold the record for most unaired pilots in FS1 history—but if I do, it will be on my terms and with substantial creative control. Because if there's one thing I've learned, it's that when I can be completely honest with my audience, good things happen. It is always interesting to me that in a field as competitive as TV, radio, and the sports media my race matters at all.

In the meantime, my identity isn't locked up in whiteness any more than a black or Hispanic or Asian person's identity is locked up in their skin color. I choose every single one of my opinions, but I didn't choose to be white with green eyes and perfect brown hair. God just blessed me with the best hair in the business, and for that, I will be eternally grateful.

We aren't just seeing the world of sports attacked by liberal political forces. The idea of sports themselves is under attack. How long before football, with its hypermasculine attributes, is sidelined? How long until cheerleaders are considered too sexist to exist? How long until it's not the best man or woman in competition, but the best man or woman from a particular background? How long until cosmetic diversity comes to sports?

I think it's not too long at all.

So, many of you reading this book right now are probably thinking: How do we take up arms against this absurdity? How do we keep sports from being overtaken by the far left in this country? How do we ensure that the country becomes more like sports and not that sports becomes more like the country?

Well, let's say you agree with everything you've read from me in this book and are convinced, like my mom is, that I'm a genius—how does sports get back to just being about sports again? To being the place where sports fans go to escape the serious things in their life? To being a uniting force and not a dividing force?

The positive thing is, I don't actually think it would be that difficult. In fact, I've got a handy four-part plan that would make sports great again.

First, don't cover athlete political opinions as major news stories. Having been to hundreds of media availabilities over the years, I can tell you that little of what an athlete or coach says at media availabilities is worth a major news story. Often there is no news at all from these events because athletes and coaches tend to speak in banal clichés devoid of anything of substance. Answering questions while saying nothing has become a coach and athlete art form.

In the past several years, many sports media companies, led by ESPN, have suddenly chosen to cover coach and player opinions on politics as major news stories. Why? My contention in this book is that this has happened because the sports media figures making decisions about this coverage agree with these coach and player political opinions and use those players as a voice to get their own political opinions out in a way that they never could have otherwise.

But that's not fair and impartial sports journalism; that's using sports to advocate for your own political views. It's made doubly unfair when athletes are praised for their left-wing political opinions, which are shared by the left-wing sports media, and that praise encourages even more left-wing political pronouncements.

Athletes are rarely, if ever, criticized for any left-wing political opinion, no matter how uninformed, uneducated, or just flat-out wrong those opinions may be. When they are criticized, they rapidly assert racism. Witness what happened when Fox News host Laura Ingraham ridiculed LeBron James's banal political opinions and told him to shut up and dribble.

Immediately the sports media reacted with outrage, defending James from an unfair attack upon his political beliefs. But all Ingraham had done was point out the banalities of James's political opinions. (Something she'd also done to San Antonio Spurs head coach Gregg

Popovich and countless entertainment figures over the years.) In fact, Ingraham even invited James on her show to discuss his political opinions. (An opportunity I've offered to Colin Kaepernick on my show as well.)

If James wants to step into the political arena, he shouldn't expect just to be praised for his political opinions. He should expect what everyone else in politics does. You have to defend your opinions against attacks from people who disagree with you.

The fact that so many players recoiled from Ingraham's criticism and immediately accused her of racism—despite the fact that Ingraham published her own book ridiculing the Dixie Chicks and other left-wing entertainers called *Shut Up & Sing*—demonstrates how coddled athletes have been by the sports media covering them. Athletes have grown used to only being praised for their political opinions no matter how childlike those opinions may be.

If Steve Kerr or Gregg Popovich or LeBron James or Colin Kaepernick have the same political opinions you do, as seems likely given what we know about the sports media's own political voting history, then covering these men's political opinions isn't fair and balanced, it's propaganda.

Why cover those political opinions at all?

Are any of these athletes saying anything different from what many left-wing political commentators have been saying about Donald Trump for the past several years? Of course not. Plus, there are plenty of left-wing political commentators doing a great job of offering a full-throated condemnation of Trump's policies. Do you really think Steve Kerr, Gregg Popovich, LeBron James, or Colin Kaepernick are saying anything we haven't heard before?

Of course not.

All these men have a right to their own political opinions, just like all of you reading this book have the right to yours too. The sports media doesn't need to provide a megaphone to broadcast those opinions far and wide while simultaneously extolling the virtues of the coach and player activism. And these political opinions certainly don't need to be considered legitimate sports media news. Again, read a transcript of a typical player or coach media press conference. You never even see 95 percent of the quotes because the media deems them not worthy of covering.

The same is true of player decisions on whether or not to visit the White House. Do we really need the sports media to breathlessly cover which players, coaches, and teams will be going to the White House and which ones won't be going? Every player has the right to share his or her decision on whether or not to visit the White House on his or her social media platforms, but, again, that's not breaking news. We don't need sports media commentators to debate whether or not players should attend the White House every time the president conveys an invitation to visit to a team that's won a championship.

The solution is to not cover the political opinions of athletes or coaches as legitimate sports news. That's not the job of sports networks or sports media.

Early in this book, I talked about my decision to take the red pill and begin to question the way I saw the sports media covering stories all around me. Once I made that decision and started to write and talk about the unfairness I saw in the sports media, I noticed something amazing: I started to get attacked all the time and branded as "controversial."

No one in the mainstream media ever said I was controversial when I was pro-choice or against the death penalty or believed in gay marriage. Or when I worked on Al Gore's presidential campaign or Democratic congressional and Senate campaigns. Or when I said I was voting for Barack Obama. The minute I started to question the liberal sports media orthodoxy, *Politico* wrote thousands of words and called me the darling of the alt-right in a headline. The *Weekly Standard* wrote thousands of words and called me the Alex Jones of sports media. Media Matters synthesized the two pieces, put me in a straitjacket in the graphics for their article, and called me a "racist conspiracy theorist" in their headline. The most interesting thing about all of these articles is that they don't actually contest any of my opinions, they just attack me personally.

Apparently, all it took to be the darling of the alt-right and to be the Alex Jones of sports media and to be a racist conspiracy theorist was to say that Michael Bennett was a liar and ESPN's politics were far-left-wing. It was amazing to see. I was immediately attacked and branded as having unacceptable political opinions all because I was willing to stand up to the prevailing left-wing orthodoxy in sports media and point out how transparently unfair it all was to average sports fans out there who look to sports as their escape from our polarized political era.

Hell, if you doubt me at all, just wait and see what my critics will say about this book. Some people in the liberal sports media will react like I've just published *Mein Kampf*. Seriously, just wait. (Of course, I'll immediately call all those critics racist and sexist—so make sure you follow me on Twitter @claytravis—so you'll see it happen.)

That's despite the fact that many, even most, reasonable people of a variety of political beliefs in America are going to read this book and agree with many of my positions. There's a clear attempt from left-wing sports media members to praise left-wing sports opinions and elevate those opinions to legitimate sports perspectives worthy of headline billing while personally denigrating anyone who speaks out against far-left-wing hegemony.

I'm sorry—LeBron James saying Donald Trump is a bum should not be a top ESPN headline. Yet, go figure, of course it was. LeBron was praised by left-wing ESPN commentators as being incredibly brave for saying it. To play a favorite game of left-wingers, let's flip the races. What if a white athlete had called Barack Obama a bum, what would have happened? He would have been called racist and publicly shamed for ever having that opinion at all. And his team might well have released him. Hell, just look at what happened to Kevin McHale for being in the *crowd* at a Donald Trump rally.

Athlete and coach political opinions are not treated equally by left-wing sports media who are biased and favoring political opinions they agree with. So my first prong is don't cover athlete and coach political opinions as legitimate news stories.

I don't think most sports fans are looking for politics from their sports figures and I don't think there's a strong business here. Put it this way: Do you really think a left-wing sports media outlet would suddenly emerge and become worth hundreds of millions of dollars?

Of course not.

Slicing and dicing sports fans into disparate interest groups isn't just bad for America, it's also bad for business. ESPN tried to turn Nate Silver's news site, 538, into a business, and guess what happened? The site cost $9 million a year and made $3 million in revenue. It lost tons of money. The same thing is true of The Undefeated, ESPN's attempt to appeal to the black sports fans online. That site is losing tens of millions of dollars, and no one is reading it despite prominent placement on ESPN.com.

The same is also true for ESPNW and every other segmented sports site ESPN has tried to develop. Those sites don't work because sports is already inclusive. Everyone wants to read the same stories regardless of their race, gender, or ethnicity. The triumph of sports is that we all care about the same top athletes. Sports, when done and covered well and fairly, unites us instead of dividing us.

There's a reason Michael Jordan sells more shoes than any other basketball player playing today. It's because he appeals to all of us, not a tiny segment of us.

So my first prong would be this—don't cover athlete or coach political opinions as news.

Second, if you are going to talk about politics intersecting with sports, have different political viewpoints involved in that discussion. This sounds simple, but it isn't happening right now. Witness what happened to Rush Limbaugh and Paul Finebaum when they challenged the prevailing liberal orthodoxy on ESPN. If you feel the need to debate anything political at all in the world of sports, you can't just feature the liberal sports perspective.

Even MSNBC and Fox News—as well as CNN—have learned they need individuals who represent both conservative and liberal viewpoints to debate issues. Otherwise, your broadcast turns into an echo chamber. If you want to "embrace debate" on sports broadcasts, then you need two legitimate sides to a debate.

How amazing is it that ESPN doesn't employ a single person who has publicly announced he or she voted for Donald Trump?

Not one person!

Those people exist, but they saw what happened to Curt Schilling. So they've kept their mouths shut. They know that thanks to Disney CEO Bob Iger, left-wing sports opinion makers get television shows and right-wing sports opinion makers get fired.

It's not just ESPN either. CBS, NBC, Fox Sports, the NFL Network—can you find one person presently employed on air at these places who has publicly stated he voted for Donald Trump?

Because I can't.

That's preposterous, because nearly 63 million people voted for Trump. Now I know some of the people who did vote for Trump and work at those places, but don't worry, I'm not going to out you guys and girls. But that's how unbalanced the sports media has become, half the country, and thirty of our fifty states, voted for Donald Trump, and he's our president right now whether you like it or not. Yet there isn't one person who feels comfortable coming out and admitting to voting for Trump in the sports media.

It's insane, and that's not a healthy marketplace of ideas.

My position is that sports TV viewers don't care who the people who talk about sports voted for, but if you feel the need to cover politics endlessly as a part of sports talk, then you need to find an entire cadre of people to debate the other side, the conservative sports fans' opinion.

There are so few people doing that in the present day that a middle-of-the-road guy like me seems like a far-right-winger in comparison to the far-left-wing obsession on sports television.

Someone needs to feel comfortable ripping Colin Kaepernick on sports TV. Even calling him an idiot for his protest. That's how real politics work. The marketplace of ideas is a brutal battlefield; you've got to be comfortable engaging in a spirited fray for the side you believe in, and you have to be willing to be insulted like crazy as part of that battle.

I believe that if you provided two different sides to each of these political debates, fans would rapidly grow tired of the protracted struggle. They tune in to sports for sports-related topics; if they want to see politics debated, they can turn on a bevy of news programming featuring the same conflicts. But maybe I'm wrong and sports fans are craving sports to be mixed with politics all day. At least then you'd get a fair fight.

We watch sports because we love to see even competitions, two great teams battling to win—no one watches one-sided blowouts. Right now, when sports and politics intersect, it's a one-sided blowout, far-left-wing sports commentators praise far-left-wing athlete opinions and the general sports fans are left out of the conversation.

Third, don't assume race is the root cause of every way that someone is treated in the world of sports. Recently Lamar Jackson, a black quarterback, went through the NFL draft process, and some teams were interested in seeing Jackson, a Heisman trophy winner at Louisville, run routes at wide receiver.

The usual suspects at MSESPN and elsewhere took to the airwaves and social media streets to pronounce this clear evidence of racism. One of ESPN's top NFL analysts tweeted: "So Lamar Jackson who won the Heisman & was CFB's most dynamic player as a QB can't play QB? Oh & THEY showed us that Johnny had 1st round QB skills! Also made sure we knew that Baker just lets his leadership & competitiveness get the best of him sometimes!! WE hear you . . . again."

As I mentioned earlier in the book, a New York *Daily News* columnist also wrote a piece titled "If Lamar Jackson were white he'd be the first quarterback drafted."

This is a transparent attempt to turn Lamar Jackson's being asked to run routes at wide receiver at the NFL Combine into an example of racism. Yet Tim Tebow, a Heisman trophy–winning quarterback at Florida, was also asked by multiple teams if he'd be willing to make a position switch at the NFL level.

Many teams were interested in Tebow playing tight end or halfback. Eventually, Tebow gave up on football and moved on to baseball rather than switch from the quarterback position.

As if that weren't enough, a Heisman trophy–winning white quarterback at Nebraska, Eric Crouch, was switched to defense to have a better shot at playing in the NFL. Defense! Matt Jones, a top SEC quarterback for Arkansas, switched his position to wide receiver before the NFL draft. As did black quarterbacks Braxton Miller and Terrelle Pryor. (Ironically, Pryor has become one of the top wide receivers in the game, banking tens of millions based on his receiving talents.)

Demonstrable evidence shows us that what is being asked of Lamar Jackson is not an uncommon occurrence for top white or black quarterbacks, even Heisman trophy–winning ones, in the modern era. Jackson has been erratic with his passes from the pocket, and NFL teams, justifiably, are nervous about whether a quarterback who hasn't demonstrated great talents passing from the pocket can survive trying to scramble in the more violent NFL.

Moreover, as I stated earlier in the book, there have been four black quarterbacks drafted number one overall since 2001. The idea that Lamar Jackson is being treated differently based on his race is transparently not true. After all, remember, one of the two greatest quarterbacks of all time, Tom Brady, a white man, was drafted in the sixth round. Predicting that any quarterback will succeed going from college to the NFL is a crapshoot, and many times, regardless of race,

NFL teams underrate or overrate a quarterback. Indeed, in the 2000 draft when Tom Brady was famously picked in the sixth round, two black quarterbacks, Tee Martin and Spurgon Wynn, were drafted before him. Was the NFL racist against Tom Brady because two black quarterbacks were taken in front of him, or was the NFL just wrong about Brady regardless of his race? Remember, Lamar Jackson was still drafted in the first round of the 2018 NFL draft and is now guaranteed millions of dollars; it's not like no one took him at all.

Yet making a false racial claim is a fast way to garner likes and retweets on Twitter, and then ESPN and other sports media networks use that divisive rhetoric to ignite debate. Debate, which is, of course, wholly based on a false narrative predicated on fomenting racial division. Worst of all, as we saw with Limbaugh, that debate is only allowed to have one side—racism is to blame.

Because here's the deal. Does anyone really think the modern-day NFL is biased against black quarterbacks? If bias did exist, wouldn't the nonracist NFL teams start black quarterbacks and win one Super Bowl title after another? The fact of the matter is this—white guys have been better quarterbacks in the past twenty-five years than black guys. That doesn't mean black guys—or Asian guys or Hispanic guys—can't play quarterback better over the next twenty-five years. It just means that white guys have been better so far. I don't claim to understand why that is, but the truth of the matter is this—there aren't very many good NFL quarterbacks regardless of race.

The NFL, like all sports, is an ultimate meritocracy. The best player, regardless of race, class, religion, ethnicity, or state or country of upbringing, will play. That's why we all like sports. Yet it has become increasingly common for race-baiting in sports to take place. And the race-baiting always takes a common form, what I've called the *A Time to Kill* of sports. Remember in *A Time to Kill*, when the lawyer Jake Brigance tells the jury to close their eyes after a stirring speech about a little girl who was raped and then says, "Now imagine she's white," and all the jurors open their eyes and they're like, "Holy hell, it turns out raping little girls is wrong! I never would have believed it if I hadn't thought she was white!"

That premise may have made more sense in 1988 Mississippi when the book came out—or even in the 1996 United States when it was released as a movie—but change-the-race narratives are all too common in modern-day American sports.

Almost always the sports figure is being treated exactly as his peers, black or white.

Yet the change-the-race narrative is a common trope that's treated far too seriously by major sports networks. And it happens *all the time.*

After white NFL quarterback Baker Mayfield was caught on camera grabbing his crotch in the direction of the Kansas sideline, ESPN's Cari Champion tweeted: "You know why it could be considered a big deal? BC Cam Newton can't dab. Because If it was Lamar - would it be okay?"

Ah, yes, we have an ESPN employee here arguing that Baker Mayfield is receiving white-crotch-grab privilege. That's even though Mayfield's crotch grab received extensive coverage and ultimately led to a half-game suspension.

Within a couple of weeks, black college players had scored touchdowns and mimicked peeing on a fire hydrant—Ole Miss's D. K. Metcalf—and mimicked jerking off on the opposing fan base—South Florida's Quinton Flowers.

Both of these celebrations happened live on ESPN or ABC broadcasts.
Do you know how much coverage they received on ESPN?
None.

How about Lamar Jackson? Champion had wondered how he'd be received if he grabbed his crotch. He started a brawl on the sideline against his state rival team, Kentucky, in the final regular season game of his college career. The brawl resulted in multiple penalties and a sideline melee.

The coverage?

Nonexistent.

Race rarely, if ever, impacts the way a story is covered in sports media when it comes to most athletes today. But when race is involved it's far more likely that white athletes like Baker Mayfield receive more criticism than black athletes would today for doing the same thing. That's because most members of the sports media are so hypersensitive to racism allegations that white players are attacked far more aggressively than their black counterparts. Far from being penalized by the media based on their race, the reverse is true. Black athletes are much less likely to be challenged because of their race because the media either supports them or is afraid of being called racist. (See Michael Bennett and LeBron James.) Flipping someone's race as a point of legitimate discussion shouldn't be a regular debate in modern-day sports. It's simply not accurate in our modern media era, and it serves to divide sports fans and artificially inflame racial tensions. I've got a crazy idea, how about we treat everyone the exact same regardless of their race?

In my opinion, the first person to accuse another person of being racist or sexist is acknowledging they don't have the power to win an argument using facts, logic, or thinking skills. Spending less time fixating on false racial divisions in sports—and rewarding those who make an entire career doing so—would also help to depoliticize sports.

Fourth, the leagues have to mandate that players not engage in political statements while in uniform at work. If you want to argue the national anthem is a political statement, you are certainly welcome to argue that position, but the vast majority of American sports fans disagree with you. Every pro sports league in America has decided having players present on the field for the national anthem is good for their business. This happens in the NFL, NBA, Major League Baseball, and the NHL.

The NBA players and coaches have been incredibly outspoken with their political beliefs, but they have all stood for the national anthem before every game. As we saw with Mahmoud Abdul-Rauf, the NBA refused to allow any player not to stand for the anthem back in 1996 and hasn't had an issue since then. There has been no controversy surrounding the NBA's on-court product other than player- and coach-related drama dealing directly with basketball itself. Ratings have not been impacted negatively; in fact, they were up in both 2017 and 2018. (NBA ratings remain, however, drastically lower than they were when Michael Jordan's reign of apolitical dominance prevailed in the 1990s.)

The NFL owners and their commissioner, Roger Goodell, could have ordered Colin Kaepernick to stand for the national anthem, as was already mandated by league rules, or face substantial financial consequences for his failure to do so. As stated earlier in the book, it's a fallacy to suggest players have unlimited First Amendment rights on the field. They're fined for inappropriate touchdown celebrations, wearing the wrong shoes or socks, and are subject to a variety of league rules while in uniform on the field. Players can even be fined for the language they use on the field, as Colin Kaepernick should well remember since he was fined for using a racial slur several years ago.

NFL players, like every other employee in the country, are subject to the rules and regulations of their workplace. If they choose to violate those workplace obligations, then NFL team owners have the right to levy fines for those decisions.

NFL owners may decide they don't want to continue the negative off-field attention and might elect to levy suspensions on players who violate league rules. That's entirely appropriate too. Regardless, the pro sports leagues have to end the idea that player political protests, no matter the cause, in uniform at work are permissible.

Sure, the negative media attention for enforcing a rule already on the books may be troubling in the short term, but the league has already created a massive mess for two consecutive years by hoping this controversy was just going to subside. The result has been nearly a 20 percent drop in ratings, which would be calamitous for any business.

If a team signs Colin Kaepernick and he agrees to stand for the national anthem, this story is effectively ended. Why couldn't a team sign

Kaepernick and agree to donate an amount equal to his salary to charities of his choice and in exchange Kaepernick agrees to stand for the anthem?

That seems like a reasonable compromise that would go a long way toward bringing back fans to the games.

I think undertaking all four of these steps would help return sports to the role that they have played for much of American history—as a unifying and not a divisive force in American life.

In 2011, I was fired from FanHouse, along with just about everyone else, when the company sold its site traffic on AOL.com to *Sporting News*. The loss of my job then turned out to be the best thing that ever happened to me because I started my website, Outkick the Coverage, that summer, and my career path has been like a rocket ship since then.

Ultimately the larger American marketplace, especially at the highest levels, is still a meritocracy; the best and most talented people rise to the top. I truly believe that. Which is why the lessons of sports are ultimately conservative: the only hand you can rely on is the one at the end of your sleeve.

Think about all the locker rooms you've ever been inside. When you lost a game, did your coach walk into the locker room and rail about the structural inequities of life, the fact that the kids you were playing against may have had better facilities than you did or more privileges in life? Did he make excuses about larger societal trends that doomed your team to lose before the game began? Or did he tell you to look deep within yourself and find the strength for you and your teammates to get better? Did he ask you to work harder and make sacrifices to succeed?

I've never met a successful coach who blamed the larger world for his team's loss. I've never met a successful athlete who did that either. That's because sports competition gets the country right, it's pure and honest and fair (Lance Armstrong and his ilk notwithstanding). Sports are about learning personal responsibility and work ethic, about the values of teamwork, about treating everyone on your team equally and encouraging everyone to succeed. It's about learning how to marshal your own talents and abilities to the best of your ability. And about not blaming others when you or your team comes up short in the end. You should have worked harder; you should have been better. You shouldn't have left the decision to an umpire or referee. You should have strived harder for perfection than you did.

In the end, we all, no matter how successful we may become, fail at sports.

It hurts to fail, but it's also ennobling.

We are a country made up of strivers, men and women who refused to accept failure no matter the obstacles before them. We, uniquely in this world, are made up of people whose ancestors weren't born here. Just about every single one of us carries the blood of a fearless warrior inside of us, someone who stepped off a ship, either voluntarily or involuntarily, onto virgin land and created the greatest and most successful democratic experiment in the history of the world.

America's not a place; it's a vision, an ideal, and ultimately what it is rooted in is two simple words: be better.

Think about those two words when you wake up and you go to bed. Was I better today than I was yesterday? Can I be better tomorrow than I was today? If your answer is yes every single day, then there truly is no limit to how high you will climb, to how far you will be able to see from the mountaintop of the American meritocracy.

Every single one of us is made up of the DNA of strivers, people who saw what was and dared to fearlessly reach for what could be. You don't conquer a continent with meek middle-management dreams, you don't reach for the stars and beyond without an existential and unending quest to be better. That's what sports is, the relentless pursuit of that which hasn't been done before, a never-ending battle against complacency, the quest to do what many believe is impossible.

Why are you reading this book right now? Because of the lessons I learned from sports long ago. We don't need to make sports look like America; we need to make America look more like sports.

With your help, I still believe, despite all the contradictions and absurdities and biases, sports can still be the one place we go in America where regardless of our races, genders, ethnicities, and sexual orientations we can all be equal.

Because in the end, victory doesn't see color and neither does defeat.

Epilogue

In the fall of 2004, I began writing online with several friends at a website one of my college classmates built. We called that website DeadlyHippos.com, and we wrote with the goal of entertaining ourselves and whatever small segment of the population might also be entertained by our daily musings.

We wrote about sports and pop culture and the things that were happening in our lives. We were a motley crew, a few friends from law school, a high school buddy and his friend from college, and a college friend of mine, Chris Shaw, who had built our website. When the website started, we were all twenty-five years old, and I was the only one of us who was married. Now we all have two or more kids and busy lives with young children.

But back then, every day when I arrived to practice law, I would check the website counter, which existed in the bottom right corner of the website. It would tick up every day, sometimes quite slowly. I vividly remember driving home from my law office one day—writing online was my escape from the drudgery of practicing law—and wishing, as deeply as a person could wish, that one day I might have a hundred daily readers. A thousand was a fanciful pipedream. Ten thousand? Pure insanity. I didn't even dare to think above ten thousand readers.

For years I wrote without making a dollar off my words.

On the day I turned thirty I accepted a full-time job at FanHouse paying me $25,000 a year. Two years later I was fired from that job— along with just about everyone else at the website—and I had a wife at home with a baby, my second son, and my yearly income was $45,000.

I was thirty-two years old, not old, but not very young either, and I had two young sons and no idea what I was going to do. I'd written two books, I had a local radio show that was doing well, but I wasn't thriving. I was stuck. Should I give up writing and talking about sports and go back to practicing law? Abandon the seven years of work I'd put in to make a small living in this world of sports?

I remember going to a minor league baseball game that spring. It was sparsely attended in my hometown of Nashville, and we sat down close to the dugout. The local team, the Nashville Sounds, were losing and a few drunken fans sat down close to the field and mercilessly trash-talked the Triple-A baseball players as they each came up to bat. Denigrating their batting averages, their weight, any and every detail was sport for the drunken revelers.

As I sat and listened to those fans' jeers, I felt just like the Triple-A baseball players. They were so close to the major leagues, having put in years and years of hard work to reach where they were, and yet they still had no guarantee they'd ever reach the promised land, the major leagues, the destination they'd been pursuing their entire lives.

Every week from 2004 to the present, as I moved from the site we founded with friends to CBS, Deadspin, and FanHouse, there had been thousands of words from me online. Every week and every month and every year over the past seven years, my audience had grown. I felt like I was a major league talent, but I certainly wasn't being paid like it. Heck, I barely even had a livable wage when you factored in my law school loans. Did it matter what I thought if no one else in the marketplace agreed?

Not long after that baseball game, I went on a sales call with my local radio station in Nashville. I was doing advertisements on our daily radio show for a hair replacement company. At that meeting, the advertiser wrote a check for six months of ads. The check was for $50,000. I remember looking at him sign that check and salivating. Here, right in front of me, was one advertiser paying $50,000, more than I'd make in an entire year, for me to do local radio ads for him.

That's the moment I decided to start my own website, Outkick the Coverage. In the summer of 2011, I started that website. I would do everything—write, edit, and sell ads. My goal was to make $60,000 that first year. If I could do that, I'd have a six-figure salary if you combined that money with my radio deal, which was my goal.

On the day I launched the site, the website crashed because we had too much traffic.

Seven years later there are days we do a million readers on the site. There are also days when millions more will listen to me on radio, watch me on TV, or check out my daily Periscope and Facebook Live shows.

In 2004, I had an audience of zero and today I have an audience in the millions.

Some of you reading this book right now were part of that initial one hundred readers, of that initial thousand, of that first halcyon day when I had ten thousand readers. When I started writing online, I could have never foreseen what Outkick would become or that a book like this might ever exist. I was, quite simply, the same as many of you reading this book are right now—a guy with a dream. I wanted to make a living as a writer and be as smart, original, funny, and authentic as I could every single day.

All of you reading this book right now have a dream of your own, but there are probably reasons you aren't pursuing that dream. Maybe those reasons even make sense. Maybe you're making too much money doing what you do now or you have young kids or you don't have the time. Ultimately all of those are excuses. And if you make enough excuses, something rotten happens inside your soul: you stop being a dreamer and, worse than not being a dreamer, you use your own fears as fuel to attack other people you see pursuing their dreams.

All of us, no matter where we live or what race, gender, ethnicity, or sexual orientation we are, have been surrounded by these kinds of people, those that aren't happy in their own lives and decide to take it out on others. Honestly that's the lifeblood of social media. Look at the people who attack you; how often are they more successful than you are? Almost never.

I wasn't born rich; neither of my parents ever made $50K a year in their jobs; and none of my grandparents graduated from college. But I was incredibly wealthy when it came to the support of my immediate family. My parents and grandparents were absolutely fabulous, and they encouraged me in everything I did.

While a parent or grandparent's support can be crucial, it can also be overlooked. My mom is still convinced I'm the best-looking person to ever do sports on television. That's nice and all, Mom, but have you seen Kirk Herbstreit and Joel Klatt? My mom is such a fan that I had to ban her from commenting on my articles because she was fighting with people saying bad things about me online. (My wife, by the way, like many wives, is the exact opposite. Every now and then she'll read one of my articles and say, "I kind of agree with the commenters. You do suck.")

So many of you, like me, probably expect and receive encouragement from your parents—and I know some of you don't, and that's just awful—but what I've found is support from people you don't necessarily expect can make all the difference.

Early in my writing career online, my uncle Hugh read one of my articles and said, "You know, I think you can make a living doing this someday."

At the time I was making $100 a week writing online. Yes, it was a family member, but my uncle made a living as a banker. He didn't give compliments just to give compliments. His opinion then, and now, mattered a great deal to me.

Shortly thereafter I was standing at a Vanderbilt University tailgate with one of my law school classmates, Kelly Worman. Kelly, who is now the best real estate attorney in Nashville, and I were drinking beers before Vanderbilt lost a football game to someone. (I don't remember the opponent, but I'm confident Vanderbilt was on the losing side because, well, they're Vanderbilt and it's football.) A reader came up to me and wanted a picture, and when that reader left, Kelly, a fan of my writing, said, "You know, I think one day you're going to make a million dollars a year doing what you do."

I remember laughing at his pronouncement.

At the time I would have signed my life away for a hundred grand a year.

But he was right.

Kelly's comment, coupled with my uncle's, are two that have stuck with me ever since. I'm sure there have been other positive comments like these two along the way, but both of those comments meant more to me than I think either guy knew at the time.

That's why I want to close the book with one more thought. Yes, there have been many opinions in these pages, and some of them may have angered you or made you want to throw the book across the room. Others you may well have agreed with. I've come to accept that in the minds of many I'm either the devil incarnate or the prince of peace because that's the world we live in today, everything is either the best or the worst, there is no middle ground.

But regardless of whom you root for or what your political persuasions are, if you've made it this far in the book, I want you to do something for me. Look for people around you who are working hard at something and tell them you appreciate their talent and believe in them. And I don't mean people like me—at this point I get plenty of love and hate every day. I mean people like me ten years ago.

There are millions of them all over this country, people pouring their heart and soul into everything they do with very few people noticing their work at all. Trust me, the right word delivered at the right time means everything, and it can be the difference between success and failure.

It's why I'm here today producing all the content I do, the guy you love to hate or hate to love.

Just a kid from Nashville, Tennessee.

Thanks to y'all I live my dream every day, and for that, and for all of you reading this right now, whether you love or hate me, I am eternally grateful.

About the Author

CLAY TRAVIS is one of the most listened to, read, and watched sports commentators in the country, with over a million daily listeners, readers, and viewers of his daily show on Fox Sports Radio, his columns for Outkick the Coverage, and his Periscope and Facebook Live show, which is the largest daily online exclusive sports show in the country. He lives in Nashville, Tennessee.